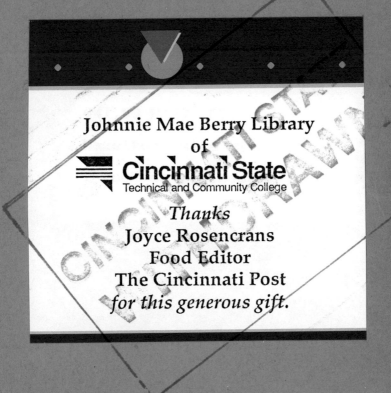

Johnnie Mae Berry Library
of
Cincinnati State
Technical and Community College

Thanks
Joyce Rosencrans
Food Editor
The Cincinnati Post
for this generous gift.

I COOK
AS I PLEASE

I COOK
AS I PLEASE

Travels, Opinions, Recipes

BY
NIKA HAZELTON
Illustrated by Lorraine Filippone

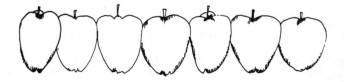

GROSSET & DUNLAP
Publishers   New York

For PRISCILLA BUCKLEY,
with much love

CONTENTS

Note to the Reader

THIS BOOK IS not a book which deals with the full range of the recipes of the countries in which I have cooked. This would be impossible, and furthermore, there are many good books which deal with these individual cuisines. I have not even necessarily included the recipes that are typical of the country mentioned. The recipes found in this book are for dishes which I like especially and which have been successful with my family and my guests.

Lest the reader, coming across the term "my then husband" in the various chapters, should think that I had different husbands in different countries, I hasten to say that this was not so. "My then husband," "my then sister-in-law," etc., were all part of a family with whom I was connected a long time ago and who are now no more than part of the tapestry of the past.

Part One

KITCHEN TALK

Chapter 1

The Current Kitchen

My KITCHEN TODAY is high over Riverside Drive in
New York City. It looks into the green trees of Riverside Park and over the Hudson at New Jersey's unlovely

skyline. But on a clear day the early morning sun fires
New Jersey into a surrealistic landscape. At night New
York's superpolluted air gives us marvelous sunsets with
such a diffusion of colors that foreign visitors congratu-
late us on the natural beauties of our city. The loveliest
sight is the ships that go up and down the river: big
freighters, tugs pulling hard at the heavily laden barges
and little sailboats looking very brave indeed.

The kitchen is small, just a kitchen to cook in. It is
by no means a display kitchen where I celebrate with
imported cookware or run a cooking school. Nor is it
a family kitchen where the folks gather for warmhearted
meals. Family meals with children are horrible, yet
children have to eat with their betters, as parents were
called in a less permissive age, to learn at least a modi-
cum of table manners. Teen-age meals are no less awful
since fights lie beneath the surface. My children have
known all this from early childhood, and even now,
when we have lived through a family meal, we all say:
"Thank God, all has gone off well."

The kitchen is practical and quite handsome, with
black formica counters, a butcher block top and pine
cabinets which get waxed three times a year and that
is it, even in dirty New York. I had silverware partitions
built into drawers, and I had deep drawers made to hold
saucepans; all the drawers are on the rollers you find in
filing cabinets and never get stuck. Another drawer holds
kitchen towels done by the laundry because ironed
kitchen towels are nice and life is too short to iron
them. It also holds aprons because it had been a hard
and fast rule in my mother's house that whoever went
into the kitchen should wear an apron, herself included.
Another drawer holds the flotsam and jetsam of kitchen
life: Hungarian pastry brushes made from goose feathers,

frames for making chocolate leaves, rubber bands, candles for blackouts, bottle tops with an artistic design on top given to me by a five-year-old child as a token of her affection, fondue forks, scallop shells, measuring tapes, and a collection of never-consulted food leaflets, including one on how to make cheese at home.

My electric appliances are at a minimum, consisting only of blender and mixer, but, had I counter space to spare, I would use my electric frying pan and deep fryer much more often. A radio stands on one counter, as well as a scale which weighs in pounds and kilos and a French pâté terrine with a terribly realistic rabbit head. The

knives hang on a magnetic wall knife board. My aluminum saucepans are very heavy, and I cook a great deal in

enameled iron casseroles that look nice at the table.

As for gadgets, and I don't call whisks or skimmers gadgets, I have but a small cherry pitter and a nut-grinder. Only a nutgrinder reduces nuts to the floury and totally dry consistency that you need for baking; if you push them through the meat grinder they will be oily. You can successfully grate nuts in a blender, but it takes ages since only a few can be ground at one time. I use the nutgrinder a great deal because I like to make nut tortes for party desserts. They are easy, spectacular, and best made a day ahead. One trick is to put plenty of freshly grated lemon or orange rinds into a nut-rich dish to pep up the rather bland flavor of the main ingredient. My refrigerator is old and creaky, but, what the hell, since the landlord won't give us a new one. However, I did buy my own kitchen range, which is a family-type stove. Some of my colleagues in the food business have the restaurant ranges that are considered chic in some circles, but I feel that the recipes you test for an unsuspecting public should be prepared on the equipment found in their homes.

I have no dishwasher and I can live without one since I don't find dishwashing nasty whereas I find making beds nasty. As I wash up, under running hot water, I muse about any number of subjects. Dishwashing is much better for musing than lying in one's bath or in bed. The thing I mused about yesterday was moral virtue in the kitchen. In a conversation with guests the night before, several people claimed that a woman who cooks well must also have a good character. I fail to see why an ability to handle food well, both in men and women, is a moral virtue. The worst bitches I've known, male and female, were excellent cooks and the truly good men and women I have come across, dull cooks, though quite as intelligent and lively as the bitches. History and personal observation tell me that almost all fine cooks are bad-tempered tyrants, and also given to excesses in their behavior. Vatel, who had to cook a dinner for Louis XIV, killed himself when the fish did not arrive on time. Some famous modern cooks that I could name, here in New York, have gone with a kitchen knife after their helpers. Furthermore, cooks lack humility. Great painters or long-distance swimmers or singers will give a certain amount of credit to their Maker for endowing them with the raw material of their success. But good cooks attribute their achievements to nothing but their own intelligence, skill, application, and exquisite sensibility. They don't admit that a delicate palate, a sure hand and culinary imagination are as much an inborn gift as a quick eye and fast foot for a tennis player. It is the sin of pride, and very boring it makes them too, as they preen themselves about their gigots with herbs.

I am not talking of the patient homemakers who produce daily food for their families. These souls have con-
siderable moral virtue because it takes a great deal of
goodwill, imagination, and stamina to come up with
noncontroversial family meals that stay within the
budget. I am talking of the men and women who will
spend hours and hours in the kitchen fiddling with food
and expecting to be admired not only for the food, but
for their zeal. Nonsense, they only cook because they'd
rather cook than play the piano or go to bingo night.
And because they want to show off; moral virtue does
not enter into their doings.

Men today are worse about this than women. There
was a time when any red-blooded American boy in his
right mind wanted to grow up to work so that he could
have lots of money for diamonds on his popsie's fingers,
neck, and ears. Then, after the day's work, our boy
would sit in the parlor, lending tone to the establishment, while the women fussed for him in the kitchen.
To the suggestion that he should cook himself, or lend
a hand, his reactions would range from rank disbelief at
this aspersion on his masculinity to leaving the house in
a marked manner to find solace somewhere else. Alas,
now, things have changed. Few of today's lads, brawnier
though less brainy than their forefathers, want to make
railroad fortunes. No, they are interested in food, that
is, making food to eat, be it in a commune or in a
kitchen as beautiful, as fancy as (I am quoting from the
New York Times) ". . . a cooking center under a hand-
crafted copper hood, combining the romance of an open
wood-burning fireplace with the built-in convenience of
an electronic oven, over a hibachi and flipover grill."
There, using the strength bred into them by gallons of

orange juice and the best meat, they will hoist heavy cookbooks and whip up wine-drenched dishes, redolent of herbs plucked at dawn, to please their inamoratas. I fail to understand that a crown roast of lamb takes the place of a diamond bracelet or serves as a substitute for an evening at the theater. Nothing is more odious than a man flaunting his skill with shrimp and garlic if he is not paid to do so. Equally odious is a man proud of not being able to heat at least a TV dinner, when every human being from the age of seven should be able to produce a meal in an emergency.

But women who do not learn to cook well are fools. Early in youth, I had observed that my mother, God rest her soul, a Roman beauty with an attractive, generous husband and scores of devoted admirers, kept close control on her kitchen in spite of her maids. I also noticed that even over the years these beaux did not fade away, whereas those of my pretty but undomesticated aunts did, leaving them with little incentive to stay pretty. When my mother, an old-fashioned Italian woman, was asked about her interest in cooking, though she did not have to cook, she would lift her eyes to heaven and say: "It is an honorable way for an honest woman to get and keep admirers." I've never seen any reason to challenge this sentiment. Nor to challenge the other thing she impressed on my mind as early as suitable, namely the obvious truth that girls and women do not stay as pretty as they once were, and that every year, every month, every week, and every day a younger and prettier number would be there, competing, competing. Any female in her senses should have other strings to her bow, and which could be better than catering to the one pleasure in life which does not pall with age—good food?

I never learned to cook in my mother's kitchen because there was no room for me there. But I did learn to cook, as we shall see later. My words of advice to young women who have asked is to learn to cook two or three dishes well. Or at least to cook with store-boughten food. There are a few rules to follow. Never buy delicatessen roast beef, which is a dead giveaway. But a rotisserie chicken, when a good one, does not betray its origin, and it is easy to make a salad of sliced

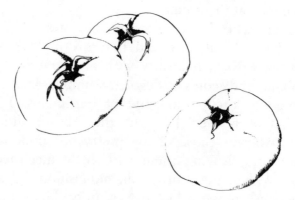

tomatoes. When relying on take-home dishes, transfer them into your own casseroles and be sure the drinks are strong. Because, when a woman has reached a certain age, she must remember that good cooks are the anchors to whom rich, middle-aged, widowed or divorced, and cynical men fasten their shattered lives.

Chapter 2

Cooking for Two and Other Thoughts

NOWADAYS MY COOKING is only for the two of us, the sons being far away with their own families. Both my husband and I have specific feelings about our daily food. He does not like leftovers, and I do not like food that is not freshly cooked. Thus, I am basically a short-order cook who has learned to throw away leftovers since he won't eat them, and I would get even fatter if I did. I must say though that it took me ages to get over the starving Armenians who would benefit from our cleaning up the plate. Where I was brought up, in Italy, food was a privilege, and to throw some away, a crime—especially bread. To this day I can throw away surplus spaghetti, bits of stew, broccoli stalks, and stale cake, but I find it awful to throw away the good Italian bread

11

we buy. I make mine into breadcrumbs in the blender, sifting out the bits that are unassimilable because these homemade breadcrumbs are so much better for all crumb-coated foods than the boughten ones. I do not use the soft bread with all sorts of milk solids, fats and other additions, but the hard-crusted Italian or French breads which contain no fat. And it is the breadiness of my homemade breadcrumbs which makes for crisp schnitzels, fried fish, and similar good two-people dishes.

I had long been puzzled by the superiority of European breaded foods, which did not seem to have anything to do with the main ingredients. When I went to Vienna I spent quite a lot of time with various hotel and restaurant schools and different chefs researching the subject of the various schnitzels. I even had several loaves of the regular American white bread airmailed to me, which my mentors and I dried out for making breadcrumbs. We were very earnest in our studies, resembling

those dedicated TV scientists discovering a better head-
ache pill, or, to stay in our field, those jacket pictures
of cookbook authors bending critically over their pots
and pans. Yes, indeed, life resembles fiction. We an-
alyzed the imported bread and the local bread, mothers
of American and Viennese crumbs, and came to the con-
clusions told above. The masters of the schnitzel also
taught me another schnitzel truth: to prepare it at the
very moment it is to be cooked, rather than follow the
American way of flouring, dipping the meat in egg yolk
and breadcrumbs beforehand, and chilling the schnitzel
for an hour or so. The American way makes the meat
soak up the coating, which thus becomes limp and wet
and stays that way even when fried; the Austrian way
keeps the coating crisp. Ah, isn't travel broadening!

It does not take very long to cook food from scratch
for two people. I usually go into the kitchen around five
in the afternoon, prepare the food for perhaps twenty
to thirty minutes, to have it ready to cook when my
husband is home and has rested up with a mild whiskey.
With the exception of frozen peas, I seldom use frozen
foods. I go in for seasonal fruit and vegetables; and I
don't have large cuts of meat which take a long time to
cook simply because we would never eat our way through
them. We are no great meat eaters. I use small amounts
of cut-up meats for Chinesey or stroganoff-type dishes,
or quickly sautéed slices of beef or veal, or pork chops,
or ground meat spaghetti sauces or meat soufflés, but
never hamburgers—a bore. There is always at least one
vegetable and usually a salad on the table, and a potato
for my old man since this is the form of starch that com-
forts him, especially when baked or creamed. Fish I cook
seldom for I loathe the smell of it, just as I loathe the
smell of food cruising through the house.

It's supposed to be a warmhearted, hospitable smell if it is fresh bread or roast meat, and low class if it is cabbage or fried stuff. I think the smell of any food in the house is off-putting, so that I cook with an open window, a closed kitchen door, and a bottle of Airwick by my side, while my husband goes through the apartment spraying, spraying, spraying with an air refresher can.

Dessert, eaten later, whenever we feel like, is invariably stewed or fresh fruit cut up into a fruit salad. Cooks underestimate the differences in taste a simple dish of cut-up oranges and grapefruit acquire with either a fresh ginger or lemon juice syrup, a pour of sherry or any other liqueur, or the addition of an assertive third fruit such as a banana or a few berries. We seldom eat a first course. Soup is a course in itself, and when I make it, only very little follows, such as stuffed eggs and a salad, or cheese and salad, for we are great cheese eaters.

Utter freshness in food is my one great fetish; quickly cooked food my second. In New York City, you cannot find food as fresh as you find in Europe, especially in France and in Italy. But by buying meats, seasonal fruits, and vegetables three or four times a week rather than once; by buying half a dozen eggs to be used quickly rather than a dozen that have to be stored; by picking up fresh bread and cheese rather than canned, frozen, or out-of-season things, you can set a good table. Admittedly, people with large families or living far from stores cannot do this. But even they can get over stuffing the refrigerator like squirrels, and much as I dislike frozen meats and vegetables, it is still better to freeze the food that cannot be used up quickly rather than to let it grow elderly in the refrigerator. But in New York and other big cities freezing is not necessary, and anybody in California—that paradise of vegetables and fruits —would indeed be delinquent not to consume them as freshly as possible. California is the only place in the United States that compares with the European vegetable and fruit markets, except for a few farmers' markets and road stands in season.

The trick is to cook vegetables quickly and to keep them crisp. I cook mine covered, over medium heat in very little liquid, and for a very short time since I don't like the French process of drowning them in oceans of hot water, bathing them in cold water, and cooking them once more; it reminds one of health fans who take alternate hot and cold showers to tone up their bodies and then anoint themselves with creams and powders. I hate overcooked vegetables as much as both my husband and I hate undercooked meats, especially lamb. The sight of American lamb—healthy, athletic adolescents compared to their little weak-legged milkfed French brothers —cooked in the French manner to be thoroughly underdone, disgusts us.

But neither must meat, especially beef, be overcooked. With the price of meat rising to such heights that it is about to become a collector's item, I weep at the thought of the innumerable fine roasts of beef that are going to be improperly cooked thanks to the falsehoods perpetuated by almost all cookbooks, meat thermometers, and various public agencies. Improperly cooked isn't really the word, overcooked is. The falsehood that is perpetuated says that an inner temperature of 140° F., as seen on a meat thermometer (the most accurate help toward roasting meat well if you ignore its judgment as to what is rare, medium, and well done), will yield rare beef. *It will not.* Inevitably, the meat will be medium rare or even medium. If you want rare beef, remove the roast

from the oven when the meat thermometer reads 120° F.
Allow it to rest in a warm place for fifteen to twenty
minutes, and it will become easier to carve because it
will be firmer. As a matter of fact, all roasted meat and
chicken should be allowed to settle down for ten to
twenty minutes, in a warm place, for a redistribution of
the juices and easier carving.

Here are the correct temperatures for roast beef as
seen on the meat thermometer, which should be inserted
into the meat before the meat goes into the oven, in
the thickest part, but away from the bone. In a rib
roast, stick the thermometer on top of the roast at a
slight angle. Remove the meat from the refrigerator one-
and-a-half to two hours or more before cooking; it should
be at room temperature.

RARE	120° F.
MEDIUM-RARE	130° F.
MEDIUM	140° F.
WELL-DONE	150° F.

We never make roast of any kind for the two of us.
It isn't only our antipathy toward leftovers, but also the
fact that small roasts simply are not as good as large
ones. A small roast of beef or veal of three or four
pounds, which is a lot of meat for two people but still
not a large roast, will dry out in the roasting process,
however much you baste it. Small roasts don't have the
inner reserves of juice of larger cuts. I loathe the sight
of the gigantic roasts that some restaurants in London,
like Simpson's or Rule's, bring around for carving to the
guests' pleasure, but I must admit that the meat is
divine. No, roast beef, when two people can afford it,
is better eaten in a good restaurant, and in our case, not

in those revolting large thick slabs covering the whole of the plate, but thinly carved.

Pork, being a fatter meat, lends itself better to smaller roasts.

Overcooking does not only apply to roast beef and vegetables. It applies to spaghetti sauce, which has a much fresher taste if it is not simmered for hours as the recipes say, but just long enough to let the flavors amalgamate, about twenty to thirty minutes or so. It applies to stews and casseroles, since far too many cooks cannot grasp that these too can be overcooked, just like steak, and that they will not wait forever for the merrily drinking dinner guests. It is all very well to follow those delicious French recipes for slow simmering daubes, fricassees, and the like, but the fact is that the recipes were for meats that really required endless slow cooking to get tender and flavorful. These meats were very different from our modern American ones that are tenderized on the hoof, so to speak, with all sorts of tenderizing medicines and therefore cook quickly, albeit with very little flavor. Larding may be necessary in Europe to make meat juicy, but it is seldom necessary with our kinds of meat that are so much fatter. Like our whole food economy, our meats are incredibly wasteful if you don't want to drown in a sea of grease; the amount of fat and gristle trimmed from a couple of pounds of beef chuck for stew is a revelation.

It seems a contradiction, but leftovers are not always necessarily due to too much food. A man may not feel like a steak dinner, preferring to gorge himself on franks and beans. He'll say the first is too much, when in fact, it is no more, and possibly less, than the second. It is his mental state that makes for leftovers of the first meal and clean plates of the second. Leftovers are also made by the type of meal served. Why must meals always be good or superb or well-balanced? Many times we are simply not up to them, craving junk food, just as many times we are not up to dressing charmingly, elegantly, or even neatly. Craving junk food may be one of the lesser instincts of man, but it sure is there. Why is it that there are never any leftovers of potato chips, franks, canned ravioli, while fine beef languishes uneaten?

I know that there are cookbooks dealing with the joys of cooking with leftovers, even with cooking for leftovers. Just as there are people who grow lyrical at the sight of those little leftover piles in their refrigerators

sitting like wallflowers at a ball. As I toss my dry leftovers into the garbage can, or into the toilet bowl if they are wet, I say, "To each his own," even if it is the Garbage Can Basse Cuisine. As I am writing this in these days of exorbitant food prices, I know that the brickbats will fly. But let me assure my critics that when cooking just for two people, it is entirely possible to gauge appetites and quantities so that there will be no leftovers, or so few of them, a spoonful or two, that it does not matter. Cooking for a family is a different thing, and one that does not concern me at the moment. I know that I spend less for food than others in my position for two reasons: one, I cook only what we will eat at one meal; and the other, I cook from scratch. When you are a short-order home cook, as I am, you can always find out if your husband is very, medium, or just a little hungry, and cook accordingly.

To get off this sordid subject, here is a recipe for

Perfect Rare Roast Beef

This is a different and very successful as well as painless way of roasting a rib roast. It was developed by Anne Seranne, a famous home economist, cookbook writer and gourmet, whom I admire immensely.

1 2- to 4-rib roast weighing   Salt
    4½–12 pounds   Freshly ground pepper
  Flour

Remove the roast from the refrigerator two-and-one-half hours before cooking. Preheat the oven to 500°F. (Preheating, essential to all oven cookery, takes twenty minutes.) Place the roast in an open, shallow roasting pan, fat side up. Sprinkle with a little flour, rub the flour into the fat, and rub salt and pepper all over the roast. Put the roast into the preheated oven. Roast according to the following chart, timing the minutes exactly. When cooking time is finished, turn off the oven. *Do not open the door at any time.* Allow the roast to remain in the oven until the oven is lukewarm or about two hours. The roast will have a crunchy brown outside and enough internal heat for serving for as long as three to four hours.

Quantities: Two servings per rib.

Number of Ribs	Weight (without short ribs)	Roasting time at 500° F.
2	4½–5 lbs.	25–30 minutes
3	8–9 lbs.	40–45 minutes
4	11–12 lbs.	55–60 minutes

(A large rib roast is better than a small one.)

Ovens: Ovens have a tendency to become inaccurate. They should be calibrated at least once a year by your friendly gas or electric or manufacturer's man. For accuracy, buy an oven thermometer, the most expensive one. Cheap ones are valueless, which is true of all thermometers.

Quick Potato Soup

(1 serving)

1 small onion, diced
1 tablespoon butter
1 medium potato, peeled
  and diced

1½ cups hot bouillon or
  water
Salt
Pepper

Cook the onion in the butter until soft and golden. Add the potato. Cook covered over low heat, stirring frequently, until the potato is half cooked. Add the bouillon. Continue to cook for five more minutes. Season with salt and pepper to taste.

Barbara's Hot and Sour Soup

(2 servings)

¼ cup dried Chinese or other dried mush-rooms
4 cups hot chicken broth
¼ cup minced leftover cooked pork
1 tablespoon soy sauce
¼ cup minced bamboo shoots

2 tablespoons vinegar or more to taste
Salt
Freshly ground pepper
2 tablespoons cornstarch
1 tablespoon water
1 tablespoon sesame oil
2 scallions, white and green parts, minced

Soak the mushrooms in lukewarm water to cover for 15 minutes. Drain, remove stems, and chop. In a saucepan, combine the chicken broth, the pork, the soy sauce, and the bamboo shoots. Bring to the boiling point, lower heat and simmer covered for 5 minutes. Stir in the vinegar and the salt and pepper and simmer for 2 more minutes. Make a smooth paste with the cornstarch and the water. Bring the soup to the boil and stir in the cornstarch. Cook, stirring constantly, for 1 minute. Remove from heat and stir in the sesame oil and the scallions.

Fried Eggs Soubise

(1 serving)

Quickly made and good for brunch, lunch, or a late supper. Preferably use individual baking dishes.

2 tablespoons butter	2 eggs
2–3 medium onions, thinly sliced	Salt
	Freshly ground pepper

Heat the butter in an individual baking dish. Over low heat, and stirring frequently, cook the onions until they are soft and golden. Make two indentations. Break one egg into each. Season with salt and pepper. Cover and cook over low heat until the eggs are set and the yolk is covered with a thin film. Serve immediately.

Piperade

(2 servings)

Serve with ham, preferably prosciutto or Bayonne ham or Virginia ham.

2 tablespoons bacon fat	Salt
3 medium onions, thinly sliced	Freshly ground pepper
2 medium tomatoes, peeled and coarsely chopped	¼ teaspoon ground thyme
2 large green peppers, sliced	4 eggs, beaten

Heat the bacon fat in a heavy skillet. Add the onions, the tomatoes, the green peppers, the salt and pepper, and thyme. Cook covered over low heat, stirring frequently, until all the vegetables are very soft and a mush. Stir in the eggs and scramble gently with a fork until just set; this is a soft dish. Serve very hot.

Yellow Chicken Curry

(3 servings)

For people who are scared of hot curries, but would like to try a mild one.

1 small chicken, cut into pieces	1 teaspoon ground cardamon
1½ tablespoons turmeric	1 teaspoon coriander seed, crushed and sifted
1 cup light or heavy cream, or coconut cream	1 teaspoon ground pepper
3 tablespoons butter or peanut oil	1 cup chicken bouillon (make with a cube)
1 medium onion, minced	Salt
½ teaspoon ground cloves	½ cup toasted shredded almonds

Take all the fat and skin off the chicken. Mix ½ tablespoon of the turmeric with the cream. Lay the chicken pieces in a bowl and pour the turmeric cream over them. Turn them over in the liquid so that all sides are coated. Refrigerate for a couple of hours, turning the pieces occasionally.

Heat the butter and cook the onion in it until golden. Do not let the onion brown. Add the remaining turmeric, the cloves, the cardamon, the coriander, and the pepper. Fry the spices, stirring constantly, for about 2–3 minutes to release their flavor. Stir in the chicken bouillon and mix well. Add the chicken and the turmeric cream. Bring to the boiling point. Lower heat immediately to simmer. Check the seasoning and add salt if necessary. Cover and simmer for about 20 minutes or until the chicken is done. Sprinkle the toasted almonds over the curry before serving with chutney and rice.

Quick Chicken, Almond and Vegetable Dish

(2–3 servings)

You need some oil for this dish, but less if you cook in a Teflon pan or wok.

6 Chinese mushrooms
1 large chicken breast,
     split
4 tablespoons peanut oil
⅓ cup shredded or halved
     blanched almonds
6 water chestnuts, drained
     and sliced
3 garlic cloves, minced
1 large carrot, cut into
     ½-inch x 1-inch sticks

6 bamboo shoots, drained
     and sliced
1 small zucchini or yellow
     squash, cut into ½-inch
     x 1-inch sticks
Salt
Freshly ground pepper
3 tablespoons water

Soak the Chinese mushrooms in lukewarm water to cover for 15 minutes. Remove the skin and fat and cut all the meat off the chicken breast and cut into strips. Heat half of the oil in a large deep frying pan and quickly fry the almonds in it. They should be golden and not browned. With a slotted spoon, remove the almonds and drain them on paper towel. Add the water chestnuts to the pan and fry them quickly until barely golden. Remove them to paper towel. Drain the mushrooms, remove stems, and cut them into pieces. Add 1 to 2 tablespoons of oil to the pan and quickly fry the mushrooms in it. Remove the mushrooms and add them to the water chestnuts. Add the remaining oil to the pan and fry the garlic and the chicken strips in it until the meat is opaque and almost done—about 3–5 minutes, depending on the size of the strips. Add the carrot, the bamboo shoots, the zucchini, the water chestnuts, and the Chinese mushrooms. Mix well. Season with salt and pepper to taste and add the water. Simmer without a cover for 3–5 minutes or until the meat is cooked and the vegetables tender, but still very crisp. Turn out on a heated serving dish and sprinkle with the almonds. Serve immediately with a rice pilaf.

Meat and Zucchini Soufflé

(2 servings)

I serve this as the main dish, followed by a tossed green salad and Brie cheese, and fruit in season.

1 pound zucchini	Any fresh or dried herb
4 tablespoons butter	to taste
2 onions, minced	Salt
½ pound ground beef, or any other meat	Freshly ground pepper
	½ cup water
¼ cup minced parsley	4 eggs, beaten

Peel the zucchini if necessary. Cut into 4 parts lengthwise and remove the core with the seeds. Cut the zucchini into ¼-inch cubes. Heat the butter in a saucepan. Cook the onions in it until soft. Add the meat and cook, stirring constantly, until it is no longer red, about 2–3 minutes. Add the zucchini, the parsley, the herb, the salt and pepper, and the water. Cook covered over low heat, stirring frequently, until the vegetables are tender. Stir the eggs into the vegetable mixture. Butter a 1-quart baking dish and spoon in the soufflé mixture. Bake in a preheated moderate oven (350°F.) for about 25 minutes or until set. Serve with Tomato or Béchamel Sauce.

Hungarian Stewed Potatoes

(3–4 servings)

A change from the usual home-fried or creamed potatoes, to go with any meats.

2 tablespoons bacon fat or lard
1 large onion, minced
2 tablespoons flour
1 tablespoon sweet paprika
6 medium potatoes, peeled and cut into ¼-inch slices

2–4 tablespoons vinegar, depending on strength of vinegar and taste
1 bay leaf
Salt
Freshly ground pepper
¼ teaspoon dried marjoram
Water to cover

Heat the bacon fat or lard in a heavy saucepan. Add the onion. Cook, stirring constantly, until the onion is soft and golden. Stir in the flour and the paprika. Cook, stirring, for about 2 more minutes or until the flour is blended into the bacon fat or lard. Add the potatoes, the vinegar, the bay leaf, the salt and pepper to taste, and the marjoram. Add just enough water to barely cover the potatoes. Cover and simmer over very low heat for 20–30 minutes or until the potatoes are tender. Check for moisture. The sauce of the potatoes should be medium thick. If necessary, add a little more water, a tablespoon at a time.

Onion and Potato Salad

(2–4 servings)

Good with cold roast beef or pork

2 large Bermuda onions,
    sliced very thinly
2 teaspoons salt
2 large potatoes, boiled,
    peeled and sliced

3 tablespoons olive or
    salad oil
1–2 tablespoons vinegar
    Freshly ground pepper
    Parsley sprigs

Lay the onion slices in a shallow dish. Sprinkle with the salt. Cover with a plate and weigh down. Let stand at room temperature for 30 minutes. Drain. Lay the potato slices on the onions. Combine the oil and the vinegar and pour over the vegetables. Season with a little more salt, if necessary, and pepper. Cover tightly and chill for 1 hour. Decorate with the parsley sprigs before serving.

Pretty Avocado Salad

(1–2 servings)

I found this in a San Antonio, Texas, restaurant

Line individual salad plates with crisp, unblemished salad greens. Cut an unblemished ripe but firm avocado into halves lengthwise. Remove the seed. Rub the cut surfaces gently with a slice of lemon to prevent darkening. Do not peel. With a sharp knife, cut, on a slight

slant, each avocado half into thin slices. Turn out one
or both avocado halves, cut side down, on the salad
greens. With the help of a knife, carefully remove the
skin, leaving the sliced halves looking intact, as though
they had not been sliced. Sprinkle a light French dressing
over the avocado halves and sprinkle with minced
parsley.

Lively Spread for Broiled Fish and Seafood

(For about 1-pound fish)

This is best on neutral fish like cod or on oily fish
like mackerel. Adjust the seasoning to your taste.

1 tablespoon melted butter or salad oil	1 tablespoon chili sauce or tomato ketchup
Juice of 1 lime or 1 lemon	½ garlic clove, crushed
1 teaspoon dry mustard	⅛ teaspoon Angostura bitters
2 teaspoons Worcestershire sauce	Salt to taste

Combine all the ingredients in a bowl and blend them
thoroughly. Or puree them in a blender. Spread on fish
just before broiling as usual.

Last-Minute Pineapple Dessert

(3 servings)

This recipe can be made with canned pineapple, but fresh pineapple is infinitely superior.

2 cups finely chopped or crushed pineapple, drained	1 tablespoon rum, Kirsch, or any favorite liqueur (optional)
1 cup heavy cream	
2 tablespoons sugar, or more, depending on the pineapple's sweetness	

Put the pineapple into a sieve and set the sieve over a bowl to let it drain for about 15 minutes or longer. This can be done ahead of time. Beat the cream until it begins to get thick. Beat in the sugar and the rum. Beat until stiff, but do not overbeat or you'll have butter. Cover the bowl with the whipped cream and chill until serving time. Just before serving, fold the pineapple into the whipped cream. Turn into a serving dish or individual bowls or dishes. Serve with plain cookies.

Note: 1) This can really be made with other fruits, such as mangoes, papayas, apricots, strawberries, peaches, figs, and the like. The main thing is to have the fruit as dry as possible, or the whole dessert will be soupy. If you are using peaches, sprinkle them with fresh lemon juice to prevent darkening.

2) This dessert can be halved or increased at will.

Chapter 3

Guests

What to Cook

"WHAT SHALL I cook for these people" is the pitiful cry that echoes through our land every day, whenever guests are expected for dinner. It's a cry as anguished as that produced by confronting the income tax one still has to pay, though somewhat less anguished than its sister cry: "Whom shall I invite with whom?"

Just as my parents' house, my own has always been a sort of Grand Central Station with its passage of guests. I like having guests for meals, because it does not bother me, since I have emancipated myself from the idea that all has to be perfect. If I think everything has to be perfect for guests (and the only reason I ever feel that way is a purely mercenary one—namely that making a poor impression would be bad for my husband's or my own business affairs), we take the guests out to a good restaurant. Those kinds of guests will be most impressed by your spending lots of good money on them in a place they can brag of later. As for the rest of the guests, I do my best and hope they will like it. If they wish to criticize, let them, it is their problem, not mine, and anyway, it is not likely that they will come again.

Inviting people for dinner is a very good test as to their behavior, and my, the surprises I've had! In Europe, you can take it for granted that people, even of the most diverse opinions, will be polite to each other at their hosts' table. Not so in New York. I've had guests who prided themselves on their enlightened liberalism insult guests who are conservative or who are practicing Catholics like myself. A recent episode sticks in the mind when the guest, who would not dare to say such a thing if she were in an Islamic country, and I suspect, not to her Jewish or black friends, asked us with utter wonderment if we really believed in God and all that nonsense. Why do I have people like that to my house? First of all, I naturally thought they would have good manners. Second, they looked or sounded interesting so that again naturally, one would like to know them better. Third, what is a dinner compared to the things you find out about people? This sort of test-inviting eliminates the duds, and makes in the end for a circle of good friends, whom I'd never have known if I'd not invited them in the first place, people being shyer with invitations than me, which does not mean that they are shy accepting them.

So, when it comes to having people for dinner, I have friends because I want to enjoy myself. I try to invite

people who have something in common or are tolerant enough to get on with opinions different from their own. I try to include some new guests at a gathering of old friends, because even the best of us can get a little tired of our own company and like to see a new face. I know one must never have two stars at one party, whether they be uncommonly good talkers, writers, experts on the same subject, or famous for something or other. About this, I remember with the greatest pleasure a party given many years ago by a magazine editor friend of mine, and I suspect, with tongue in cheek, where Evelyn Waugh and Salvador Dali were both guests of honor. In the large living room, each celebrity had established himself at opposite ends, holding court there. Between them was a vast, empty no-man's land, crossed hastily and somewhat furtively by guests switching celebrities. As far as I could see, the celebrities totally ignored each other. The whole thing was great.

Since the hostess, even more than the host, is respon-

sible for insuring harmony under her roof, there are two schools I know on how to insure it. One is that if a guest the hostess does not particularly like or is boring has to be invited, he might be fitted in with beloved guests. This way, the hostess will be in a sunny mood and therefore act more cordially toward the moot guest. Or else have all the questionable, but obligatory guests together in one heap. This applies especially to bores, who are good at entertaining each other, I have noticed. I try not to waste my amusing friends on them, because the bores won't know the difference but the amusing friends might find it hard to forgive me. As for bores at someone else's party, never encourage them by listening.

One indispensable factor for any dinner party, small or large: at least one decorative and amusing woman. She will make the men more attentive.

"Guests, however inconvenient, must be honored" was one of the things I learned at my mother's knee, along with the idea that every woman should have a private little nest egg. At my father's knee, I learned that a good digestion and good servants are the foundations upon which to build a pleasant life. How right they both were! Had I but lived by their admirable precepts! *Ehu fugaces!*

The basic way of honoring guests is to feed them well. Nothing else will do: neither Picassos on the wall nor candles amidst the roses on the table; neither tempting female/male morsels at one's side, nor chic ambassadors from the emerging countries will prevent a guest from feeling deprived if his dinner is not good. But why people tear their hair about what to cook for company is something I don't quite understand. It seems to me that in case of doubt, you'd cook something you and your husband like so that at least somebody will be satisfied with the meal.

When it comes to making guest menus, one must rid him/herself of a number of preconceived ideas. Such as that one has to keep up with the Joneses, whoever these mysterious, mystical people are. The only Jones I ever knew was such a sink of iniquity, as well of depravity, and an ocean of nastiness that one would have to be one of Satan's assistants to want to keep up with him. Honoring guests is very different from inviting them in order to put them down, the habit of all too many hosts. What you can do I can do too, is the leitmotiv, and thus we had the fashions in food. There was a year of the Stroganoff and the Beef Wellington; the year of the Bourguignon and the Quiche; now we are deep in Crepes and Chinese cooking. It is all so boring, this food tit-for-tat, when the fun of going out to dinner is to eat something you don't cook and eat at home.

Another idea to throw to the winds with a yell is that a guest meal should be elaborate or gimmicky or long. A meal can be simple and short, with a main dish and perhaps a starch, a salad, fruit and cheese, or a dessert, good bread and butter. Now that people are so diet conscious, I don't think that starters are any longer desirable, unless they are very simple, such as a cup of hot soup with a cold meal. The little goodies served with drinks are quite sufficient for that sort of thing, but more about this later.

Another conception to emancipate oneself from is that it is necessary to serve one or two vegetables, unless they are part of the main dish, as in a boiled dinner. The main dish, French-fashion, can appear perfectly well by itself, if it is handsome. A potato or two, a spoonful of noodles or rice or barley, are quite sufficient if a stretcher is wanted. For that single touch of beauty, a few parsley sprigs will suffice to decorate the dish. All that timing and dishing up of vegetables that don't get appreciated anyhow is a waste of time, energy, and money since the hostess is not a dietician responsible for the health of her charges.

If a vegetable is served because it is particularly good, such as fresh asparagus or new peas or artichokes or fennel, serve it as a course of its own, or best, as a valid first course. If a salad, let it be a splendid, fresh one, not gunked up with fancy dressings, but plainly seasoned with olive oil, vinegar or lemon, and salt and pepper. But let the mixed greens be bone dry by keeping them—washed and drained thoroughly and swaddled in a clean kitchen towel—in the refrigerator for several hours. And if cheese is served, let it be in large hunks so that it is fresh. Better a hunk of Swiss or a slab of Brie (one cheese will do) than half a dozen miserable little pieces of different cheeses, which on a platter look like small orphans abandoned on an empty plain.

The most objectionable of preconceived ideas on how to treat guests well is that the home kitchen has to rival a good restaurant kitchen. Books, magazines, cooking schools all have done their best to make people believe that anybody can be a gourmet restaurant cook. No greater falsehood was ever perpetrated on the gullible aspirers to instant chefdom. It is not possible unless you have undergone a chef's training and have a chef's resources at hand. Even Julia Child—who, heaven knows, has slaved long and probably bitter hours anticipating anything that might go wrong in her recipes, so as to make them even more explicit—does not succeed in making a body master the art of French cooking if the body has not mastered something of the art of cooking before. Cooking is a matter of feeling from experience whether a dish is right, and knowing how to make the inevitable adjustments when the flour does not absorb a liquid the way the recipe says, when the cream does not thicken enough, when the tomatoes are too watery, or when the size and shape of a saucepan are such that a liquid evaporates too quickly or will not evaporate quickly enough.

Home cooks lack not only a chef's skill, but they also do not have access to ingredients needed for gourmet cooking. Take meat and chocolate. The best beef is reserved for fine restaurants, but even when you can get it, which is seldom, a home-cooked roast of beef will never be as flavorful as its restaurant counterpart simply because at home you have small quantities of meat compared to the quantities cooked in a restaurant, which preserve the meat's juiciness. The superb chocolate cake of New York's Four Seasons restaurant cannot be made at home because it needs a special machine to roll out thinly enough the special kind of chocolate needed for the covering. And think of all the other ingredients available in a restaurant kitchen! Shrimps and oysters for decoration of fish dishes; aspics; the various basic sauces, that are combined into other sauces; varieties of vegetables and fruits and so on and on. If a home kitchen can provide all that is necessary for the *haute cuisine*, which poor, deluded gourmets think they can make at home, it is no longer a home kitchen, but a professional one. But such is the vanity of some people that they'll believe anything, including the likelihood of becoming instant Escoffiers.

Mine is the European point of view that those who want to eat fine restaurant food should eat it in its native habitat. In a home, I think, if you want to please true gourmets, serve them the dishes that are best made at home, such as unusual soups like peanut, sorrel or *homemade* chicken noodle soup, now a rarity; pasta or rice cooked just before it is to be eaten and served with fresh vegetable sauces; chicken fricassees; pork chops with home-fried potatoes and homemade hot applesauce spiced up with a little fresh horseradish; boiled dinners with vegetables, each cooked separately rather than in the common pot to preserve their individuality; unusual meat loaves, aromatic with herbs or picturesque with a stuffing of ham; hard-boiled eggs and pistachios as well as marvelous custards poured over ripe, fresh pears; melting rice puddings and all the lovely, homey fruit desserts that go under the name of Apple Betty, Blueberry Grunt, and Summer Pudding. Naturally all must be cooked with more than usual care, timed to perfection, and served at that moment. And the ingredients must be of the freshest, the best to be had, for when you cook simple food, not masked by sauces, not only your care, but the goodness of what you cook is what determines success. And in most cases, goodness means utter freshness, for which there is no substitute.

One of the ways of pleasing guests is to cook the food of their childhood for them. When I do this, I know that for the dish to be successful, I must recreate the remembrance of it rather than the literal dish. If the stuffing in the roast chicken was the memorable thing, I make up an extra batch that is even more flavorful to bake along with the bird, so that I can pile it on the guest's dish. If there were a few raisins in his childhood apple pie, I put in a handful and stress the spices.

Another way of pleasing guests is even simpler. It consists of specializing in a few, well-done nonrestaurant dishes. If they are really good a cook need not look further; guests will be sorely disappointed not to get Melissa's Minestrone or Gustav's Real Creamed Onions or Linda's Cherry Pie and other simple foods.

How fascinating and delicious a nonresturant-type home meal can be was brought home to me and to my fellow guests when a New York hostess, named Alice, prepared a Chinese meal for us. The lady is an expert cook of true Chinese food from all the provinces and on that night she cooked and served to us, in proper consecutive Chinese style, no less than seven courses. None of the guests present, all inveterate Chinese-food fanciers, had ever eaten a single one of these dishes in a restaurant, and they were very different indeed from even the lesser-known pearls of Chinese cooking served in good Chinese restaurants. As admirable as the food was that fact that our hostess was hardly away from the table though the dishes had to be readied at serving time only. How she did it I shall never know; everybody present agreed to the dinner being one of the memorable ones.

When it comes to making the menu, the starting point is the people who will eat it. It is folly to cook anything one is not completely sure of, having done it over and over again. It is equal folly to go in for exotic experiments, no matter how enticing, unless you know your public. Else you may find yourself with the uneaten remains of a great Turkish buffet for sixteen people. A discovery I have also made is that unless I know my guests' tastes, it is unwise to serve fish or seafood as the main course. I once took a poll on this among everyone I knew, and the results came as a great surprise since I thought that everybody would like shrimp, lobster, or sole.

Another thing I have learned is that there are guests and guests. I would never dream of serving lobster, steaks, filet mignon, and the like to the well-heeled, since this is the food they eat mostly anyway. For them are peasant stews, chili, curries, sauerkraut, and sausages. But poor students and struggling couples do get the most expensive food I can afford.

As for desserts and drinks, that is for another chapter.

When I make a menu for guests, I try to imagine what the food will look like. I start with the main dish and imagine it in its full glory, including the platter on which it will be served and the dishes on which it will be eaten. And I keep it simple, with as few garnishes as possible to keep the food appetizing, since overdone garnishing brings to the inward eye busy little fingers that leave no inch of food untouched in their beautifying effort.

Another idea to toss away is that every dish for guests must be home cooked. What matters is perfection, and perfection is largely a matter of money. It can be bought in the form of Scottish smoked salmon and imported fresh truffles to strew over a dish of creamy noodles or scrambled eggs; of a ready-baked big puff paste vol-au-vent from a good bakery, which needs only to be filled with a superlative creamed chicken or whatever one fancies in the way of fillings; of real turtle soup or superior ice creams and pastries. Hostess-cooks in those heavens of good eating—France, Belgium, Switzerland, and Italy—would be considered cheap if they did not buy their pâtés or galantines or antipasti or desserts from the best shops in town, since everybody would know that some good things are beyond any home cook.

I do not go in for formal entertaining because I think it an affectation if you have no servants in the kitchen or serving at the table. In all my life, I've only known one woman, a lovely Belgian girl called Betty, who could alone manage a formal dinner party for twelve, with some help from her husband. But there is a difference between having a friend or two coming to eat with us and having a dinner party. When I can bear it, which is not always, in spite of the practicality of the idea, I have two dinner parties in a row. The house is clean and so is the silver, the flowers are bought and there are always a good many usable leftovers in the form of cheese, crackers, fruit, and what not. It is much simpler to cook the same meal twice, and also less expensive.

What else do I cook for guests? If I want a simple

meal, I make an Italian one. Not lasagne or any of the
heavy pasta dishes; in fact, no pasta at all if there are
more than four people because I just don't have that
many large spaghetti pots, and even if I had them, I
could not manage. If there is a first course it will be a
simple soup—a mushroom broth, a light vegetable soup,
not a minestrone; or a well-seasoned salad of tomatoes
in season, mozzarella, and black olives; or a simple antipasto of prosciutto and melon, or peeled red or green
peppers with anchovies; or a vegetable and egg dish; or
a little cheese soufflé. These come to my mind first.
Sometimes I make a pilaf-type risotto laden with vegetables, the kind that you prepare beforehand and bake
rather than the Milanese risotto. For that you have to
stand at the stove pouring broth and stirring while the
rice cooks. When you are cook and hostess at the same
time, you cannot have dishes that can only be cooked
at the last minute; all you have time for then is to put
the food together. Who likes a hostess slaving in the
kitchen and appearing among her guests with the patient
air of a tired saint?

This first course will be followed by an Italian roast,
a pork or veal Arista, or a chicken dish, with a vegetable
and, if there are very hungry people, an Italian potato
dish. Then, unless we had salad as a first course, a salad
of mixed greens dressed only with olive oil, vinegar, salt
and pepper, sometimes accompanied by cheese, usually
Brie—the cheese depends on the guests and the menu.
Then a choice of desserts, one of which is always some
kind of fresh fruit salad, or fruit in season; the other,
something like a chocolate cake, a Zuppa Inglese, or a
Tart Lemon Cream.

Having cooked this kind of meal all my life, I have

become bored with it. Now that so many people are, or think they are, French gourmet cooks, I have even fewer desires to go in for French cooking, except for some favorite dishes like *ratatouille*, *piperade*, and so on. Not only French, but almost all European cooking bores me, with the exception of Russian and Eastern Mediterranean food. Thus, sometimes I cook a big Ukranian borscht, with homemade kwass, a fermented souring ingredient, which makes all the difference to this truly meal-in-one dish. With this, one needs only a salad, cheese, and dessert.

I am not a lover of casserole cookery, but certain dishes do have to be cooked that way, albeit not over-cooked. For a larger number of guests—eight or ten or twelve—I often make a curry, with its entourage of chutneys and relishes, things I love to make, or another spicy dish like a Moroccan casserole or chili which can be made in advance. This will be followed by a salad and cheese and dessert.

Depending on how I feel (which is not a way of speech, but a reality with me since I have had two total hip replacements, after years of walking on two sticks and crutches and being practically immobile), I make a buffet or sit the people, with placecards around the table. The food is on the sideboard, for each to help himself; the salad, cheese, and plates on a little table, and the dessert comes in after my husband and I have cleared the table down to the salt and pepper, with the help of a little rolling serving cart. I hate to have people help me do this, as they so often do, meaning it kindly when they see my distress, especially when they will stack the dishes at the table. One of the things I learned at my mother's knee, and my own children learned at my knee, is that stacking plates at the table is disgusting. Even if it takes ages, dirty plates have to be carried out, one in each hand, or at worst, piled on top of each other on the cart where they are at least not so visible. All my life I have had a horror of sitting and looking at a plate one has finished with; the sight has ruined many a dinner party for me.

After we've finished eating, plates and food go back into the kitchen, there to stay late at night or until the morning when I feel like washing up. Coffee and liqueurs are brought in on trays that I have readied beforehand, and then the kitchen door is closed. All this is neither difficult nor laborious since I've gotten over wanting to impress my guests. After all, even for the fanciest of guests, homecooked meals do not have to be the equivalent of the wedding luncheon of President Grant's daughter, held at the White House on May 21, 1874, with the following menu: Soft-shelled Crabs on Toast; Chicken Croquettes with Green Peas; Lamb Cutlets with Tartar Sauce; Aspic of Beef Tongue; Woodcock and Snipe on Toast; Salad with Mayonnaise; Strawberries with Cream; Orange Baskets Garnished with Strawberries; Charlotte Russe; Nesselrode Pudding; Blancmange; Ice Cream Garnished with Preserved Fruits; Water Ices; Wedding Cake; Small Fancy Cakes; Roman Punch, Chocolate and Coffee.

Champagne Oysters

(1 serving)

Luxury restaurants serve this dish which, unlike almost all luxury restaurant dishes, can be made at home without much trouble. You need not use a vintage champagne, but it should be a good, *dry* one. It is the flavor that makes the dish, not the bubbles.

6 fresh raw oysters, opened
⅓ cup dry champagne
1 shallot, minced
1 bouquet garni (½ bay leaf, 2 sprigs parsley, and ¼ teaspoon dried thyme tied in a cheesecloth bag)

2 tablespoons butter, at room temperature, cut into pieces

Preheat the oven to slow (300°F.).

Drain the oyster juice into a small saucepan. Arrange the oysters side by side in a shallow baking dish. To the oyster juice, add the champagne, the shallot, and the bouquet garni. Cook over medium heat until reduced to about one-half. With a wire whisk, beat in the butter. Keep hot over lowest possible heat, if necessary on an asbestos pad placed over the source of heat. Place the oysters in the oven. Cook for about 5 minutes or only until they are warm and starting to plump. Remove from oven. Strain the sauce through a small wire strainer directly over the oysters. Serve immediately, with the remaining champagne as a drink.

Note: Or use a split which holds about ¾ cup and drink what is left over while you cook.

Cream of Lettuce Soup

(4–5 servings)

2 tablespoons butter
1 large head Romaine
    lettuce, trimmed,
    washed and shredded
12 spring or green onions,
    sliced
6 cups chicken
    consommé

Salt
Freshly ground pepper
2 tablespoons cornstarch
2 tablespoons water
2 egg yolks
⅓ cup heavy cream
2 tablespoons minced
    parsley or chervil

Combine the butter, the lettuce, and the spring onions in a deep saucepan. Over medium heat, and stirring frequently, cook for about 5 minutes or until the lettuce is wilted. Add the consommé and season with salt and pepper to taste. Bring to the boiling point. Lower heat to simmer. Cook covered for about 15 minutes, stirring occasionally. Mix the cornstarch with the water to a smooth paste. Stir into the soup. Cook without a cover for 3–4 minutes longer. Puree the soup in a blender or strain through a foodmill. Return to very low heat and heat through. Beat together the egg yolks with the cream. Stir a couple of spoonfuls of the hot soup into the egg mixture. Stir the egg mixture into the soup and heat through for a minute or so. Do not let the soup boil. Serve hot, with the parsley sprinkled over the soup.

Yogurt Soup

(5–6 servings)

This is a thin, tart soup, good with a dinner that features roast meats. It should be served very hot.

2 cups plain yogurt
6 cups very hot beef
    bouillon
1 tablespoon butter
1 tablespoon flour

2 tablespoons chopped
    fresh mint or 1
    tablespoon dried
    mint

Stir the yogurt into the beef bouillon. Keep hot but do not boil or the soup will curdle. In another small saucepan, melt the butter and stir in the flour. Over very low heat, cook, stirring constantly, for about 2 minutes. This removes the raw flour flavor. Do not brown. Stir the flour mixture slowly into the hot yogurt–bouillon. Bring to one quick boil—no more—stirring constantly. Just before serving, sprinkle with mint.

Mushroom Soup

(6 servings)

4 tablespoons butter
4 tablespoons flour
8 cups hot chicken
    bouillon
Salt

Freshly ground pepper
1 pound fresh
    mushrooms, minced
¼ teaspoon ground
    cardamon or nutmeg

Heat the butter in the top of a double boiler and stir in the flour. Cook, stirring constantly, for about 2 minutes. Stir in the chicken bouillon and salt and pepper to taste. Cook, stirring constantly, until the soup begins to thicken. Add the mushrooms and the cardamon. Bring to the boiling point. Set the top of the double boiler over the bottom, filled with simmering, not boiling hot water. Cook covered, stirring occasionally, for about 20 minutes. Serve as is or puree in blender.

Salmon Baked in Champagne
(6 servings)

Use a good, dry champagne, but do not use a superior vintage which is too good for cooking. These are champagne bottle sizes and contents: Split (6.4 oz.) about ¾ cup; Tenth (⅖ pt., 12.8 oz.) about 1½ cups; Fifth (⅘ qt., 25.6 oz.) about 3 cups; Magnum (52 oz.) about 6½ cups; Jeroboam (104 oz.) about 13 cups.

The cooking time for salmon steaks varies according to thickness. Steaks 1-inch thick cook for 20 minutes in a preheated slow oven (325°F.) and steaks that are 2-inches thick for 30 minutes.

6 fresh salmon steaks, weighing 2½ to 3 pounds	¼ cup butter, cut into pieces
Salt	1½ cups dry champagne
Freshly ground pepper	½ cup heavy cream

Place the steaks in a buttered shallow baking dish. Sprinkle with salt and pepper. Dot with the butter. Pour the champagne over the fish. Cook in a preheated slow oven (325°F.), according to thickness as specified above. Baste the fish frequently with the pan juices. Keep a serving dish warm in or on the stove. When the fish is just tender, remove it carefully to the serving dish. Cover the dish and keep hot. Pour the pan juices into a

small saucepan. Bring to the boiling point and cook
until reduced to about one-half. Reduce the heat and
stir in the cream. Simmer until the cream is just heated
through but do not boil. Check the seasonings and pour
the sauce over the fish. Serve immediately, with parsleyed new potatoes.

Mango Chicken

(4–6 servings)

A mildly exotic dish which will not frighten those
who do not like exotic food. Apricots or papaya may be
used instead of fresh mangoes, but fresh mangoes are
best. They can be bought in Latin groceries and at most
fruit markets.

1 4–5 pound roasting
   chicken, cut into
   pieces
2 tablespoons butter
2 tablespoons oil
2 large or 4 medium
   onions, thinly sliced
1–2 mangoes, depending on
   size, peeled and
   chopped (about 2–3
   cups pulp)
or
2 cups fresh or canned
   and drained, stoned
   mashed apricots or 1
   cup dried apricots,
   plumped in
   lukewarm water for
   1 hour

or
2–3 cups peeled, seeded,
   and diced papaya

¼ cup mango chutney
⅔ cup chicken bouillon
   or water
Salt
Freshly ground pepper
⅛ teaspoon ground
   nutmeg
Rind of 1 lime or
   lemon, green or
   yellow part only
Juice of 1 lime or
   lemon

Remove every trace of fat from the chicken. Remove the skin. Wash and pat dry. Heat the butter and the oil in a large skillet. Cook the chicken in it until all the pieces are golden brown on all sides. Transfer them to a heavy casserole. Add the onions to the skillet. Cook over low heat, stirring frequently, until they are very soft but still white. Add the mango or other fruit and the mango chutney. Raise the heat to medium and cook, stirring all the time, for about 3 minutes. Stir in the chicken bouillon. Season with salt and pepper to taste and add the nutmeg. Pour the sauce over the chicken and add the lime rind. Cover. Cook in a preheated moderate oven (350°F.) for about 45 minutes or until the chicken is tender. Clear the chicken pieces free of the fruit and onions and transfer to a hot serving platter. Keep hot. Puree the sauce in a blender and stir in the lime juice. Pour the sauce over the chicken pieces. Serve with Yellow Pilaf and Puree of Broccoli, with assorted relishes on the side.

Note: You may serve the dish without pureeing the sauce, but it is better with a pureed sauce. You may have to adjust the sauce in cooking. If it is in danger of scorching because too thick, add a little more bouillon or water.

Chicken Pilaf

(4–5 servings)

Easy and good for unexpected guests

2 tablespoons minced onion	½ teaspoon pepper
½ cup butter	¼ teaspoon ground coriander or thyme
2 cups cooked chicken, cut into strips (canned chicken is fine)	2 cups rice
	4 cups boiling chicken bouillon
⅓ cup walnuts, coarsely chopped	2 medium tomatoes, peeled, seeded, and chopped
1 teaspoon salt	

Sauté the onion in the hot butter until it is soft and golden. Add the chicken and cook 3 minutes over low heat, stirring constantly. Add the walnuts and cook 2 minutes longer. Season with salt, pepper, and coriander. Add the rice and cook over medium heat 5 minutes, stirring constantly. Pour in the boiling chicken bouillon and stir in the tomatoes. Cover tightly and cook over the lowest possible heat about 20 minutes or until the rice is cooked and the liquid completely absorbed. Turn off the heat and let stand 5 minutes before serving.

Spicy Moroccan Lamb Casserole

(6 servings)

This dish has the virtue of being easy to make (ahead of time so that it only has to be reheated), of being different, and of being inexpensive. Serve it with a pilaf of either rice or cracked wheat (bulgur, to be bought at

Eastern groceries) and leeks vinaigrette (poached leeks—wash them many times, cut into finger lengths, cover with French dressing, and chill).

2 tablespoons butter
2 pounds lean boneless lamb, cut into 2-inch strips
1 large onion, minced
2 garlic cloves, mashed
2 tablespoons flour
1½ cups chicken or beef consommé
½ teaspoon saffron
½ teaspoon cardamon seeds or ground cardamon
½ teaspoon ground ginger
1 teaspoon ground cinnamon
1 cup golden raisins
Salt
Freshly ground pepper
2 or 3 small yellow or zucchini squash, peeled and cut into small cubes
Juice of 1 large lemon

Heat the butter in a skillet. Place the lamb in it and brown well on all sides. Transfer the lamb to a three-quart casserole. Cook the onion and garlic in the skillet juices until the onion is soft. Stir in the flour and cook, stirring constantly, for three more minutes. The mixture should be medium brown. Add to the casserole together with the consommé, the saffron, cardamon, ginger, cinnamon, raisins, and salt and pepper to taste. Mix well. Simmer covered, over very low heat, stirring occasionally, for about 30 minutes or until the meat is almost tender. Add the squash and cook until the meat and squash are tender. Remove the casserole from the heat and stir in the lemon juice.

Note: If you are preparing this ahead of time, cook until the squash should be added. Refrigerate, heat up gently at serving, put in the squash, and finish cooking.

Jean Hewitt's Fresh Ham

(15–24 servings)

1 10–14 pound fresh
   pork leg (fresh
   ham), skin removed
1 bottle dry red wine,
   about 3⅓ cups
¾ cup vinegar
3 carrots, cut into 1-inch
   pieces
2 small onions
4 whole cloves
6 shallots, finely chopped
4 garlic cloves, finely
   chopped

1 teaspoon grated lemon
   rind
2 ribs celery, cut into
   1-inch pieces
4 sprigs parsley
3 bay leaves, crumbled
2 teaspoons ground
   thyme
½ teaspoon ground
   marjoram
12 whole peppercorns
6 juniper berries
3 teaspoons salt

Slash the fat down to the meat level in lines about 1 inch apart and pierce with a fork down into the flesh between the fat and on the underside.

Combine the remaining ingredients in a saucepan and bring to the boiling point. Boil 5 minutes and cool.

Place the fresh ham in a large pottery bowl or porcelainized iron kettle or casserole (do not use aluminum), and pour the cooked marinade over the ham. Cover and refrigerate at least four days or up to a week, turning twice a day.

When ready to cook the ham, preheat the oven to slow (325°F.).

Drain the ham and scrape off all the vegetable or herb pieces. Wipe dry with a paper towel. Place on a rack in a shallow roasting pan and roast about 35 minutes a pound or until the internal temperature is 185°F. (5½ to 7½ hours). If the fat begins to brown too much, it can be protected with a tent of aluminum foil. Serve hot or, if preferred, cold.

Marinade for Indifferent Roast Beef

(About 1 cup for a 3–4 pound roast)

½ cup light soy sauce
¼ cup salad oil
½ cup dry sherry
 6 scallions, chopped
 2 large garlic cloves,
      chopped

2 bay leaves
1 beef roast, weighing
      about 3 to 3⅓
      pounds

Combine all the ingredients in a bowl (do not use aluminum) and mix well. Soak the meat in it for from 4 hours to 2 days, turning occasionally to make sure that all sides are well coated with the marinade. Drain and strain marinade and reserve it. Remove any clinging pieces of scallions, garlic, or bay leaves from the roast. Roast in the usual manner, basting occasionally with the reserved marinade.

Note: This marinade is also good for any skewered meats.

Flemish Asparagus

(3–4 servings)

During the fresh asparagus season, I often serve my guests asparagus as a main dish, followed by cheese and salad and a substantial dessert such as a chocolate cake. It goes without saying that there should be lots of asparagus for each diner—at the least, ¾ of a pound.

3 pounds asparagus, evenly stemmed	Freshly ground pepper
4 hard-cooked eggs, shelled and mashed	1 tablespoon fresh lemon juice
1 cup butter, melted Salt	2 tablespoons minced parsley

Trim the asparagus and peel the stems with a rotating vegetable peeler. With kitchen string, tie 6–10 stems, depending on thickness, into bunches. Fill the bottom of a double boiler with 3–4 inches of cold, lightly salted, water. Place the asparagus bundles in it; the water should reach halfway up their stems. Invert the top of the double boiler over the asparagus. Or use a saucepan deep enough to let the asparagus stand upright. Bring to the boiling point. Cook until just tender but still crisp. Lift the asparagus bundles out with two forks and drain on paper towel. Line a serving platter with a linen table napkin. Place the asparagus bundles on it and cut the string. Throw away the string. The napkin will absorb any remaining moisture. Keep warm. While the asparagus is cooking, make the sauce. Combine the mashed eggs, the butter, salt and pepper, the lemon juice, and the parsley in a small saucepan. Over low heat, heat through thoroughly but do not boil. Pour into a sauceboat and serve with the asparagus.

Broccoli Puree

This is a practical and delicious restaurant idea. Restaurants have trouble serving vegetables because these must be freshly cooked to be good, and this is not always practical. A pureed vegetable stays appetizing and looks pretty. This method applies to other vegetables such as carrots, spinach, green beans, peas, lima beans, etc. You may add any flavoring herb you wish; I don't, because I like the pure vegetable flavor.

Broccoli	Cream (optional)
Boiling water	Freshly ground pepper
Salt	Butter

Wash and cut the broccoli into very small pieces. Put them into a saucepan and add boiling water to cover. Bring to the boiling point, lower the heat, and cook covered until the broccoli are very soft and mushy. Check the moisture; there should be just enough water to prevent the vegetable from sticking and burning. Puree the broccoli and their cooking liquid in the blender, or force them through a food mill. If the broccoli are too thick to puree, add a little cream or milk, but not too much or the puree will be soupy. Return to the saucepan and season with salt and pepper. Add a tablespoon or so of butter. Heat through and serve very hot.

Note: If the broccoli puree is soupy, cook it over medium heat to dry it out. Stir constantly. The vegetable will form little volcanoes and spatter as it dries out.

Watercress, Belgian Endive, and Mushroom Salad

(4–6 servings)

1 large bunch watercress
4 large Belgian endives,
    cut into long thin
    strips
6–12 fresh mushrooms,
    depending on size
Juice of 2 lemons or
    more to taste

⅓ cup olive oil or more
    to taste
1 teaspoon Dijon
    mustard
Salt
Freshly ground pepper

Wash the watercress and trim off all the big stems. Shake dry. Place the watercress on the bottom of a salad bowl. Wash and drain the endives and lay them on the watercress. Slice the mushrooms and put them on the Belgian endives. Combine the lemon juice, the olive oil, the mustard, and salt and pepper to taste and mix well. Pour the dressing over the salad. Toss at the table.

Cucumber Bhurta

(4 servings)

This may be as mild or as hot as you like

4 cucumbers   1 cup yogurt
   Salt   Tabasco

Peel the cucumbers and slice them wafer-thin. This is best done with a vegetable slicer. Put them into a bowl and sprinkle them heavily with salt. Cover the bowl and let stand at room temperature for 2 hours or overnight in the refrigerator. The salt will draw the water from the cucumbers and make them crisp. Drain the cucumbers. Rinse them under running water to get rid of excess salt. Drain and squeeze them dry. Put into a serving dish. Add the yogurt and Tabasco to taste and mix thoroughly. Refrigerate for at least 4 hours to let the cucumbers chill and crisp.

Tart Apple Chutney

(About 12 cups)

2 pounds tart green
   apples (must be tart
   green apples),
   peeled and cured
4 medium onions (about
   1 pound), peeled
   and chopped
4 garlic cloves, peeled
   and chopped
½ pound glacé orange
   peel, chopped
1 box golden raisins
   (about 1 pound)
1 box currants (about 1
   pound)

1 pound dark brown
   sugar
1 quart cider vinegar
1–3 tablespoons curry
   powder, or to taste
1 3-inch piece fresh
   ginger, peeled, or 1
   tablespoon ground
   ginger
1½ teaspoons ground
   cloves
1 teaspoon ground
   cinnamon
1 tablespoon salt

Combine the apples, the onions, the garlic, and the
orange peel on a chopping board. Chop together with a
heavy knife or an onion chopper until the mixture is the
size of small lima beans. Or push through the coarse
knife of a meat grinder; I prefer the former method for
texture in the finished product. Put the chopped mixture
into a large kettle. Add all the other ingredients and mix
well. Bring to the boiling point, stirring to prevent burning. Lower heat to very low. Simmer without cover for
1 to 2 hours (two is better) or until the mixture is
thick. Stir frequently to prevent sticking. Pack into sterilized jars and seal. Or keep in the refrigerator. Let the
chutney age for one week for a better taste.

Dried Apricot and Date Chutney

(About 10 cups)

1 pound dried apricots,
    or 2 pounds fresh,
    stoned
2 pounds stoned dates
¼ pound fresh green
    ginger, peeled, or ½
    pound preserved
    ginger, with syrup

3 garlic cloves
3 tablespoons salt
1 pound golden raisins
1 pound white or brown
    sugar
    White or cider vinegar
    to cover

If the apricots are dried, soak them in water to cover for 2–4 hours or until soft and plump. Chop together into fairly small pieces the apricots, the dates, and the ginger. Crush the garlic and mix it with the salt. Turn the fruit, the garlic salt, the raisins, and the sugar into a saucepan. Mix thoroughly. Add the vinegar and mix well again. Bring to the boiling point, stirring frequently. Lower heat immediately to simmer. Cook the chutney without a cover over low heat until thick and transparent, about 2 hours. Stir frequently. Store in sterilized or refrigerator jars.

Mango and Banana Chutney

(About 5 cups)

3 mangoes, each
   weighing
   approximately 1
   pound
1 medium onion, minced
1 garlic clove, minced
1 cup golden raisins
5 large bananas, sliced
2 tablespoons finely
   chopped fresh ginger
   or 1 tablespoon
   ground ginger or
   ginger to taste

1 cup sugar
1 cup cider vinegar
1 tablespoon salt
½ teaspoon Tabasco or
   hot sauce to taste

Peel the mangoes, remove the flesh from the pit, and chop into pieces. Put the mangoes, the onion, the garlic clove, the raisins, the bananas, and the ginger into a heavy saucepan. Dissolve the sugar in the vinegar and stir in the salt and Tabasco or hot sauce. Pour the mixture over the fruit and mix well. Bring to the boiling point and lower heat to simmer. Cook, stirring frequently, over very low heat for about 2 hours or until the mixture is thick and cooked down.

Note: Instead of mangoes you may use 1 pound tart cooking apples, peeled, cored, and chopped, or hard pears, peeled, cored, and chopped.

Desserts for Guests

IT's BEEN MY experience with guests that many will tell me that they don't eat desserts. Yet even these Spartans will plunge in with the best when they are confronted with a delicious concoction. Granted it must be a worthwhile dessert. Otherwise it is a waste of time to make and a waste of good calories to eat, calories that would be far more amusingly spent on liquid cheer.

Even the people who say they never eat dessert, and heaven knows, they might be truthful, feel deprived if you don't give them dessert at a dinner party, or at least, offer them the chance of turning it down. Usually, after some decorous reluctance, they will take a little piece or a spoonful of dessert at first, and then come back; I am talking of sophisticated eaters, not of guzzlers. I think this shows that dessert is a totally different eating experience—an emotional, sensuous one—since one has the freedom of choice because it is not a course that must be eaten for nutrition's sake. Eating dessert is rewarding oneself, eating for fun, so much so that many people will hold off eating dessert until they are less full and can enjoy it to the last morsel.

Making desserts is an equally pleasurable experience to most women, including myself. It is creative because desserts rely largely on eye appeal rather than on the aroma which makes nondessert courses mouthwatering— that of fresh bread, roast beef, coffee. Stew is an unattractive-looking dish, but it captivates with an odor which promises flavor. But a messy-looking chocolate cake, mashed-up strawberries (one of the few desserts that have aroma), even if we know that they will taste good, will not attract us. I believe that with food, you have to have either aroma or appearance in a dish.

If desserts fill an emotional need in the eater and in the maker, it is interesting to note that favorite desserts usually have to contain something creamy, soft, and yielding. Apple pie is served à la mode with ice cream; ice cream is the favorite of all desserts; icings soften cakes; and whipped cream goes wherever possible. Fruit is the exception in this wish for creaminess, but fruit is combined with soft puddings and gelatins, all yielding foods.

Dessert, like other cooking, seems to have narrowed down to simple things for everyday—puddings, gelatins, box cakes, boughten pies, ice cream, cookies, and refrigerator cakes. Company is another deal—here we create looks as much as flavor, demanding attention and love from those for whom the dessert was made because we ourselves put so much attention and love into making it. Few women expect to be loved for a pot roast, but they will be disappointed if they are not loved for their cake. And on the occasions when domestic love has to be shown with a bang—on birthdays, anniversaries, weddings, holidays—it is shown with a dessert, namely a cake, one of the very oldest forms of festive food. It is also interesting to note that the "company special" most women have in their cooking repertoire is usually a dessert, made from a recipe rather than memory. Of course I'm talking of the majority of American women, not the select souls who find fulfillment in knowing how to bone a chicken.

Over the years, I've also noticed that far too many

so-called educated women underestimate the power of
a good dessert on their men. Not for nothing does the
song inquire if she can bake a cherry pie. Almost all men
are natural dessert lovers. Desserts are part of the lower
and truer nature of men; that does not mean they will
always confess to this fact. No, they like to be coaxed
and they like to have it pointed out to them that the
stupendous creation before their greedy little eyes was
made for them alone. Women are far more straightforward in their approach to desserts. They'll say that
they darn well know they shouldn't, but that they will
and let it go at that.

Great desserts do not have to be complicated. Some,
made with fruit, are extremely simple. I am thinking of
fresh pineapple sprinkled with sugar and Kirsch, the perfect finale for a rich or exotic dinner, or of a dish of
fresh strawberries coated with fresh or even frozen raspberries pureed in a blender. Heavy unwhipped and unsweetened cream is good with this, as with a compote of
fresh pears cooked in a vanilla syrup. Marvelous too are
fresh dark cherries, pitted, of course (there are cherry
pitters on the market, descendants of those invented by
the Shakers), sprinkled with a little sugar, and brought
to a quick boil to set their juices flowing. This instant
way of cooking fruit is also excellent with fresh purple
plums. These fruit desserts should be served ice cold,
with heavy, barely sweetened cream for those who like it.

A man I once knew, a true dessert lover, had an interesting theory on the subject. He said that desserts are
closely linked with sex. Every good meal should be followed by a sweet and by dancing girls, the latter practice
well-known to the gourmets among the ancient Egyp-
tians, Greeks, Romans and to the Persians and other
bon vivants of the Near East. Now that dancing girls are

not easy to come by in most households, however hospitably inclined, the stress has to be put on dessert, which should be rich and preferably chocolate, the sexiest sweet of them all. Indeed it is true that no people in the world are as preoccupied with sex as Americans, and no other country loves and makes so many chocolate desserts as the United States, where chocolate is the number one flavor for sweet things. An American-style, many-layered, thickly frosted devil's food cake will establish one as a lovable homebody. Chocolate mousse, on the other hand, will give one the air of a cosmopolite, and so does the French chocolate cake and mousse for which recipes follow. Both are easy and nearly foolproof.

Dark Chocolate Mousse

(6–8 servings)

To succeed, this dessert must be made and chilled at least twelve hours, but preferably twenty-four hours before it will be eaten. Otherwise it will not have the right consistency.

4 squares (4 ounces) unsweetened baking chocolate	¼ cup water or coffee
	5 eggs, separated
¾ cup superfine sugar, preferably, or ordinary sugar	1½ teaspoons vanilla flavoring, or 1–2 tablespoons brandy, rum, or Kirsch

Combine the chocolate, sugar, and water or coffee in the top of a double boiler. Cook, stirring all the time, over—not in—boiling water until the chocolate is melted and smooth. Remove from the heat, but leave top in double boiler. Beat in the egg yolks, one at a time, beating well after each addition. Remove top of double boiler from the bottom and cool. When cool, stir in the flavoring. Beat the egg whites until stiff but not dry. Fold the egg whites gently into the chocolate mixture. Pour into individual little white soufflé dishes (the classic way) or into a serving bowl. Cover the dishes or the bowl with plastic wrap so that the mousse won't absorb the refrigerator odors during its stay there. Chill no less than 12 hours.

Note: The mousse may be served with a sprinkling of chopped salted pistachios—the salt brings out the chocolate flavor. Or with a dollop of sour or sweet whipped cream. Or, best, as is.

French Chocolate Cake

(6–8 servings)

A rich, rather flat, and dense cake

4 squares (4 ounces)
    unsweetened baking
    chocolate
4 tablespoons water or
    coffee
½ cup sugar
½ cup (1 stick) softened
    butter, cut into
    pieces
4 eggs, separated
⅓ cup finely ground
    blanched almonds

1½ teaspoons vanilla
    flavoring or 1
    tablespoon brandy,
    rum, or Kirsch
⅓ cup sifted all-purpose
    flour
1 cup heavy cream,
    whipped with 1
    tablespoon sugar
Candied violets

Set the oven to medium, at 350°F. Grease and flour two round 8-inch layer cake pans. Put the chocolate in the top of a double boiler, add the water and sugar, and cook over hot, not boiling, water until the chocolate is completely melted. Stir frequently. Remove the double boiler from the heat, but keep the top over the hot water. Stir the butter, piece by piece, into the chocolate, but do not add the next piece of butter until the preceding one is totally melted. Remove the top of the double boiler from the bottom and cool the contents. Add the egg yolks, one at a time, beating well after each addition. Blend in the nuts and the flavoring. Gradually stir in the flour and mix well. Beat the egg whites until stiff and fold them gently into the batter. Spoon the batter into the prepared cake pans. Bake for about 20 minutes or until a knife (or a cake tester or a skewer) inserted in the middle of the cake comes out clean. Do not overbake; the cake should be on the moist side. Cool the layers in their pans for about 5 minutes; turn out of the pans and cool completely. Just before serving time, whip the cream with the sugar. Spread about ⅓ of the whipped cream on one layer and top with the other. Spread the remaining whipped cream over the top and sides of the cake. Decorate with the candied violets, which can be bought, imported from France, in any gourmet store.

Note: The layers may also be sandwiched together with a tart jam or jelly, such as red currant or apricot, and ice with the following frosting:

Glossy Chocolate Frosting

(About 2¼ cups)

3 tablespoons butter
3 squares (3 ounces) unsweetened baking chocolate
2 cups sifted confectioners' sugar

¼ teaspoon salt
¼ cup milk
1–2 tablespoons brandy, rum, or Kirsch

Combine the butter and the chocolate in a saucepan. Over very low heat, stirring constantly, cook until melted. Stir in the sugar, the salt, and the milk. Beat until smooth and remove from heat. Place the saucepan with the frosting into a pan filled with water and ice. Beat the frosting until of spreading consistency. Stir in the liqueur. Spread over 1 layer, top with the second layer. and spread over top and sides of the cake.

Mother Hazelton's Tart Lemon Pudding

(6 servings)

Lemon puddings are no rarity; the trick is to use lots of freshly squeezed lemon juice so that the pudding will be tart.

3 large or 4 small eggs, separated
Grated rind of 1 large or 2 small lemons
½ cup sugar
½ cup fresh lemon juice
1 tablespoon (1 envelope) unflavored gelatin

¼ cup water
1 cup heavy cream, whipped
Candied violets, strawberries or mandarin orange slices for decoration

Beat the egg yolks until light. All of the beating is best done in an electric blender. Beat in the lemon rind. Beat in the sugar, 2 tablespoons at a time, beating well after each addition. Beat in the lemon juice. Sprinkle the gelatin over the water and stir to mix. Let stand a few minutes, then set over hot water to liquefy. Stir into the egg mixture. Chill until just beginning to set. Fold in the whipped cream. Beat the egg whites until stiff and fold into the cream. Chill thoroughly before serving in a pretty dish, decorated with either candied violets, fresh strawberries, or mandarin orange slices.

Brandy Alexander Pie

(6–8 servings)

One of the favorite desserts of *New York Times* readers, for which they keep on asking.

1 envelope unflavored gelatin	¼ cup crème de cacao
½ cup cold water	2 cups heavy cream, whipped
⅔ cup sugar	1 nine-inch graham cracker crust
⅛ teaspoon salt	Chocolate curls for garnish
3 eggs, separated	
¼ cup cognac	

Sprinkle the gelatin over the cold water in a saucepan. Add ⅓ cup of the sugar, the salt, and the egg yolks. Stir to blend. Place the saucepan over low heat, stirring all the while until the gelatin dissolves and melts, and the mixture thickens. Do not boil. Remove the saucepan from the heat and stir in the cognac and the crème de cacao. Chill until the mixture is getting thick and starts to mound slightly. It must not be too firm. Beat the egg whites until stiff. Gradually beat in the remaining sugar. Fold the egg white mixture into the thickened gelatin mixture. Fold in 1 cup of the whipped cream. Spoon into the crust. Chill several hours or overnight. At serving time, garnish with the remaining cream and chocolate curls.

Brandy Cake

3 large eggs
1 cup sugar
1 teaspoon ground mace
Grated rind of 2 lemons
1 cup fine dry
    breadcrumbs

¾ cup good-quality
    brandy
1⅔ cups ground, blanched
    almonds

Beat the eggs and the sugar until light. Beat in the mace and the lemon rind. Stir in alternately the breadcrumbs and the brandy. Beat in the almonds. Turn the batter into a well-greased and floured 8-inch springform pan. Bake in a preheated moderate oven (350°F.) for 30 to 35 minutes or until the cake tests done. Loosen the sides of the springform pan and cool the cake. When cool, remove the pan bottom. Ice the cake with Lemon Icing (1 cup), and if wanted, decorate with toasted almond halves.

Lemon Icing

For each cup of sifted confectioners' sugar, stir in gradually 1 to 2 tablespoons fresh lemon juice, beating to spreading consistency.

Mango Fool

(8–10 servings)

Impressive, beautifully golden, popular, and easy

5 ripe mangoes (each weighing approximately 1 pound)
2 envelopes unflavored gelatin
¼ cup hot water

Juice of 1 lemon or lime, or more to taste
½ teaspoon ground ginger
Sugar to taste
1 cup heavy cream, whipped

Peel the mangoes and strip the flesh off the flat stone which sits in the fruit's middle. You need a sharp knife for this. Do the job over a bowl to catch the juices. Chop the mangoes and put half of them into a blender container. Dissolve the gelatin in the hot water and add it to the mangoes. Add the lemon juice, the ginger, and a few tablespoons of sugar. Blend and pour back into the bowl. Blend the remaining mangoes and add them to the first mixture. Mix thoroughly. Taste; add more sugar and more lemon juice and ginger if needed. Mix again thoroughly. Fold the whipped cream into the mangoes. Pour into a glass bowl. Cover and chill thoroughly before serving. Serve with dry cookies or cake.

Note: Since this is a rich, creamy mixture, the cookies should best be bland almond or nut crisps.

Apple Betty

(8–10 servings)

Easy, totally delicious hot apple dessert

3 pounds tart apples
(about 9 medium
apples)
Water with lemon
juice or salt
10 tablespoons butter (1
stick plus 2
tablespoons)

10 tablespoons sugar
1 cup fresh white
breadcrumbs
Grated rind of 1 lemon
Heavy cream or vanilla
ice cream for 8–10
people

Peel the apples, core them, and cut them into thin slices. As you prepare the apples, drop the ready pieces into a bowl with water and about 1 tablespoon of lemon juice or salt, to prevent them from turning dark. Melt 8 tablespoons (1 stick) of the butter and pour it into a bowl. Drain the apples. Add the apples and toss them to coat with the butter. Add 6 tablespoons of the sugar and half of the breadcrumbs. Toss thoroughly. Turn the mixture into a 2- or 2½-quart baking dish. Combine the remaining sugar and breadcrumbs and grated lemon rind and sprinkle them over the apples. Cut the remaining 2 tablespoons of butter into small pieces and dot the apples with them. Bake in a preheated hot oven (400°F.) for about 40 minutes. Serve with cream or vanilla ice cream.

Dried Apricot Pineapple Compote

(4–6 servings)

If the dried apricots are soaked in water or in other liquid (orange juice, apricot nectar, pineapple juice, etc.) for a long enough time, they soften sufficiently and don't have to be cooked. This way, they are far more flavorful.

1 cup dried apricots
1 cup water
1 cup orange juice
1 fresh pineapple
1 cup sugar

Grated rind of 1 large
   orange
¼ cup Kirsch, rum, or
   brandy (optional)

Soak the apricots overnight or for 24 hours in the combined water and orange juice. Peel and cut the pineapple into bite-sized pieces. Drain the apricots. Measure their liquid. There should be 2 cups. If there are not, make up the difference with water. Combine the apricot liquid and the sugar in a saucepan. Cook over low heat without a cover for 2–5 minutes. Remove from heat and stir in the orange rind and the Kirsch. Combine the apricots and the pineapple in a glass serving dish. Pour the hot liquid over the fruit. Chill thoroughly before serving with macaroons.

Drinks for Guests

IF LIFE HAS taught me anything, it has taught me that I am not the person to give drink parties. Cocktail parties are fine for hostesses who can have the whole affair catered so that they can be guests at their own parties. To begin with, for more than eight or ten people you have to have a bartender. Since no host can keep up with the consumption of liquor, your party will soon be a shambles without a bartender. If the guests pour themselves, they will invariably overpour, which would be all right if this did not slosh them sooner than seemly, whereas the bartender can make judicious mixtures. Then consider the food, of which there is seldom enough in quantity and kind. The horror of making cocktail party food is great and really a complete waste of time since the food serves only as a blotter for the booze. But it has to be, and the more substantial, the better. I applaud hostesses who serve good solid stomach liners, like roast meats, savory pies, ready-made open sandwiches, stuffed eggs, cups of robust soups, and best still, baked potatoes in their jackets ready to eat with plenty of butter, salt and pepper. Protein foods are needed for drink parties if the guests are not to succumb to alcohol, and they should be passed around constantly.

These hard-drink parties are not for me, since I have no social obligations that can be paid off this way. I find drinking sessions at best depressing, having been brought up in the unalterable axiom that men do not get drunk in front of women, and that women certainly do not get drunk themselves. I have learned to make compromises of course, since I live in America, and I no longer regard a certain alcoholic jollity, even in myself, as the crime of crimes as I used to. But still . . .

I invite people only for dinner, any number from six to ten. Naturally, they do get whatever they want to drink, following the old rule of the first drink strong, the other ones weaker. Strong drink is needed to break the ice between strangers, and it is not a bad idea either when I think of all the European dinner parties I've sat through, when a mild aperitif did not break the ice between strangers. My concession to cocktail goodies is minimal since there will be a good dinner to follow and since most people feel it is better to consume liquid rather than cocktail-food calories. But that is only half the reason: the other half is that I loathe making petty little foods that show the tender loving care of my industrious hands. Thus, at best, I may serve Stuffed Raw Mushrooms, which are no sweat, or a boughten pâté spread on crackers, or nuts, fritos and the like, and just as often, nothing at all.

Another reason for the absence of cocktail nibbles in my house is that I serve dinner after, let us say, two drinks, and I think it is better that guests save their appetite for the real food. More and more hostesses are coming to this conclusion, apart from the universal calorie-consciousness that has engulfed the nation. Also, I am not the only one horrified with those dinner parties where dinner is served hours late, when the desperate guests have nibbled themselves sick with itsy-bitsy cocktail stuff to enable them to make their way to the dinner table without falling down as soon as they stand up. Roughly speaking, I let half to three-quarters of an hour pass from the arrival of the first guest to sitting down to dinner, and I do not wait for people. Waiting for tardy guests who could not bother to phone the reason for their lateness is rudeness to the guests who were polite enough to come on time. The places of the latecomers at the dinner table remain empty, and if they come at salad and cheese time, this is what they get, since I would have to have a very good explanation to serve them what is left of the earlier courses.

Other verities I have learned the hard way: it is not worthwhile to cook delicate, subtle food for heavy cocktail drinkers, nor serve them superior wines. They simply are not in a position to really taste them. For the three-and-more-before-dinner drink man or woman, hearty, strongly flavored stews and other patient dishes which will wait without going to pieces completely. And good, robust wines—anything else is a waste of money, and worse, of wines that others would truly enjoy.

Guests or no guests, we always drink, and always have drunk, a glass or two of wine with our meals. Naturally, when we have guests, we serve better wine than the ordinary, European-type of table wine from California we usually drink. We have found that the California variety of these vin ordinaires, especially the Almadén ones, are usually much better and certainly more reliable than the European stuff sold at comparable prices. Unfortunately, we are not in the financial position of serving great vintages to our guests and for that matter to ourselves as I would like to, because I think it infinitely more interesting and pleasant to spend money, and if need be, lots of it, on wine rather than on food. Not for me gastronomic pilgrimages to three-star restaurants, but for me vinous pilgrimages to France, the Moselle, Italy, and Spain, and if I could, to the vineyards of Yugoslavia, South Africa, and Australia.

I seldom serve two kinds of wine at dinner, and the glasses I use are the simple, clear tulip-shaped all-purpose ones. As for champagne, I think it is the best of all drinks as an aperitif and dessert wine (bone dry or sweeter). I could drink it first thing in the morning, last thing at night, and all the time in between.

Having written about food and wine myself I shouldn't knock the subject, but when it comes to food and drink, I find it touching that so many people put so much faith in the words of writers like myself. They wish to be told in unmistakable terms about things which, after all, are matters of taste and opinion and which they can settle for themselves with a rather small outlay and little trouble. I can see that the voice of ultimate authority is desirable in the purchase of a washing machine or a painting for investment. But in matters of wine, horrendous as the prices now are, and mounting, mounting, mounting, you can start to experiment and form opinions of your own with an outlay of $2 to $50. Even the super bottles for scores and hundreds of dollars are a *kulturni* (very cultural) bargain compared to what it would cost to be able to talk as connoisseur of pre-Columbian objects.

As for the drinking, you'd think that this would be no more difficult than pouring the contents into some sort of vessel, lifting the vessel to the lips, and taking a swallow, the way it has been done for thousands of years. But no, not in this our land of plenty. Here the citizens wait, nay expect, the word from the wine pundits before they can enjoy a glass of the stuff. And the wine pundits give their opinions with all the moral assurance of the Assembly of the Church of Scotland and the undeviating line of a Communist Party presidium.

Of course, the real problem is how to describe wine,

which like all matters of taste, is basically indescribable. So a nomenclature has been set up, with words like smooth, mellow, crisp, clean, springly, full- or light-bodied, brisk, lively, fatigued, and so on. All this would be very well if these words meant the same to all the people who read them. But they don't. What is lively in Ashtabula is not lively at Cheetah, what is brisk to young conservatives in New York is not so to Alabama Democrats. As for softness, opulence, grace, elegance, finesse, rich, fleshy, flashy, round, ripe, sick, and/or gallant, these are fighting words, with vastly different meanings which depend on the social class, economic background, age, lustfulness, frustration, avariciousness, and other attributes of the user. Yet these are the words that our trusting readers wish to be guided by, *poveri innocenti*, as we say in Italy.

Thus, we writers often plunge into purple prose. Ah, those ecstatic descriptions relating to landscapes, works of art, mystical visions, wonder-of-it-all, and the spiritual and physical attributes of men and women, such as the nostalgic smell of the floor wax in the parlor of the cloistered nuns of Medina Sidonia, or the sight of the wash fluttering on a barge on the Rhine, or the crooked little finger of a maiden partaking *un coup de rouge* with a blue-smocked old man in a bistro in the Charente. Then there are the technical writers, who instruct with all the grace of computer programmers. Do not dare to question them, for theirs is the infallibility of the technical expert, the god of our age. They will tell you what vintage is right, what wine is right with what, what glass is right, what bottle opener and wine cradle are right. And then the wine historians, men of immense erudition—at the sight of a bottle of South African port, they will be reminded of the grapes the younger Darius

planted in Lower Slobodia, which played such a deci-
sive role in that country's revival of Manichaeism in
the eighteenth century. They make you feel even more
unworthy by remarking that only civilized man can
appreciate a glass of *vin ordinaire*. The Wine Snobs will
tell you nothing but the gossip associated with certain
wines. They will say: "Ah, that old *blagueur* of Ponte-
nouilli with his great spats and his new presses! But his
wife, who was born a Debrouillarde, got the better of
him, although she always sipped her wine through a
veil."

Equally interesting are the Wine Debunkers, with
their robust and frank attitudes. They will describe a
white wine as 'lark's piss" and a red one as "redolent
of subway-in-the-rush-hour atmosphere." The Vintage

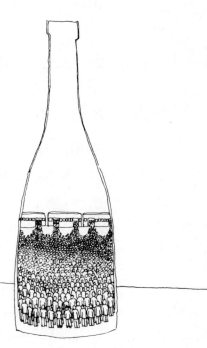

and the Label Snobs will always tell of a wine that is better than the one that they are supposed to describe: the *right* wine was grown four vineyards up the river, and by the man who owns the other part of the vineyard, on the southeast corner. Then there are the Rare-and-Precious-Wine writers, who are full of the Château Auslese 1879 of which only five and a half bottles could be made because of an early frost. The Great-Little-Wine-Find writers will steer you to a liquor store in Upper Troy, where they found that delicious sour red they so enjoyed in a sailors' tavern in Toulouse. As for the Foreign-versus-American-, and American-versus-Foreign-Wine writers, they use language that one would not dream of reproducing in a family book like this one.

So what is a reader to do when he wants to find out about wine? When personal experimentation is not possible, go after the words of a writer who uses them in the same sense you do and whose opinions you like or hate; either will clarify your own. Above all, enjoy, enjoy. What else is the purpose of drinking the stuff?

Stuffed Raw Mushrooms

(6 servings)

1 pound fresh medium mushrooms

Juice of 1 lemon ⎱ combined
1½ cups water ⎰

1 herbed Boursin cheese or 1 cup mashed, heavily seasoned, and herbed cottage or cream cheese, softened to spreading consistency with a little sweet or sour cream

Parsley sprigs

Wash the mushrooms very quickly under running cold water. Drain thoroughly and pat dry between paper towels. Remove the stems and save them for soup or sauces. As you remove the stem of each mushroom, dip it into the lemon water to keep it white. Shake dry. Spread the cavity with a little of the cheese, smoothing it off. Serve as soon as possible after making, on a platter decorated with a few sprigs of parsley.

Creamed Camembert

Serve on crackers with drinks or with fresh apples or pears for dessert.

1 ripe Camembert cheese (it must be ripe) at room temperature Dry white wine	Sweet butter, half the weight of the cheese, at room temperature

Scrape the cheese and place it in a deep glass or china dish; do not use metal. Pour just enough wine over the cheese to cover it—no more. Let stand in a cool place for 12 hours, but do not chill. Drain the cheese if necessary. Mash the cheese with a silver fork. Blend in the butter and mash and stir until the mixture is smooth. Reshape it into a round. Let the cheese harden a little, but do not chill it or it won't spread.

Fried Zucchini

To serve with drinks

8 medium zucchini	2 cups salad or olive oil
1 tablespoon salt	Salt
1 cup flour	Freshly ground pepper

Wash the zucchini and trim off the ends. Cut into narrow strips lengthwise. Sprinkle with the tablespoon of salt and place in a colander. Let stand about 1 hour to drain off excess moisture. Dry between paper towels. Coat with the flour and shake off excess flour. Heat the oil in a large frying pan. Fry the zucchini in it until golden and crisp. Drain on paper towel. Line a serving dish with a napkin. Place the zucchini on it and sprinkle with a little salt and pepper. Serve immediately.

Variation

Use eggplant instead of zucchini. If the skin of the eggplant is very thick and coarse, peel the vegetable before cutting it into strips.

Amusing the Guests

GIVING A DINNER party in New York or in another large city is very different from giving one in the suburbs or in a small city. The reason is that in New York you can have guests with a variety of occupations and life-styles who, provided they don't get into fights, make for liveliness. As somebody has put it: "When you go out to dinner in New York, you never know whom you are going to meet." In the suburbs and in small towns, however, the same people see each other all the time. With all the affection and goodwill in the world, finding something to talk about with people you see constantly, year in, year out, is not easy unless you can get together on some iniquity; being doleful together about life makes for a strong common bond even among strangers. But even taking umbrage palls after a time, when everybody has had his and her say. That's where the party with a theme comes in. It can be just food built into a typical meal—French, Indonesian, or what have you— or a dinner composed of soup and seven desserts, one of the most successful ones I've ever given. This was followed by an equally successful dinner, for the same people, of seven soups and one dessert. Or you can have a party with a theme carried out in appropriate decorations, just as with a children's party, and just as appreciated if prettily done. Imagination is what counts here, not money. If you have a house that is large and pretty enough, have your party all over the house, drinks in one place, main course in another, and dessert in a third one, or you can have a dinner party followed by games like the following, guaranteed to make waves and keep things lively:

1) *Russian Sledges*. Everybody writes down the same list of a dozen common friends, including present people. Then each of us imagines himself crossing the Siberian steppes with all of them in a sledge pursued by packs of hungry wolves, and has to throw them out, one by one. You have to decide who to throw out first, second and so on; number the names on the list accordingly, in the order in which you would throw out your friends to be torn into pieces. You may not throw yourself out. The game provides useful statistics, for all the marks given to each person are added up afterward. The person who gets the fewest is, of course, the least popular of our friends.

2) *Qualities or the New Confessions.* Each player first assesses himself and then the other players on the qualities below. The qualities are: beauty, brains, charm, taste, discretion, tolerance, willpower, sense of humor, moral sense, sensibility, sensuousness, tact, sincerity, humility. Of course it is possible to add to these qualities or change them according to the occasion. The results are invariably interesting. Full marks are twenty for each.

I find that in my own house, after the ice has been broken with the first drink, people have no trouble talking to each other. After all, my husband and I know every one of our guests, and we can do something about getting the conversation started. This carries through dinner, when thanks to the lubrication of much wine, conversation holds up through the evening. But oh, the pangs suffered at some dinners, when conversation simply would not get going. This prompted me once to run a competition in *National Review* for the best dinner-table conversation starters with uncommunicative partners. Money, politics, and religion were banned as subjects, and harmless remarks along these lines were encouraged: "Do you like string?" and "If you had to make a final choice, which would you take, sex or books?"

The contest was a huge success. There is a lesson to this. Herewith I offer some of the entries, hoping that they will be useful to my readers in a similar predicament. "If you had your life to live over again, would you have come tonight?" "Do you think if snow were a darker color, it would make the earth look smaller?" "Do you think the alphabet does any good?" "Is ground glass shiny after being cooked?" "How do you stand on the Great Lakes?" "Does a snake curl or coil?" "Describe yourself in three simple, declarative sentences." "Longing is a great force, but possession emasculates; how do we resolve this?" "How old do you think I think you are?" "Where will it ever end?" "Would you resent being called Kafkaesque?" "Do you think orphans can be psychoanalyzed?" "Have you ever thought about falling pyramids, and if not, what have you thought of?" "How many people do you know?" "Describe the taste of water." "Are you for or against anything?" "Are you traveling incommunicado?" "Does a woman sag with age or get more pliable?" "Do chickens have lips?" "Are horses smarter than pigs?" and "Are plastics really here to stay?"

As you can see, harmless nonsense remarks all, because anything else would be offensive and not further the harmony every hostess hopes to achieve. But they work, they are tiny straws to grope for in order to break that stifled silence between two people who sit next to each other throughout a meal.

Like any hostess I wish to project the image of a serene woman, gentle of speech and to the touch, easy-going but supremely competent, a woman who, without apparent effort, always does right by her guests. Thus I am an avid reader of etiquette books, such as Vogue's Book of Etiquette, which offers four and a half pounds of advice on situations that range from Manners in General, Monograms and Initials, House Guests, Money Matters within the Family, When Your Friends Travel, Religious Ceremonies (including Mormon weddings and Quaker funerals), and Difficult Times. This latter chapter deals with all aspects of Divorce, Expulsion from School or College, Out of a Job, Mourning, and the Return to a Normal Life. The book ends triumphantly with Formality and Protocol, which shows you a chauffeur in a double-breasted winter overcoat (regulation); the chauffeur should also be clean-shaven. You can also find out *all* about formal entertaining, including the Order of Precedence of Officials, the last of whom are Special Ambassadors not accredited to the United States (but to the UN), who are preceded by the Secretary of the Senate and the Assistant Chiefs of Protocol. Should you be worried about seating the Bishops of Washington, the Secretary of the Smithsonian or the Chairman of the Interstate Commerce Commission, your trusty *Vogue* etiquette book will tell you. The last entry is devoted to the Choice of Words, which tells you that lady and woman and gentleman and man are not interchangeab'e words, nor lunch and luncheon.

The book makes utterly fascinating reading. But certain problems present themselves. Since situations that require etiquette-ous behavior are apt to crop up in a totally unforeseen manner, what do you do? Do you memorize the whole book the way people made their children memorize the Bible, to be forewarned and forearmed, so to speak? Do you look up the parts that refer to a possible social situation that might crop up, copy them in shorthand on your shirt cuffs or your handkerchief and sally forth, thus prepared to deal with the worst? Or should hostesses have the etiquette book ready in the ladies' and gents' rooms, propped up like an encyclopedia, so that worried guests may consult their mentor unbeknownst to (at least) the opposite sex. It is all so difficult when one wishes to behave in the proper manner.

Reading *Vogue's Book of Etiquette* I had an uneasy feeling that this noble volume ignores, or is above, many *real-life* situations that keep on happening among the people I know. To spare my readers any possible social humiliation, I have tried to draw up a realistic code of behavior and some practical answers to a few of them.

When your husband/wife has too much to drink: Remove him/her without making any remarks about his/her condition, since others, well-lit themselves, may not have noticed it. If he/she doesn't want to come, feel ill suddenly and ask him/her to take you home. It works; I once saw a woman throw a fainting fit to stop her husband from making a fool of himself with an important fellow guest.

If your husband/wife tells a long, boring story: Look entranced and eager. Chances are that the others will think the story fascinating. Gossip: Don't stop it; it's about the only way to find out what others think of you.

To someone rude: "Don't you find your manners a handicap in your work/social life?"

Apologies for male/female party misbehaving: A bunch of flowers, with a card saying "You were marvelous, as always."

When you want to meet that tall, fascinating stranger: "Do you know lots of people here?" or "Didn't we meet at Percival's party for the Curator of Turtles of the Bronx Zoo?" or "Aren't you *the* Bill Buckley/Johnny Cash/Phyllis Diller/Jane Fonda?"

When you're asked to comment on somebody's painting: "You know so much more about art than I do" or "I admire the spirit of the painter."

When being offered pot: "Thank you, not today" or "I'm not ready yet."

When your hairpiece comes off in his hands: "You can't rely on anything these days" or "It was my last defense, you know."

To the man who propositions you, refusal: Say what

you want to say beforehand, and nicely: you never know. You can't say no in bed, it's too late then.

Wife swapping: "I wouldn't like you to be disappointed, old boy" or "Let's stay friends."

To shed someone, after: "Tell me, do you have a lot of trouble with your work?" or "You made me think of my Aunt Nellie, I loved her as a child."

When your friend's husband/wife makes a pass at you: Take it or leave it, but *shut up tight* about it.

Safe conversation with someone richer than oneself, who does not know it: Proclaim the pleasure of the new Woolworth.

When someone innocent at a party introduces you to your most-hated enemy: Don't hiss, but smile sweetly and say how glad you are to meet such an interesting person. Then leave a) to get a drink, b) to go to the bathroom, or c) to lie down because you don't feel well.

How to annoy a rude taxidriver: Get out of the right side of the cab and leave the door open; he will have to get out to close it.

Impressing your social betters: Don't bother, they won't believe it anyway.

Chapter 4

Why It Tastes Different
Over There

A subject about which I've had endless (and on the whole, useless) conversations is the touchingly optimistic belief of only too many Americans that anything that is good somewhere else will be just as good in the United States. This is not necessarily so for anything, let alone food. When I think of all the traveling gourmets who've made a heck of a nuisance of themselves separating European chefs from their recipes, working themselves to a frazzle in their own kitchens to reproduce them, with a zeal worthy of a longer-lasting cause! When I think of their wails: "Why, oh why is this not what I ate on the banks of Lake Annécy or in Bologna? What, oh what, did I do wrong?"

On the contrary, chances are that the cook did nothing wrong. But the ingredients he or she had to work with, no matter how much money they cost, are not the same as they are in Europe, and there is nothing anybody can do about that. The taste of food is determined by often very subtle differences, hidden ones. So let us begin at the beginning, with the water, which is one of the basic ingredients of all food. Mountain water from the Rockies, spring water in Sweden, reservoir water in Croton, and Rhine water may all be water, but the flavor is different. Roman fountain water is a delight

to drink, New York tap water horrid. Dublin beer is superlative, and so is the tea, because of the local water. With coffee, the water is less in evidence since the coffee flavor covers up a multitude of sins.

Direct food such as vegetables and fruits, and indirect foods like meat and milk, are extremely influenced by the water that is in them. The earth, in its turn, is influenced by the weather, and American weather, with its extremes of temperature, is very different from the more moderate climates of Europe—which after all, is the mecca of good food. This is nowhere more evident than in the case of wine. You can transplant all the *pinot noir* and other grapes from Europe to California and work the wine just same, but you will invariably have a different wine from that of Burgundy. The strawberries grown in the lingering spring of England, the apples of Germany, the vegetables maturing in the temperate climates of France, are by nature more flavorful than those of our American continent. Even the Pacific coast and Northwest, which do not have the excessive temperature changes of other regions, are much more excessive in drought or rain than their European counterparts, and our best stuff comes from there.

Aside from basic growing conditions, many food categories are quite different in Europe. Take butter. French butter, and Danish butter, which I think even better, are made from cream treated differently from ours; it is somewhat acidulated. Ours starts with sweet cream, and there are no limits to its water content. The water content affects the spreading consistency of butter, which in its turn affects the way it handles in things like Danish pastry or puff paste, which consist largely of butter. This more plastic foreign butter makes for a featherlight texture which you simply cannot achieve with our own butter, no matter how faithfully you reproduce a recipe. That's why Danish pastries are quite something else in Denmark than here.

The basic difference is even more pronounced in the flavor of meats. The best-tasting lamb in the world is the French *pre salé*, and Norwegian lamb similarly fed on the grass of salt-water farms, since this grass offsets the slight taste of tallow found in all sheep. The deliciousness of French and Italian veal is determined by the fact the animals are really milk fed, that is, they have never grazed but only drunk their mama's milk, which gives their flesh its pale, almost white, fine-grained quality. American veal is ruddy-hued and coarse, since it comes from athletic teen-agers that were left to gambol in the meadows or barns. Furthermore, the best European veal is never more than six weeks old—babies, never adolescents. Those delicious suckling pigs of Spain are infants no heavier than a couple of pounds (and better not seen hanging up in the butchers' shops if one has feelings about the slaughter of innocents). But they taste mighty good and delicate, and very different from the greasy ten-to-twelve-pound porkers that are used for roast whole pig in this country.

Cream and flour, ingredients of the great sauces, are also something else in Europe. The French *crème fraîche*, which is out of this world spooned over fruit, can be reproduced after a fashion—just barely—by combining our heavy cream with buttermilk or sour cream. But the result is different because first of all, our milks are pasteurized and theirs are not, and second, because a naturally acidulated cream will thicken a dish whereas the reproduction will not. Thus the French cream is used as is to thicken a sauce, but we will have to add, horror of horrors, more egg yolk. However, all this changes not only the consistency, but also the character of a sauce.

We also treat our foods differently. European agriculture is not as commercialized as ours when it comes to table produce, where we irrigate, fertilize, and spray with abandon. And anybody who has ever eaten a fruit that was left alone to mature knows that there is no substitute for time, natural sunshine, wind, and rain. Or why do people flock to farmers' markets?

Cheese is another example of what happens when everything is made safe and standardized. American milk is pasteurized all over the country, which is wonderful because no matter where you are it will be safe and clean. But pasteurized milk does not make great cheese, since all the bacteria are controlled like robots, and they are what give cheese its flavor. American-made cheese is uniformly good but never great. Only cheese that is cooked, so to speak, like Parmesan or Swiss, can be reproduced here, since the manufacture kills all bacteria. (As an aside, I've never heard of anybody in Europe getting undulant fever from cheese, but I've heard of it in this country, and that's why I think the pasteurization of milk may be sad in one way although very, very good in others.)

Finally, there is a respect for fresh ingredients and a spontaneousness of cooking not found here. Freshly ground spices are the secret of good Indian curries, but the importing of the spices unavoidably detracts from their freshness. Frozen foods, however convenient, will never be as good as fresh ones, as best seen in the case of berries, fish, and poultry. And however Americanized Europeans may be becoming, I doubt that they would think that a product called Dream Whip could take the place of fresh cream. Its ingredients, as listed on the box, are: "Sugar, hydrogenated vegetable oils, with BHA added as a preservative, sodium caseinate, propylene glycol monostearate, hydroxylated lecithin, and artificial flavor, and color."

All of this means merely that food grown in America, though good, will seldom taste quite the same as its European or Asian equivalents—because conditions are different. Why else would foods be imported? It is interesting to note that a baking company in New York, in order to cater to the demand for real French bread, imported the French baking ovens and uses the same combinations of flours as are used in France. Excellent as many other French and Italian breads may be, they still are not exact replicas of their European counterparts, for the reasons realized by the above-mentioned baking company.

Even with the same raw materials, food will taste differently depending on who cooks it. The flavor of a dish comes from a combination of many small factors that spring from that particular cook's technique. Chopping a little more or a little less, the degree of golden-brown in sautéeing, the amount of stirring—they influence the end results a great deal. A dish is not only made by the ingredients and the flavorings, but by the way it is prepared, in France, in China, in America, everywhere.

What is wrong with things being different in different parts of the world? It seems to me a case to welcome this and say "Vive la différence." However, it has been pointed out to me that not everybody thinks as I do, not that this comes as news. I herewith offer a few recipes which will taste over here remarkably as they do over there.

Barley Soup

(4–6 servings)

3 tablespoons butter	Salt
1 medium onion, minced	Freshly ground pepper
1 celery stalk, minced	½ cup heavy cream or
½ cup medium barley	more, according to
1 tablespoon flour	taste
7 cups hot chicken consommé	

Heat the butter in a large deep casserole. Add the onion, celery, and the barley. Over medium heat, and stirring constantly, cook for about 3–4 minutes or until the onion is golden and the barley opaque. Reduce the heat to low. Stir in the flour and consommé. Stir to mix. Season with salt and pepper to taste. Simmer covered for about 1 hour. Just before serving, stir in the cream.

Note: This soup may be made ahead of time and reheated with perfect success. The cream, however, must be added only at serving time.

Mushroom and Artichoke Sauce for Spaghetti

(Enough for 1-pound pasta)

This tastes reasonably like its Italian prototype

2 big artichokes, trimmed and sliced as described on page 171
2 tablespoons butter
2 tablespoons olive oil
1 large garlic clove, minced
1 large ripe tomato, peeled and chopped
3 large scallions, sliced, green and white parts

Salt
Freshly ground pepper
½ teaspoon ground marjoram or thyme
½ cup hot water or hot chicken or beef consommé
½ pound mushrooms, sliced
Cooked pasta
Grated Parmesan cheese

Dry the sliced artichokes on paper towel. Heat together the butter and the olive oil. Add the artichokes, garlic, tomato, scallions, salt, pepper, the marjoram or thyme, and the water or consommé. Cook covered over low heat until the artichokes are almost tender. Add the mushrooms and cook until the vegetables are tender. Pour over cooked pasta and serve with grated Parmesan cheese.

Crabmeat Charentais

(3–4 servings)

This dish will taste as authentic as possible away from France (even accounting for the different American butter) if a dry white wine imported from France is used. These wines are easy to come by—such as Pouilly Fumé, Pouilly Fuissé (the first from the Loire, the second from Burgundy), Sancerre, Chablis. A good French cognac is imperative; the flavor of the dish depends on the wine and spirit used.

1 pound freshly cooked crabmeat, carefully picked over	½ cup dry white wine Salt Freshly ground pepper
¼ cup sweet butter	2 teaspoons fresh tarragon, minced, or ½ teaspoon dried tarragon, crumbled
6 small spring or green onions, thinly sliced, white and green parts	
½ small green pepper, minced	⅓ cup cognac 1 tablespoon minced parsley

Separate the crabmeat into small lumps. Heat the butter. Cook, stirring constantly, the onions and pepper in it for about 3–5 minutes or until soft. Do not brown them. Working carefully so as not to break the lumps, add the crabmeat, wine, the salt and pepper to taste, and tarragon. Over medium heat, cook until heated through thoroughly—about 5 minutes. Stir frequently and carefully with a fork and do not break the lumps of crabmeat. Warm the cognac in a ladle or small saucepan. Flame it and pour over the crabmeat. Sprinkle with parsley. Serve with buttered boiled rice or on hot buttered toast.

Beef Bourguignon

(4–5 servings)

Like all stews, this dish reflects a cook's individuality. But essentially, the flavor of Beef Bourguignon depends on the combination of salt pork, Burgundy wine, cognac and if possible, dry Madeira, a wine much used in French cookery. All these ingredients are obtainable in the United States.

½ cup salt pork
2½ pounds lean beef,
     trimmed free of all
     fat and gristle, and
     cut into 1½-inch
     cubes
¼ cup cognac
2 tablespoons butter
2–3 medium onions,
     chopped fine
2 tablespoons flour
   About 2 cups imported
     good-quality
     Burgundy wine

Salt
Freshly ground pepper
Pinch of nutmeg
Bouquet garni (1 bay
     leaf, 3 parsley sprigs,
     1 teaspoon ground or
     dried thyme tied in a
     cheesecloth bag)
Hot water
¼ cup dry Madeira
     (optional)

First, blanch the salt pork to remove excessive saltiness. Place the pork in a bowl and pour boiling water to cover over it. Let stand for 15 minutes or until bland; saltiness in the pork varies. Drain, dry, and mince. Place the minced pork in a large, heavy casserole and render. When all the fat has run out, remove the bits of pork with a slotted spoon. Over high heat, brown the meat in the pork fat, turning it constantly to let it brown heavily on all sides. The meat should be almost black, but not be scorched. Remove from heat and pour off any excessive fat. Pour the cognac over the meat and flame. The browning in salt pork fat and the flaming with the cognac will give the meat part of its characteristic flavor.

In a separate frying pan, heat the butter. Cook, stirring constantly, the onions in it until they are soft and beginning to brown. Add the onions to the beef and mix well. Return the meat to medium heat and stir in the flour. Add enough wine to cover two thirds of the meat. Mix and season to taste with salt, pepper, and the nutmeg. Add the bouquet garni and just enough water to cover the meat. Bring quickly to the boiling point and lower heat immediately to lowest possible. Simmer covered for about 2–3 hours—the slower the heat, the better—or until the meat is tender. Check occasionally for moisture and if necessary, add a little more hot water.

Half an hour before the meat will be ready, remove the bouquet garni and throw away. Stir in the Madeira. Simmer covered for 30 more minutes. Serve with buttered noodles or best of all, with plain boiled new potatoes.

Note: Some people add ¼ to ½ pound sliced mushrooms sautéed in a little butter, 10 minutes before serving. I don't but this is a matter of taste, and as I said, Beef Bourguignon can be made many ways.

Veal and Peppers

(4–5 servings)

Since this dish does not require the tenderest veal such as found in France and Italy, but seldom in America, it can be made successfully with the more mature American veal. This is a Roman dish well-liked by Americans and a favorite in Italian restaurants in America. Serve with parsleyed potatoes and a salad.

3 pounds boneless veal, trimmed free of all fat and gristle and cut into 1½-inch cubes
Flour seasoned with salt and freshly ground pepper
⅓ cup olive oil
1 garlic clove
4 sweet green or red peppers, trimmed, seeded, and cut into strips

1½ cups dry red or white wine
20 stoned black Italian or Greek olives (optional)
2 teaspoons dried crumbled basil
Salt
Freshly ground pepper

Coat the meat with the flour and shake off the excess. Heat the olive oil in a deep saucepan. Add the meat. Over high heat, brown the meat on all sides. Lower the heat to medium and add the garlic and peppers. Cook, stirring constantly, for 2 minutes. Add the wine, the olives, and the basil. Season with salt and pepper to taste. Bring to the boiling point. Lower the heat to simmer. Cook covered for about 25–30 minutes or until the meat is tender. Do not overcook. If the meat looks too dry, add a little hot water, a few spoonfuls at a time.

Venison Steak Mirza

(2–3 servings)

Serve with stewed apples and/or cranberry sauce and buttered noodles or parsleyed potatoes.

1 1½-in-thick slice venison, weighing about 1½ pounds	Flour
Salt	4 tablespoons butter
Freshly ground pepper	1 cup dry red wine
2 teaspoons paprika	½ cup heavy cream
1 tablespoon fresh rosemary, chopped, or 2 teaspoons dried rosemary, crumbled	

Rub the venison on both sides with salt, pepper, the paprika, and rosemary. Coat lightly with flour and shake off excess. Heat the butter in a deep frying pan. Brown the meat quickly in it on both sides. Add the wine and bring to the boiling point. Turn the heat to low. Simmer covered until the meat is tender; cooking time depends on its age. Transfer the cooked meat to a heated platter and slice. Keep it hot. Stir the cream into the pan juices and bring to a quick boil. Pour the sauce over the meat and serve immediately.

Note: Pork may be cooked in the same manner. All the fat and gristle should be trimmed off before cooking.

Red Cabbage With Apples

(4–6 servings)

Unlike other vegetables, American red cabbage tastes pretty much like European red cabbage. Serve with pork or roast duck or goose.

2 tablespoons bacon fat or lard	4 tart cooking apples, peeled, cored and sliced
6 slices lean bacon, minced	1 tablespoon sugar
2–3 large onions, thinly sliced	⅓ cup water
1 firm head red cabbage, thinly sliced (about 8–10 cups)	Salt
	Freshly ground pepper
	¼ teaspoon ground nutmeg

In a heavy casserole, combine the bacon fat, bacon, and the onions. Cook over low heat, stirring frequently, until the onions are soft. Do not brown. Add the cabbage and mix well. Lower heat to lowest possible; if necessary, place an asbestos plate over the source of heat. Cook covered, *without stirring,* for 10 minutes. Shake the casserole frequently to prevent scorching and check the moisture. If the cabbage looks too dry, add 1 or 2 tablespoons water. Add the apples, sugar, water, salt and pepper, and nutmeg. Mix well. Simmer covered over low heat for 1½ hours, checking the moisture and stirring occasionally.

Note: The long, slow cooking is essential to the flavor of the dish.

Belgian Endives Au Gratin

(4 servings)

Since the endives are imported, they taste here as they taste over there. Serve as a separate first course or with ham.

8 large Belgian endives	Salt
3 tablespoons butter	Cayenne pepper to taste
2 tablespoons flour	½ cup fine dry
1½ cups milk	breadcrumbs
½ cup heavy cream	2 tablespoons melted
½ cup grated Swiss	butter
cheese	

Wash the endives and trim them. Place them side by side in the bottom of a buttered 2-quart baking dish. Heat the butter in a saucepan. Stir in the flour and cook, stirring constantly, for 2 minutes. Stir in the milk and cream. Continue cooking and stirring until the sauce is smooth and thickened. Remove from the heat and stir in the cheese. Season with salt and cayenne pepper. Pour the sauce over the Belgian endives. Sprinkle with the breadcrumbs and drizzle the melted butter over the crumbs. Bake in a preheated moderate oven (350°F.) for about 30 minutes or until the crumbs are golden and the sauce bubbly.

Variation

Add 1 to 1½ cups cooked chopped crabmeat or cooked, shelled, and chopped shrimps to the sauce.

Cherry Compote With Wine
(4 servings)
Serve with macaroons

2 pounds dark sweet
  cherries, stemmed
  and pitted
¼ to ½ cup sugar,
  depending on the
  sweetness of the
  cherries
½ cup red currant jelly
1 cup full-bodied dry red
  wine, such as Pinot
  Noir or Burgundy

¼ teaspoon ground
  cinnamon
Peel of 1 lemon, yellow
  part only

Combine all the ingredients in a deep saucepan. Bring to the boiling point and stir. Turn off the heat and cover the saucepan. Let the cherries stand for 10 minutes. Turn the fruit into a deep serving dish. Chill thoroughly. Remove the lemon peel before serving.

Chapter 5

About Cookbooks

COOKBOOKS ARE ANOTHER of the subjects I muse about as I wash dishes or perform the hundred and one mindless occupations that are part of kitchen life—putting away dishes, cleaning silver, lining kitchen drawers with clean paper. I write cookbooks myself, endeavoring to earn a living, but it still beats me why people buy so many new cookbooks when they could cook just as well from the ones they have. I presume it is for the same reason that makes people go in for Zen—to become more spiritual when they could do this perfectly well by taking their Christian or Jewish backgrounds more seriously. Everybody likes a painless kick in the pants which does the work of becoming a better cook or a noble mind without having to make an effort of one's own.

The trouble with the American obsession with cookbooks is that rather than getting one out of the kitchen doldrums, it widens the chasm between one's higher culinary aspirations and one's daily cooking. The cookbooks may be read, or grace the coffee table as a proof of I prefer not to say what, but we still remain stuck at one level, be it the steak or fishstick one, which is just as deadly in the long run as a voice with no inflections. Practically everybody is bored with their own food and too lethargic to try making new things. The reason for the success of the many exotic convenience foods which are flooding the markets is that they conveniently satisfy the human craving for a change. But a safe, comfortable Americanized change, such as a canned Chinese dinner or a frozen Mexican one.

American eating patterns are changing rapidly. The sacred three-meals-a-day pattern is on the way out. How many families eat a real breakfast any longer, or want to? For harassed parents, it is a boon when the little ones are big enough to get their own cereal and milk in the mornings while their parents gulp down some fruit juice (maybe) and coffee (yes). Lunch is certainly up for grabs by whosoever is hungry, except on weekends when it gets to be the all-purpose meal of brunch. Now, dinner is fading out too as a sit-down meal of family togetherness. Soon it will survive only as a part of entertaining or ceremonials. First it was TV which kept the kids quiet, but made conversation impossible. Then came the various activities of the various members of the families, all timed differently, and far more important to those involved than yet another family meal. Another factor is that the increased level of culinary sophistication, due to the increased level of all-round sophistication produced by TV, foreign travel, new life-styles, makes the sameness of family food even more boring. When each one in the family wants their own

thing in food, there is not much point in cooking a
dinner for all, especially when parental authority is no
longer strong enough to enforce the old dictum: "You
eat what's on your plate." More and more food manufacturers, as one sees in the ads and more importantly,
in the supermarkets, take this into account with single-
helping food products, boasting that now every member
of the family can be suited both as to food tastes and
eating times. TV dinners started this trend, to which
there is no end.

The way things go, women cook with the minimum
of effort for their families, while they will put themselves
out for company. Not only the overwhelming role of
convenience foods is proof of this, but the runaway
success of quick food chains and take-home food parlors,
the last on all levels, from the local Chinese restaurant
to expensive fancy ones. All over our vast and beautiful
land, mothers and fathers pile the kids in the car on
Saturday night or on Sunday and treat them to a hamburger or fried chicken dinner from a roadside stand.
Family harmony reigns supreme because mother doesn't
have to cook, father feels good because he's treating the
folks for not much money, and the children are blissful
because they can eat what they really like, with lots of
French fries and condiments. All this while the guardian
angel of happy, old-fashioned family meals steals out,
wings folded over his eyes, weeping over a nation of
snackers.

Yet cookbooks proliferate. Gluttony, in our permissive and commercial society, is no vice; on the contrary,
it is pandered to from every angle. The libel laws forbid
me to say what I think of the majority of cookbooks
which I see, which leave no gimmick unturned, even to
pornography and homosexuality. Who writes and buys

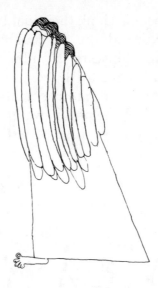

all these books, and why?

Professional food writers and some professional cooks write cookbooks for the same reason anthropology professors publish anthropology papers, namely because it is their job. Cookbooks are good for keeping one's name before the public eye, leading to reviews, radio and TV appearances. All this reminds magazine editors, manufacturers who need consulting work connected with food, and advertising agencies who dish out TV and radio commercials where the talent lies. The professionals usually turn out good, useful books and though cookbook writing is a chore, they do it well because their living depends on it.

As for the nonprofessionals, some write cookbooks because they have found that some food ideas and recipes work out well or because they have a good contemporary idea. Very often these are one-shot books, even excellent ones. But most cookbooks, as far as I can see, are written because it is so fashionable and *kulturni*. Cooking is like

writing; most people think they could do it better if they
had just a little time. From the cookbook trash published
in profusion over the years, it is obvious that the writers
knew they didn't have to study nutrition, discover new
food combinations or improvements on old ones, or
think up a genuinely helpful new angle to get their book
published. They did not have to test the recipes as long

as they read more or less properly to their editors, a
fallacy that shows up in baking recipes where you have
to be accurate or the whole thing won't work. A book
that has accurate baking recipes (a bother to test) is
never wholly bad because the author had a conscience,
rare thing in many cookbook authors. If a cookbook
writer dreams up a catchy theme, such as "Food to
Shoot Geese By," or "Fairy Dishes on the Continental
Divide," or now, in our age of nostalgia, "The Best-
Loved Recipes of 1872 in Their Original Form," he or
she is in with many publishers. The next step for these
cookbook writers is assembling the recipes. These come
from books, magazines, advertising giveaways, and publicity releases, on the principle that if it is in print, it's
ours to make our own.

Every respectable cookbook writer knows and admits the trading of recipes. But at least he or she admits the source, or changes a recipe so that it tastes differently. Unrespectable cookbook writers take the recipes as is, with all their mistakes, if there are any. How often does one not recognize a recipe of one's own, which wasn't quite right because of ignorance, in somebody else's opus! Or one meets another product of one's own, with a little change such as making a quarter of a teaspoon of mace into one of allspice, or using two onions instead of four. Well, at least that shows a certain amount of endeavor. But what I particularly resent are the advertising and publicity recipes that constitute the body of many cookbooks, obtained for free, naturally, since they are to be publicized. Any food publicist will tell of the calls for recipes from somebody who wants to write a cookbook. Making somebody pay for something that is free to all comers is a fraud. Equally fraudulent are the plethora of cookbooks with recipes that don't come out. Cookbooks are technical manuals, how-to books, which should be written by experts, and not by celebrities in search of publicity. If they could be returned to their manufacturers, like any faulty merchandise, the publishers would make certain that the quality would improve with enough protests. But you shell out ten or fifteen or twenty-five bucks, the book wastes your time and money, and you are stuck.

However, I must admit that mistakes happen to all who write recipes, out of ignorance or haste; I hang my own head in shame. And as for all of those printer's mistakes—horrors.

Contrary to what most people think, cookbook writing is not a well-paid profession compared to the money earned by people in the food business, such as home economists and publicists. Of course there are the stars like Julia Child, Craig Claiborne, and Jim Beard who have become well-to-do with their books, as stars in any profession. This applies also to the owners of standard cookbooks, such as *The Joy of Cooking,* of which the paperback rights have been sold for one and a half million dollars.

Cookbook authors cash in on their work in other ways. It is supposedly irresistible to see one's name in print, to go on one of the standard radio shows—TV appearances being a rarity for cookbook writers—to be taken for lunch by the editor, the standard treatment for any author. But a cookbook writer feels he or she is with it in this age of preoccupation with food and diet. It does not even spare the communes, where, according to one expert, neither sex nor politics are the main topics of conversation but food. Cookbook writing brings the author a certain amount of lagniappe, such as occasional invitations to food publicity lunches and even edible or drinkable gifts. The real manna though falls very heavily on the magazine and newspaper food writers, since they reach a far larger public than the most successful cookbook writers. Nevertheless, it is more than the cookbook writers would get if they worked as tie salesmen or accountants.

Cookbook writing is an agreeable occupation, which can be done at one's convenience, at home. The results give pleasure to one's friends, or at least they will think you an interesting person. It always amuses me how even the most unlikely people react when you tell them you are a cookbook writer. Their greedy little eyes light up and at once they embark on long and usually very boring descriptions of how they or their friends ate this or that,

or worse, how they cook. Only a few will ask technical
advice or want an honest discussion; mostly these bores
want to hear the sound of their own voices and feel they
are terribly clever. I react to this with all the interest of
a lethargic camel.

Cookbooks are mostly bought as escape literature, not
to cook from. As *kulturni* it is to write them, it is even
more *kulturni* to have the tonier ones lying around,
casual-like. And cookbooks are easy and fun to read,
which cannot be said of many other kinds. If you want
to judge flower painting on porcelain, or the glissandos
of a harp player, you have to know something of the
techniques of these divertissements. But with cookbooks
you can be instant judge because almost everybody has
cooked something or other at one time; besides, all of
us eat. After all, cooking is one of the few subjects left
where you can safely discuss outrageous opinions without getting into trouble with the FBI, the Mafia, and
the Media. What more can anybody want? And why do
I write cookbooks? Because it is my profession and I
like it.

I happen to cook from cookbooks, including my own.
This is hardly surprising—since if I didn't like the food,
I would not have put it in a book in the first place. That
is, most of the food. When writing cookbooks dealing
with specific national cuisines as I have done, one has
to include recipes that are typical, even if not personally
liked. My memory is poor, that is why I look up recipes,
and because it bores me to cook the same things all the
time.

What cookbooks do I like and use? Ah, this is my
secret. Those among my readers who really like to know
may read the cookbook reviews in the Book Review Sec-
tion of the *New York Sunday Times*, where I have re-

viewed cookbooks for the last eight years. But though I own more than two thousand cookbooks, I cook from a score or less. An informal survey revealed that women use very few cookbooks even if they have them—three to five is the average number they consult regularly. But we cookbook users are the exception because the majority of women do not have cookbooks, except maybe the standard volume received as a wedding present, a few volumes bought at the supermarket or as a premium, or put out by local charitable organizations as money raisers. Even if most women wanted to buy cookbooks they would have a hard time doing it. There are so few general bookstores in the United States, about 2500 for a population of over 200 million, compared to Germany, with 61 million people and about 5300 bookstores, and to England, with 55½ million people and about 3000 bookshops. No wonder that mail-order bookselling is a profitable enterprise.

Thus I believe that having cookbooks, or at least, reading cookbooks, is entirely a middle-class thing, which does not concern the female population in general. This does not mean that women do not have recipes. On the contrary, they have lots of recipes, "collections" of them, as they put it when asked. Where do they come from? They are recipes from magazines, newspapers, publicity releases, friends, relatives, free recipes—irresistible to clip or rip out and keep. The keeping is not done in lovely orderly files, card indexes, scrapbooks or what not, but the collection is dumped into a big or small drawer, a shoe box, an envelope, helter skelter. I keep mine in a covered basket (bought in Vermont when my sons were in camp there because it looked pretty), in the same total disorder as anybody else's. Like my sister recipe collectors, I say what we all say, that one day when we have time, when the kids are out of the way, when the house is clean, when it rains and we have nothing else to do—that will be the day when the recipes will be sorted and filed, when the chaos will be transformed into dazzling order. A likely story, but we can dream, can't we? However, this does not mean that we do not consult our recipes when we think of it, rummaging through the pickings, recognizing favorites by their battered and stained condition, starting to read long-forgotten ones, and usually finding something quite different from what we started to look for.

Recently I did just that and found out to my surprise that recipes date just like other things. I mean not old-fashioned recipes, but recipes of the last ten years, which today would be written differently. Recipe writing is more of a skill than one would think, making things clear and yet not bogging instructions down with so many details that the cook loses her way. When not obvious, one should make clear if a dish is to be cooked covered or not; in what size container if this matters; over what kind of heat; if it is necessary to follow instructions down to the last half teaspoon, as in baking; and finally, what the finished dish, if it is an unfamiliar one, should look and taste like. It is always a matter of total surprise to me how often even the best cookbook writers do not tell you the latter and how cookbook editors do not pick up this omission. But then, how many cookbook editors really know food and editing, for that matter—just let us tiptoe away from this scabrous subject.

Not telling a cook if the unfamiliar dish in question is hot or mild, thick or soupy, and so on is especially infuriating with *haute cuisine* and exotic recipes. If the cuisine is to be *haute*, it has to be just so, or else it falls down with a plomp to *basse cuisine*, a waste of ingredients and time. With exotic recipes such as curries, for instance, composed of strange, hard-to-get ingredients, how on earth do you know what it will taste like, and if it's worth taking all the trouble? For that matter, not telling you specific uses of a recipe comes up in domestic cookery as well. How many cookbooks, giving you several recipes for pie crust, tell you what each one is especially suited for? There is also the fudging over quantities and costs in the so-called economy cookbooks. A certain quantity of meat, for instance, should serve so many people, as the recipe says. But what it does not always say is that some meats are very wasteful, and that when you cut away a fourth or even more in unappetizing fat and gristle, the dish will no longer serve the number of people claimed and is therefore no longer inexpensive. Lamb's neck, riblets, and other cuts are described as cheap, but how much meat versus fat is there on what allegedly saved you money? Recently I trimmed an 8½ pound leg of lamb for curry, removing about 4¼ pounds in fat and bones, as weighed on my kitchen scales. Whereas beef and pork fat can be rendered, lamb fat is horrid, so that one of the important things to do when you serve lamb hot is to have really hot plates. When you serve it cold, cut off any smidgen of fat.

Diet cookbooks have their place in life, if nothing else because they make their authors a little or a lot of money. But diet books which promise that you can have French *haute cuisine* or other gourmet cooking with diet cooking methods are just hot air. The very taste and texture of some cuisines depend on lavishness with high-calorie ingredients. If these are not used, the results may be good, but it is not what is claimed. Better to eat a dish whose nature is sparse, but which is the real thing rather than those fakes.

Cookbookmanship has become the new national pre-occupation. Bookstore shelves bulge with cookbooks, and new ones on every conceivable gastronomical subject keep appearing in a steady stream. Which brings up the question: what is a good cookbook and how do you recognize it? The answer depends on several very different and very personal factors.

First you should ask yourself what you want the book for. Are you going to use it as a straightforward instruction manual—which a standard cookbook should be? Are you especially interested in the food of foreign countries? Are you looking for ideas for entertaining or barbecuing? Or do you merely want to satisfy your curiosity about a personality's or a group's food preferences, or to indulge in some fun bedtime reading? There are first-rate cookbooks in all of these categories, although few perfect ones.

The most difficult to recognize is the good standard cookbook. It should have a great deal of basic and advanced information about cooking methods and techniques; a certain amount of information on foods, the table, and wines; all the basic recipes that are the cornerstone of daily eating, plus some festive and original dishes and menus. A standard cookbook emphatically does not need to go deeply into such sidelines as nutrition, medical diets, and current food products like mixes—subjects which are better left to experts and are likely to be outdated in a short time. There should be no more than the most general information and advice for special techniques such as freezing and preserving. It is obviously neither possible nor desirable to cram every known kitchen fact into one single book.

I find it almost impossible to judge a cookbook without actually testing some of the recipes, preferably those relating to baking. You can't fool with an exact chemical process like baking as you can with a stew, and if the recipe comes out as promised, the chances are that the others will work, too. But since it is impossible to test before laying out the often large sum many cookbooks are now selling for, I suggest that to prevent disappointments you take the following precautions. Before buying any cookbook, especially by an unfamiliar author, make a detailed list of all the things you hope to find in it. Then check if the answers—or at least some of them—are there.

For standard cookbooks, look for these points:

1. Does the book have the kind of recipes you want? Some standard cookbooks place undue stress on desserts and baking at the cost of other recipes.

2. Do the ingredient listings specify both the quantities and the nature of the food? For instance, "one onion" may be very misleading, since the taste of a dish will obviously be affected by the onion's size; it should be listed as small, medium, or large. When almonds are called for, are they to be blanched or unblanched? Are tomatoes to be peeled and seeded? Is the flour to be all-purpose flour, and is it to be sifted or not? While it is not necessary to sift 1 tablespoon of flour for thickening a sauce, the flour used in baking must be sifted before measurement in order to get the accurate quantity by volume.

3. Are the sizes, depth, or measurements of the equipment clearly specified? This is essential information for baking, since a cake or soufflé depends for its success on the proper-sized pan. Are you to roast on a rack or not?

4. Are you told what to do with the equipment? Should the baking dishes and cookie sheets be greased or ungreased? At what speed do you use the blender or mixer, and for how long? Are the oven temperatures given, and just as important, are you reminded to pre-heat the oven before using it?

5. Is the cooking information complete? Are you told what type of top-of-the-stove heat you need, and what distance the food should be from the broiler flame? Should you be simmering or bringing to a quick boil; stirring constantly or occasionally; basting, and if so, at what intervals? Are cakes to be cooled in pans or on racks? Are you given the length of cooking times? Since foods and heat can vary considerably, is there an additional, alternate description of how the food should look at a certain stage? (A *gratin* bubbly on the top, a cake shrinking from the sides of the pan, gelatin thickened to the consistency of unbeaten egg whites, egg whites beaten until they stand in stiff peaks.) Are the number of servings in each recipe specified?

Ideally, all these points should apply to all cookbooks. But in foreign cookbooks, the main thing to look for is the authenticity of the recipes and information. Books which adapt recipes "for the American table" or use American shortcuts and convenience foods may produce palatable dishes, but not the real thing. Some so-called foreign cookbooks at least admit to such practices, but a great many more sneak them in, and that I consider dishonest.

If a book is wanted for a special purpose, look at it closely to see if it gives the proper information and is not padded with extraneous recipes. A book for entertaining should fit your circumstances, style, and budget, and also give you the necessary background information about shopping, serving, and general organization. A book on outdoor cooking should point out pitfalls, one on picnics be specific about the matter of transporting foods, and one on boat cookery be realistic about the space of the galley.

The choice of personality cookbooks and bedtime escape reading is obviously not dictated by the desire to cook. If the recipes are good and usable, so much the better. Here your taste is the only real criterion.

Chapter 6

A Place to Soothe,
to Heal, and to Cheat

When I was young and foolish, I thought the kitchen was the place to cook meals in, and that was all there was to it. Life has taught me differently: I now know that the kitchen is also the place where wounds are healed, the stricken comforted, and fraud perpetuated.

As I write this, in the month of March, which comes around every year, "Dies Irae, Dies Illa" is the unhappy cry echoing through the land because it is the time when sins of omission are about to be bared before the Feds. Tax time is the time to have a good cry and get it over and done with. But crying in itself can be an upsetting rather than a calming process. It is also an unbecoming one, except in the case of very young, beautiful women, so that it is far better to cry *into* something than weep and curse at random. The easiest thing to cry into is booze, but it is not the best, not at all. It is far better to cry into food though not quite as simple.

I am under no illusions about food solving problems, except the problem of hunger. On the contrary, eating in sorrow brings overweight and even more problems. But a little dish of something can spread balm upon a wounded psyche, restore balance where there was despondency, the way a gentle spring rain makes the dusty world sparkle again. And there are ways of dealing with these illicit snacks which will make them not too disastrous.

I have worked out two basic and different kinds of food to cry into, to suit different temperaments. One demands food that is gentle and prepared quickly and without effort; food that is vaguely rich but soft and bland, so that it will make no demands on an already overtaxed system. In other words, it must be the food that we give to little children, for in this our hour of need, we are little children demanding comfort. Cereals, hot or cold, especially oatmeal with brown sugar and a few drops of cream, are excellent to spoon while the tears of self-pity drip. Staunch souls may use skimmed milk, but the richer liquid is not fatal. Yogurt, French toast, omelets, poached or scrambled (but not fried) eggs are good also, but hard-boiled eggs are disastrous. Crackers and milk and milk toast are also most soothing. Soups, especially cream soups, are splendid for the purpose, and so is plain spaghetti or noodles with butter and cheese, or boiled buttered rice. If none of these appeal, I suggest going back to our childhood favorites. My husband likes to spoon cold baked beans from a can, and a rugged professional footballer eats sweet condensed milk with a spoon. A stockbroker friend, prone to melancholia, stuffs himself on bananas. Two eminent female food editors turn respectively to collard greens and homemade fudge. And a famous museum director I know eats plain red Jell-O.

The second approach is radically different. The foods here are not very simple, but extremely complicated. The idea is to force oneself to spend as much time as possible preparing them, and the longer the better, to expunge one's grief. A variety of pretty, little open-faced sandwiches, with different kinds of breads cut into fancy shapes, spread with different butters such as lemon, herb, anchovy, and garlic, topped with dainty little morsels from the delicatessen, will consume hours and hours. Especially if a little homemade mayonnaise decoration is added, piped in artistic patterns from a pastry tube, and the whole then assembled as a Roman mosaic or the Unicorn tapestry or the illuminations of the Très Riches Heures du Duc de Berri. As for giving you exact details on how to do this, I am no help since such an enterprise would enormously increase my own grief rather than decrease it. I suggest you consult a standard cookbook or better still, invest in an hors d'oeuvres cookbook of the fancy kind, which is full of ideas and recipes for this sort of thing. It may cost a few dollars, but they are well spent under the circumstances. You'll have occasion to use it over and again.

For deep grief, such as back taxes, galantines and pâtés are eminently desirable. I don't make the first because life is too short, but I have read plenty of recipes which indeed are complicated, beginning with the boning of the chickens or ducks. This is an art which does not appeal to me, but it may to others. However, I do make pâtés. The activity soothes me, and the results are useful.

For medium grief, I recommend working hard for every bite, which can be done by peeling tiny shrimp or filleting sardines. Lovers of French fries can try cutting a hundred or more into absolutely even-sized pieces; this takes ages. Or one might flute a whole three-pound basket of mushrooms or make Cassoulet, which also takes time and patience.

The pitfall of this approach to food to cry into is that one is apt to get good and sick of these fiddly propositions before one is through. But one should not give up at that point, unless one is sure of having conquered one's emotions. Another pitfall: most of the foods in this category are fattening, which is not good. This can be mitigated by blunting one's appetite before the food is ready to eat. Endless glasses of soda water, low-calorie soda and best, plain water, will serve the purpose, as will the munching of raw celery. The sufferer will be so full that he will be able to throw or give away at least half of what he was going to cry into, which may be a waste, but is all to his good. Or else the sufferer, having got over his sufferings, can save the food and give a party.

Here are a few recipes which have been balm for my own wounds and which have helped friends.

Milk Toast

(One serving)

Toast one slice of bread lightly and spread both sides with butter. Sprinkle with salt, or alternatively with a little sugar and cinnamon. Heat one cup whole or skimmed milk. Put the toast into a bowl and pour the milk over it. Cover tightly and let stand for two to three minutes.

Cream of Mushroom Soup With Sherry
(6 servings)

This soup is best made with homemade White Veal Stock, which makes an excellent base for soups and sauces. As far as I know, it cannot be bought frozen or canned. Cream of mushroom is a good party soup, and it should be very light.

⅓ cup water
⅛ teaspoon salt
1 tablespoon fresh lemon juice
1 tablespoon butter
½ pound very white, very firm mushrooms, thinly sliced
2 tablespoons butter
2 tablespoons flour
6–8 cups hot White Veal Stock (see below) depending on how thick a soup is wanted

Salt
White pepper
⅓ cup light dry sherry, or more to taste
½ cup lightly whipped heavy cream

In a glass or enamel saucepan, bring the water, salt, lemon juice, and the 1 tablespoon butter to the boiling point. Do not use a metal saucepan which will darken the mushrooms which must remain very white. Add the mushrooms and stir to cover the mushrooms with the liquid. Simmer covered for 5 minutes, shaking the pan frequently to prevent sticking. In another saucepan, heat 2 tablespoons butter. Stir in the flour. Cook stirring constantly for 1–2 minutes. Gradually stir in the hot veal stock. Simmer covered for 10 minutes, stirring frequently.

Season with salt and pepper to taste. Add mushrooms and their liquor and heat through. Remove from heat and stir in the sherry. Pour the soup into a heated tureen and top with the slightly whipped cream. Or pour into individual bowls and top each serving with a little whipped cream.

Note: In a pinch, use chicken consommé instead of the veal stock.

White Veal Stock
(About 2½ quarts)

The stock will keep in the refrigerator for about 3–4 days, and it may be frozen.

5 pounds veal bones, including knuckle, cracked	3 quarts water
	2 celery stalks, with tops
	1 large onion, sliced
1 pound veal, cut into pieces	1 large carrot, sliced
	3 parsley sprigs
4 chicken backs	2 teaspoons salt

Place the veal bones, the veal, and the chicken backs into a deep kettle. Add water to cover. Bring to the boiling point, and boil gently for 5 minutes. Drain into a collander. Rinse bones, veal, chicken backs under running cold water to remove the scum. (Veal produces a great deal of scum and this is an easy way to remove much of it; the taste of the stock is not affected.) Rinse the kettle free of all scum. Return the bones, meat, and chicken backs to the kettle. Add the 3 quarts of water and all the remaining ingredients. Bring to the boiling point. Lower heat to lowest possible. Simmer covered for 3–4 hours, skimming as necessary. Strain the stock through a fine sieve lined with a triple layer of cheese-cloth. Chill and remove the fat. Store covered in the refrigerator.

Note: The stock must really simmer, with barely a bubble or two on the surface.

Buttered Spaghetti
(One serving)

Cook as much spaghetti as you think you can eat in plenty of salted rapidly boiling water *al dente,* that is, still firm to the bite. Drain and quickly place in a big, *very hot* bowl. Stir in the butter, cut in pieces, and the grated Parmesan cheese. Toss very thoroughly to coat the spaghetti evenly. Serve immediately on a hot plate, or better still, eat from the bowl.

Use as much butter and cheese as you like. The proportions, roughly speaking, are half as much butter and cheese as spaghetti. That is, for 1 pound spaghetti use ½ pound butter and ½ pound grated Parmesan cheese; for ½ pound spaghetti use ¼ pound butter and ¼ pound grated Parmesan cheese.

What is *important* is to use good, preferably sweet butter and freshly grated Parmesan cheese. The butter should be cold, but not chilled, and cut into slices, for the best flavor. If wanted, season with more salt and freshly ground pepper.

Buttered Rice

Proceed as above, but use boiled rice.

Pâte Fernandé

(10 servings)

This is the kind of pâté served sliced on a bed of lettuce, as a first course. It comes from Madame Garvin, a Bordeaux wines expert.

1½ pounds pork liver, trimmed
1½ pounds lean pork, trimmed of fat and gristle
¾ pound salt pork, blanched
2 eggs
1 teaspoon salt

¾ teaspoon freshly grated pepper
¼ teaspoon ground thyme
1 bay leaf, crumbled fine
2 tablespoons finely chopped onion
2 tablespoons cognac
½ pound sliced bacon

Chop the pork liver, the lean pork, and the salt pork as finely as possible, or push through the finest blade of the meat grinder. In a bowl, combine the meat with the eggs. Mix thoroughly until very well blended. Stir in the salt, the pepper, the thyme, the bay leaf, the onion, and the cognac and blend thoroughly. Line a 9-inch loaf pan with half of the bacon slices. Fill with the meat mixture. Cover with the remaining bacon strips. Place the loaf pan in a pan filled with water; the water should be about ½ inch up the sides of the loaf pan. Bake in a preheated moderate oven (350°F.) for 2 hours. Cool in the pan, unmold, and chill before serving.

Note: To blanch the salt pork, cover with boiling water and let stand for 10–15 minutes. Drain and dry before using.

Cassoulet
(8–10 servings)

4 cups dried pea beans
2 quarts water
1 tablespoon salt
2 cloves garlic, minced
2 carrots, quartered
2 onions, each stuck with
    4 cloves
    Bouquet garni (parsley,
    celery, bay leaf, and
    thyme tied in a little
    bag of cheesecloth)
½ cup diced salt pork
2 tablespoons duck
    drippings or salad
    oil
1½ pounds lean pork,
    cubed

1 pound lamb, cubed
    (trim off all excess
    fat)
2 large onions, chopped
1 cup chopped shallots
1 cup thinly sliced celery
1 6-ounce can tomato
    sauce
1 cup dry white wine
2 Italian or Polish
    sausages
1 roasted duck, boned
    and cut into bite-
    sized pieces or 1
    roasted goose, boned
    and cut into bite-
    sized pieces

Combine beans, water, and salt in a large kettle. Boil for two minutes, take off heat, and let stand for one hour. Add garlic, carrots, onions, bouquet garni, and salt pork. Bring to a boil, then simmer covered over low heat for one hour. Skim as needed. Heat drippings or salad oil in a deep skillet. Add the pork and lamb, and cook over high heat, stirring constantly, until the meats are browned. Add them to the bean mixture.

In the same skillet, cook the chopped onions, shallots, and celery until they are tender. Add the tomato sauce and wine and simmer for five minutes. Add the mixture to the beans. Add the sausages and simmer covered over low heat for about one hour or until the beans are tender. If it looks as though it is drying out, add more hot water, a little at a time. Skim off excess fat. Discard bouquet garni. Check the seasoning and add salt and pepper, if necessary.

Transfer the mixture to a large casserole. Add the roast duck or goose and mix. Bake for 35 minutes in a preheated medium oven (350°F.).

Note: For a party, serve this dish with a tossed salad and fruit and cheese and a chilled, very dry white wine such as Italian Verdicchio di Jesi.

Japonais Torte
(One 8-inch torte)
An elegant and very good Swiss confection

CAKE:
- 5 egg whites, at room temperature
- ¼ teaspoon cream of tartar
- ¼ cup superfine sugar
- ¼ cup sifted flour
- ⅞ cup blanched almonds (4 ounces), grated fine

FROSTING:
- ½ pound sweet butter
- 2 cups sifted confectioners' sugar
- 2 tablespoons instant coffee
- ½ cup hot water

NOUGAT:
- 3 tablespoons sugar
- ⅓ cup coarsely chopped blanched almonds

DECORATION:
- 2–3 squares semisweet chocolate
- 16 whole blanched almonds
- ½ cup heavy cream, whipped with a little sugar

Line two cookie sheets with aluminum foil. Mark out four 8-inch circles on the foil, using the bottom of an 8-inch layer or pie pan as a pattern. Butter the aluminum foil circles. Preheat oven to hot (425°F.).

Beat the egg whites with the cream of tartar until stiff. Sift together the sugar and the flour. Fold it into the egg whites. Fold in the almonds. Divide the mixture evenly between the four buttered circles of aluminum foil. Spread out the mixture to the edge of the circles, keeping the layers as even as possible and keeping the edge of the layers thicker than the middle. Bake for 8–10 minutes or until the tops of the layers are golden brown. Cool for 2–3 minutes on the cookie sheet. Turn the layers upside down on a cake rack and carefully strip off the foil. Cool the layers on the rack.

To prepare the frosting, cream the butter until soft and fluffy. Gradually beat in the sugar and the instant coffee, beating well after each addition. Then slowly beat in the hot water, 2 tablespoons at a time, until the mixture is of spreading consistency. Spread the frosting between the layers and top with the fourth layer. Spread the top and sides of the cake with the frosting.

To prepare the nougat, melt the sugar in a small, heavy frying pan until the sugar liquifies and turns golden brown. Watch carefully because the sugar burns easily. Stir in the almonds. Turn out the mixture on waxed paper, spread it and let it stand until it has hardened. When cool, crush with a rolling pin into a fine powder. Sprinkle the nougat powder over the top and on the sides of the frosted cake. Carefully place the torte on a cake platter. Chill until ready to serve.

Before serving time, melt the chocolate over lowest possible heat. Do not scorch. Dip each almond halfway into the melted chocolate. Lay dipped almonds on a cake rack so that they will dry on all sides. Place the cream into a pastry tube with a small nozzle. Place the chocolate-dipped almonds around the cake in a pleasing pattern. Pipe whipped cream rosettes between the almonds. Chill again until serving time.

A Place to Heal

ANOTHER TIME WHEN the kitchen has to help the stricken is New Year's Day and other day-after mornings, or rather, mournings, when there is a heap o' sorrow piled upon one's loved ones. As Byron said in *Don Juan*: "Let us have wine and women, mirth and laughter, Sermons and soda-water the day after." I think that sermons are uncalled for, and unchristian. But soda water and other medicine, yes indeed. Once, in the spirit of brotherly love, I compiled a list of hangover remedies from friends who shall be nameless, but who do know. Not that I want to imply that anything stronger than Seven-Up touches their lips most of the time, but there are occasions when even saints fall from grace. My collaborators on this project were kind people, who could not resist the men and women with stricken eyes who approach them saying: "Help me, please, help me."

The proper help, the help of brothers who have gone through the same sufferings, should begin before the disaster. Prevention of drunkenness is the first step of the cure. Don't let your friends get stoned in any case, is what I feel. When they are on the way, I shamelessly water or pour away their drinks, distract them (or at

least try to) from going back for more with any means
at hand—conversation, other people, and so on. That is,
when there is a connection between myself and the in-
cipient drunk so that I care. Otherwise I walk away, and
if he can't get home by himself, let him rot in the gutter
for all I care. If I am stuck with a drunk in my own
home, I sit it out only if he/she is a very, very good
friend or business connection. For the latter, I show
that I am not amused; for the former, I have the patient
air of a tired saint. In either case, I don't feed him because that would make him sick, and I get him home
as soon as I can, with any means at my disposal, from
cajoling to threatening. It can be done because nobody
has to put up with other people's drunkenness, if one
really does not want to. I also provide my friends with
hangover cures and suggestions, in the interest of friend-
ship and charity.

Basically, there are two kinds of hangover cures: one
so shocking to the system that it bounces back into
shape through sheer fright, and the other, working with
gentle persuasion over a longer period of time. To the
first category belong a slug of Tequila seasoned with
lemon juice and salt, or a slug of any whiskey, neat, or
a Nikolashka. This is the frightening remedy of my
father's youth, made with a large glass of pure vodka
covered with one slice of salami which has been spread
with a good sharp mustard and sprinkled with pepper.
You sip the vodka through the salami and finally swallow
this too. Other system shockers are tomato juice purple
with Angostura and burning with Tabasco or hot red
peppers, and the classic Prairie Oyster, a nasty concoction of a raw egg yolk pepped up with at least 1 teaspoon
of Worcestershire sauce, ½ teaspoon vinegar, a dash of
Tabasco, and plenty of pepper. Above all shines Fernet

Branca, the most fearful, the most potent of all bitters, made in Italy from an awesome, secret mixture of herbs and bitters. Fernet indeed is effective for the ailments of the stomach, but my husband says that not all people are strong enough for it. Fernet, which really cures a hangover faster than any other remedy, can be spiked with a little gin or vodka for comfort, and taken either straight or with soda. It can only be described as an experience.

Milder hangover remedies are Nelson's Blood, equal parts of brandy and port; Black Velvet, equal parts of champagne and stout; British Blood, equal parts of champagne and brandy; a mean Bloody Mary; sauerkraut juice, spiked or unspiked; Coke syrup from the fountain diluted just a little with soda; a strong Campari and soda, apple juice, Vichy or Perrier water; a milk punch made from ¼ cup brandy and ¾ cup ice cold milk; and, of course, endless cups of black coffee preceded by aspirins and Alka Seltzers.

In my inquiries, I found that most sufferers favor a little food with their hangover medicine. Sour herring and beer are the classic combination; sauerkraut soup is favored by those of Russian and Hungarian ancestry and hot boiled rice with nothing but lots of lemon juice is recommended by the man who runs about the best restaurant in New York, the Coach House. The most terrible of all cures advocates a quart of salted water taken upon arising.

My research also shows that some people cautiously drink 3 pints of water before going to bed, or 1 pint of milk, both followed by aspirins. Even wiser ones take 1 tablespoon of olive oil, a glass of milk or cream, or they eat some cereal or a sandwich to line the stomach against the assault to come. In any case, my own experience with the sufferings of others has taught me to cut short their complaints with remedies such as nourishing soups, a herring snack, chili or curry (found elsewhere in this book), a goulash, and when I can afford it, a great big steak. And I read to them the excellent advice given by Satchel Paige, the baseball pitcher: "Avoid fried foods which anger the blood. If your stomach disputes you, lie down and pacify it with cooling thoughts. Keep the juice flowing by jangling around gently as you move. Go very lightly on the vices such as carrying on in society—the social ramble ain't restful. Avoid running at all times. Don't look back; something may be gaining on you."

Here are a few healing recipes.

French Onion Soup With Wine

(6 servings)

Ali Bab, greatest of all modern French gastronomes, recommends this soup as invigorating.

2 tablespoons butter	6 cups hot beef consommé
2 tablespoons salad oil	
1–2 pounds onions, thinly sliced (quantity depends on whether thicker or thinner soup is wanted)	2 cups dry white wine
	Salt
	Freshly ground pepper
	French bread, sliced
1–2 tablespoons flour	1 cup freshly grated Parmesan cheese

Heat the butter and the oil in a large saucepan. Cook the onions in it, stirring constantly, until they are browned. The onions should be dark, but not burned. Stir the flour into the onions. Add the consommé, the wine, and salt and pepper to taste. Simmer covered over low heat for about 1 hour.

Place slices of French bread in a tureen or in individual soup bowls. Pour the soup over the bread, which will rise to the surface. Sprinkle the bread with the Parmesan cheese. Run under the broiler or place in a preheated hot oven (450°F.) until the cheese is melted.

Sauerkraut Soup

(4–6 servings)

2 tablespoons butter
1 medium onion, chopped
1½ pounds sauerkraut, drained (reserve the juice)
2 tablespoons flour
6 cups hot beef consommé
Salt
Freshly ground pepper
2 bay leaves
½ to 1 cup sour cream

Heat the butter and cook the onion in it until it is soft and golden. Add the sauerkraut. Over medium heat, stirring constantly, cook the sauerkraut for 5 minutes. Be careful not to scorch. Stir in the flour and add the consommé. Season with salt and pepper and add the bay leaves. Simmer covered for about 30 minutes to 1 hour; the longer cooking improves the taste. The soup should have a sharp flavor, which depends on the sauerkraut. If it is not nippy enough, add the reserved sauerkraut juice. Pass the sour cream separately.

Cauliflower Soup
(5–6 servings)

1 medium cauliflower	5 cups hot chicken
Boiling salted water	consommé
2 tablespoons butter	2 cups hot milk
2 tablespoons grated	Salt
onion	Freshly ground pepper
2 tablespoons grated	1–2 egg yolks
celery	⅓ cup heavy cream
2 tablespoons flour	2 tablespoons dry sherry

Trim the cauliflower. Cook it in rapidly boiling salted water until just tender. Drain, divide into flowerets. Reserve about one-fourth of the flowerets. Strain the remaining cauliflower through a foodmill or sieve or puree in a blender with a little of the chicken consommé. Heat the butter. Cook, stirring constantly, the onion and celery in it for about 2 minutes. Stir in the flour and cook 1 minute longer. Gradually stir in the consommé and the cauliflower. Mix well and stir in the milk. Season with salt and pepper to taste. Cook over medium heat, stirring constantly, until the soup coats the spoon. Beat the egg yolk or yolks with the cream. Remove the soup from the heat. Stir a little soup into the egg mixture. Then stir the egg mixture into the remaining soup. Return to heat and heat through, but do not boil. Remove from heat and stir in the sherry and the reserved flowerets. Serve very hot.

Katerfruehstueck

(Herring snack for hangovers)

(4–6 servings)

8 salt herring	1 cup cider vinegar
3 cups milk	1 cup water
3 medium onions, thinly sliced	½ cup sugar
	1 teaspoon pepper

Skin and bone the herring. Slice in half lengthwise. Soak overnight in the milk; this will make them glossy. Drain herring and rinse in cold water. Cut fish into ½-inch pieces. Place alternate layers of herring and onions into deep bowl; do not use aluminum. Combine vinegar, water, sugar, and pepper. Pour over herring; they should barely be covered. Refrigerate for 2–4 hours. Serve with pumpernickel and sweet butter and beer.

Goulash

(4–6 servings)

2½ pounds beef chuck, trimmed of fat and gristle and cut into 1½-inch cubes	2 tablespoons sweet paprika or more to taste
Salt	1 tablespoon flour
Freshly ground pepper	Hot water
¼ cup sweet butter	1 cup sour cream
4 large onions (about 2 pounds), thinly sliced	

Season the meat with the salt and pepper. Heat the butter in a large saucepan. Over high heat, brown the meat in the butter. Push the meat to one side of the saucepan. Reduce heat to medium. Add the onions and cook, stirring constantly, for about 2–3 minutes. Stir in the paprika and cook, stirring all the time, for 2–3 more minutes. Stir in the flour. Add enough hot water to just cover the meat. Bring to the boiling point and reduce heat to lowest possible. Simmer covered for about 1½ hours or until the meat is tender and the onions have cooked down to a pulp. Stir in the sour cream and heat through. If part of a dinner, serve with buttered noodles sprinkled with caraway seeds.

A Place to Cheat

KITCHENS, MOST AMERICANS think, are the heartland of all that is good, honest, heartwarming, family-conserving. Alas, not always so. Kitchens are also the places where people are made to think they can do things which they cannot do. Food for photography and TV is prepared in kitchens—the glorious food you see in the ads and on the screens, the food that makes you drool, and hopefully, rush out to buy the cake mix, the gelatin, the mayonnaise, the fried potatoes, and so on, which will make such splendid dishes. It doesn't, as so many of us find out to our chagrin. I have been one of those whose dreams of culinary magnificence have turned out to be dust and ashes, or rather, were deflated into culinary mediocrity.

There was a time when I was both ambitious and innocent, when I thought that I could reproduce the even-domed pâtés en croûte, the vivacious, multicolored sculptured gelatins, the puddings hidden under baroque swirls of whipped cream of breathtaking symmetry, and the cakes, so tall, so glorious that their sight made my knees go weak—all of which I had seen on TV, in the magazine food pictures, and in the food ads. But however closely I followed the instructions I could not, or only very seldom, reproduce such beauty; my finished dish simply looked so much less than its prototype. As time went on and I got deeper into the food business, I learned the cruel truth: food for photography and food for eating, made at home, are not the same thing. Naturally there are exceptions, especially among magazines, some of which photograph their food just as it is described in the recipe, without any tricking up. But even then the food looks better because the person who fixed it up for photography has more skilled hands than most home cooks.

People who sell food, like those who sell cosmetics, deal in dreams. When photographed, reality in the shape of a nice-looking woman or a cake made according to directions does not look like very much. In fact, thanks to the innate cruelty of the camera, they both seem much less interesting than they appear to the naked eye. Why should anybody imitate or spend money for such plainness? Reality, be it lipstick or roast beef, has to be made into an ideal image to be desirable.

Hundreds of thousands of dollars are spent yearly on food photography, on tons of food of every kind and on the endless hours needed to fix it up for the camera.

And once photographed, most of the food has to be thrown away. The food in the pictures has to be real food, says the Federal Trade Commission, aware that imitation foods would very often look the same or better and be far easier and cheaper to handle. A cake made of styrofoam and frosted with library paste or shaving cream looks like any real cake, and real ice cream looks either too hard or too runny. But the FTC has no laws I am aware of that prevent you from gussying up the food for photography until it is no longer edible.

Food photography is an incredibly skilled kind of photography, for which those who are masters get paid anything from $500 to $3000 and more for a color picture in an important ad. Preparing the food for photography is both an art and a skill, performed by experienced home economists. They may get a couple of hundred bucks a day for their work and even more, but aside from knowing what will look good under the camera and how to make it look good, they must have a peaceful disposition and a patience greater than Job's.

Color photography begins with a layout made by the art director of the magazine or the ad agency who pays the photographer, plus all expenses such as the home economist's fee, that of the person who gets together the props, the expenses for the food, for the maid who cleans up the studio kitchen. All of this is billed to the client. By the day of the picture, the photographer's prop girl, called a stylist, has behind her a lot of running around to get the various accessories needed for displaying the food and creating an atmosphere—special dishes, figurines, distinctive table accessories, posters, and what not, not forgetting vases and flowers or plants. The home economist has prepared whatever food she could in advance, using her own kitchen, arriving early at the studio

to finish her work in the ᴋᴛchens that all food photog-
raphers must have as part of their studios. Large grocery
orders from shops specializing in food for photography
have arrived, such as fish, meat, vegetables, fruits, and
beverages. The photographer is fussing around with his
assistants, getting the lights set up and everything else
ready. If the picture is important, the food editor of the
magazine (or one of her assistants if it is not of first-class
importance) or the art director of the agency is also on
the spot. Shooting begins usually around 10 A.M. and the
end is open. A very important color picture can take
one and even more days to shoot, if the first pictures
taken were not satisfactory. In any case, the best you can
do is to shoot two color pictures a day, one in the
morning and one in the afternoon. Black-and-white
pictures take less time; publicity food pictures, which
are inexpensive, get shot quickly.

The amount of food needed for one photograph is
hardly believable for a layman. This cannot be avoided,
much as those who work with it and pay for it, would
like. The reason is that a number of stand-ins have to
be played around with to determine the perfect angle,
the amount of food needed, the size of each helping or
quantity put intc the dish, the relation between the
food and the things that set it off, like parsley sprigs or
chocolate curls. Before the set-up is ready to be photographed, it has been arranged many times for the best
angle. This is done by making each set-up different from
the other—greatly different or just a little—so that the
photographer can look into his camera and decide.
Imitation foods may be used for these mock-ups, but for
the final shot the real thing has to be made to look
like the model mock-up.

Cakes are among the most difficult foods to shoot,

along with meat and ice cream. It may take as many as thirty-six layers for one picture, as I know from experience. All I am saying here is based upon my own experience. To look tall and ample, picture cakes are baked with more batter than in the original recipe, in deeper pans than those usually used in home kitchens. To look even, the slices of cake have to be trimmed and cut, neatly. Tapemeasure in hand, measuring on all sides, the home economist does her best to produce even slices, but cakes have a life of their own, and like to go in for individual contours no matter how similarly they were cut. To make cakes, especially chocolate cakes, look moist, they may have to be spread with water; to make them look glossy, with lacquer, as with women's hair. Those appetizing crumbs on the dish are painstakingly assembled with toothpicks, chosen for even color and deposited with tweezers where they are wanted; no cake ever crumbles attractively if left to itself. The filling between layers must be smoothed out so as not to look like an open trench in the photograph; the frosting may have to be fortified with flour, sugar, cornstarch, gelatin, and what not to keep it from running under the hot lights. If coconut goes onto a cake, the shreds have to be of fairly even lengths, or the whole will look messy. And those shreds have to be picked out from the contents of package upon package of coconut. And all of these tricks are done not only once, but again and again to get the piece that will look best. Once the perfect stand-in has been produced, it has to be copied exactly for the final shot. This is usually late in the afternoon, and if the art director or the photographer does not like the shot because of the lighting, or because, after all, it is not what he had in mind, the whole thing begins over again, and if not finished, goes on the next day.

Unless you've been there, you cannot believe how the heat of the lights affects the foods. Gorgeous gelatin dishes are fortified with enough extra gelatin to qualify them as footballs, to prevent melting. Carrot curls and cucumber slices lie down limply like dying swans unless their backbone is stiffened with spray or supported by a leaf of lettuce or some other more solid food. The heat plays havoc with all protein foods, cooking them beyond the stage that is right for the picture. Thus fish, in order not to look like foam rubber, is cooked barely to the opaque stage. All birds are roasted for a few minutes, just until the skin is firmed and the goosepimples have disappeared, and their delicious golden brown color is painted on with Kitchen Bouquet or Angostura bitters, the appealing gloss applied with spray or oil.

Kitchen Bouquet and Angostura are invaluable in food photography and are frequently used for the making of photogenic coffee, soup, and liquor drinks. Meat, so as not to look grayish, is roasted to barely rare. The mouth-watering red juices of a roast of beef may be its own or a mixture of food coloring and oil. Tomatoes and radishes at times lose their anemic looks with a little red nail polish, and all salads become dewy with applications of water or spray.

Ice cream is one of the photographer's greatest headaches. For the final shot, the ice cream, which has been kept in containers at temperatures that permit scooping, is molded in the desired shape and frozen for good. When it just begins to melt at the edges, and this takes a fraction of time, it is photographed, so as not to look either like ice or sauce. It takes gallons to get the perfect shot, and even more when the ice cream is rippled or filled with fruit. Then it has to be put together in orderly patterns—and orderliness is the first rule of food photography—and frozen again. Compared to this, stuffing a pâté or pie with foil to achieve a perfect dome over a top layer of filling, or lining a soup dish with marbles for that inviting, brimful look (neither of these permitted now), would be child's play.

Obviously, a color photograph has to be prepared with greater care than a black-and-white one. But food in black-and-white is seldom appealing, as we can see from TV food, since our reactions to it depend on color and color associations. If you don't think so, try serving blue spaghetti or purple mashed potatoes, using food coloring. Since colors, under the camera, have their quirks, they have to be considered in food fixing. But who cares as long as the cake on the box looks twelve inches tall and as glossy and soigné as a fashion model? We can dream, can't we?

Part Two

KITCHEN WORK

Chapter 7

My Mother's Kitchens

Rome

No man, unless he was a tradesman, ever entered my mother's kitchens in Rome or Milan. My father was a man whose shoelaces got ironed each time he changed shoes, which was often, as well as his newspaper, because he did not like a creased newspaper. The idea of going into the kitchen would have surprised him as much as a wife who did not set a good table. He did not even know how to make coffee. When my mother and I went away summers to escape the heat, elaborate arrangements had to be made with the *portiera*, the caretaker's wife downstairs, to have her come up to prepare his coffee, iron his shoelaces and newspaper, and serve all these to him. He never ate anything in the morning.

149

My mother was an excellent cook, though she did not cook regularly because she always had two maids and extra help when needed. But she liked to take a turn at the stove, like a painting teacher touching up his pupils' efforts here and there. When a meal was very important, she would cook the main dish herself. Since my father was a German and my mother Italian, we had both Italian (mostly) and German food at home. My father liked simple dishes, such as scrambled eggs, home-fried

potatoes, and cucumber salad; my mother only liked underdone beef and salad. Our main meal was at one, in the middle of the day, and the usual Italian meal: antipasto or pasta or rice, roast or broiled meat, a vegetable or a salad, and cheese and fruit. Supper, at eight, was a light meal of cold cuts, or eggs, cheese, and invariably, soup, with fruit for dessert. No one in our family had anything for breakfast except black coffee made in a turn-upside-down coffee maker—Napoletana it is called and now just as common in America. Yet the tiled floor of my mother's kitchen was scrubbed three times a day, after each meal, and by scrubbed, I mean scrubbed on knees.

My mother hated the picturesque and there were none of the artifacts of some kitchens in her own—strings of onions and garlic, clay pots, and the like. Quite the contrary, she banished her old inherited copperware to the house in the country because it took the maids too much time to keep it shiny. Shiny it had to be kept and shiny it was kept, by a child who belonged to one of the peasants. My mother cooked on heavy aluminum-ware which even then were better designed than the ones we now have in America, with rounded bottoms and sloping sides. The pots were shined with fine steel wool until they shone like silver.

My mother went in for modern gas stoves, trading in her model for a new one every two years. She did the same with the gas water heater, an enormous, gleaming white enamel thing which heated the water for the many taps in our apartment in the days when each Italian apartment dweller was responsible for his own hot water. The original water heaters were made of copper, and I have the results of the switch from copper to enameled steel still with me in the form of three big copper kettles and an enormous, silverplated salad bowl decorated with Renaissance scrolls. These objects had come about because my mother, not about to throw out a wealth of expensive copper, had ordered one of the numerous Roman artisans to transform the heater into these lovely things, which please me sixty years later.

Since in Italy, to this day, you buy all your own kitchen furnishings except the sink, one wall of our kitchen was occupied by an enormous dresser with more drawers, shelves, pull-outs, and hooks, a creation worthy of Louise Nevelson. The kitchen dishes and silver were kept here as well as whatever saucepans did not hang from the wall, plus the few canned goods we used, such as tomatoes and fruit, sardines, anchovies, and jams. Pasta, rice, flour, and the starches like beans lived in a little cabinet of their own, next to the icebox. Even by modern standards, our icebox was big; the iceman filled it every day, except Thursdays, when it was scrubbed with hot water and household soda to remove all odors.

The dining room had an oval table which could be expanded to seat sixteen and often was. The walls were covered with a dark green cotton damask, as were the straightbacked chairs. On the walls hung Piranesi prints (I still have them on my walls) and on the sideboard stood a display of silver bowls, bonbon dishes, and the like, grouped around a silver coffee and tea set, all of which were polished every other day by a woman who came to polish the silver and wash my father's shirts. Another woman ironed the shirts, as well as the fancy linens used for parties, which were masterpieces of convent embroidery.

We had three sets of dining-room dishes. The best was an old Meissen flower pattern, inherited by my mother and sufficiently precious that she personally supervised its washing. It was used for my father's official entertainments. The second best, for ordinary company, was Nymphenburg, a white pattern with rococo roses. The everyday set was Italian cream china with blue and gold by Ginori, a firm which now has a shop on Fifth Avenue. Once, in a fit of nostalgia, I asked for the pattern but alas, it was no more. The kitchen china was blue and white, a willow pattern, and even as a child I thought it pretty. When many years later, I came to America to set up house on very little money, I remembered my mother's kitchen china and I scouted around New York for it. Indeed I found it, at Georg Jensen, and all smiles, I was prepared to buy a kitchen or rather dining room full of it. I've never forgotten the nasty shock on discovering that my mother's kitchen china was the No. 1 pattern of the Royal Danish Porcelain Factory, that country's traditional pattern and very expensive. I think my mother did not consider it elegant, and that she must have bought it for far less than we pay now.

As I said, my mother knew how to cook extremely well, but she did not do so, except on special occasions. Her maids, trained in her ways, also could not stand anybody in their kitchen, with the result that I never went near the kitchen. But Italian households, even grand ones, are never as remote from the kitchen as equivalent English or American ones. I've never met, nor can I imagine an Italian woman of any age who would be incapable of making some simple food, whereas I have met many American women who literally did not know how to boil an egg.

Streams of visitors, some of them houseguests, passed through our homes. If they stayed with us, they had to adjust themselves to the basic house rule of breakfast in their rooms. My mother hated having the maids' meticulous early-morning housecleaning interrupted by underfoot guests who, to boot, had to be waited on for breakfast when it was so much simpler to send in a tray. Now, having breakfast in one's room seems to me the only civilized way of having it, but not so to others, especially Germans. They were used to sitting down at a prettily laid breakfast table, with special china, tea cozies for the tea or coffee, and tiny cozies for the soft-boiled eggs to keep them warm, plus a bunch of flowers. Of course their loving wives had to be present; some German husbands insisted that the wives butter their bread, offering it to them in small pieces, as if pacifying a difficult household god with small gifts. This repulsive

connubial habit is not only German, but also still to be
seen in Denmark and in Sweden. The treatment of the
German guests, whom my father had to have because
of his position as a diplomat, was an eternal bone of
contention at home.

"Guests, however inconvenient, must be honored,"
said my father, and my mother agreed, but not to the
point where they had to be honored at certain hours of
the day, like breakfast in the dining room. She won out
and I can still see the giant tray going into a bedroom,
crowded with boiled eggs, sliced ham, toast, butter, jam
and honey, fresh rolls, and a blossom in a bud vase to
give that single touch of beauty, all being lugged by a
maid in a blue-and-white striped cotton morning dress.
If the guest was male, and without a wife, he had been
warned by my father to be decently clad when breakfast arrived, which meant a dressing gown hiding every
inch of pajama. An unfortunate incident had brought
this warning about, when a lightly clad elderly and very
famous German writer had become so entranced with
the fresh rural charms of the maid who brought his
food that he clasped her to his bosom, though fortunately only after she had set down the tray. It turned out
that the maid, hoping for a large tip, had not been
averse to this show of affection, but my mother, whose
room was nearby, had heard something of the commotion. She burst into the guest room, yanked out the
maid, and pushed her back to the respectability of the
kitchen; then she told the guest, bursting into his room
again, what she thought of his morals.

The worst among our guests, and one of the most
prominent, was Richard Strauss, the composer, or so
my mother claimed. Strauss had come with his wife to
Milan to conduct some works of his at the Scala and they

stayed with us a few days until they could find a hotel to their liking. They were a difficult couple. The maestro was lugubrious by disposition, but he had the habit of command. Frau Strauss, a former actress and a lively woman, defended her husband's willfulness as the divine right of composers, which did not sit well with my mother. The maestro was also very fussy about his food, and his wife had the habit of presenting her hostesses with the menus and even recipes of what he wanted to eat. My mother paid her back by having the Strauss dishes prepared just as they liked it, but only for them; we and the people who had been invited for various meals to meet them ate whatever my mother had decided on. I still have a recipe for barley soup which came from Frau Strauss, which I think rather good. My own memory of the Strausses is not that sunny either. The maestro never spoke to me (I was a teen-ager) and his wife, whom I had to guide around on her passionate shopping trips, never stopped haggling, even in Milanese luxury shops—because "that's what you do in Italy," were her words.

As I said, I never cooked in my mother's kitchens, though I was allowed to do one dish, fresh fruit salad

for parties. Fruit salad had become a favorite dessert after my mother had come back from England, and it had to be made with a great variety of fruit— peaches, fresh pineapple, apricots, greengages, strawberries, oranges, and grapefruit, whatever fruit was seasonable. My mother treated this as a great discovery, why, I do not know; "macedonia di frutta," as fruit salad is called in Italy, is one of the standard dishes. The fruit had to be peeled and pitted carefully—even grapes—and it had to be cut into neat, even pieces. Rather than plain sugaring the fruit, we made a thick sugar syrup in which we cooked the yellow peel of several lemons for a subtle, haunting flavor and poured the hot syrup over the fruit. The lemon rinds were removed before serving, and the juice of a lemon stirred in to point up the flavors. The fruit salad was served from a silver bowl, icy cold and accompanied by a bottle of Kirsch for those who liked it on their fruit. Cherries did not go into fruit salad because they would have discolored it. They were cooked and served separately, pitted, of course, and boiled up just once with sugar and no water and then chilled.

The only reason I was allowed to make fruit salad for parties is that it takes a good deal of time to make it properly and neatly, so that my mother felt the maids had better things to do. Otherwise desserts were ordered at the best local pastry shop, spectaculars like Saint Honoré or Religieuses—a tower of tiny, differently flavored puffs hidden behind a veil of spun sugar. This was, and still is in Italy, considered far more elegant than a homemade dessert, with the exception of Crème Renversée, which my mother occasionally made herself, turning it out on the crystal dish without a crack.

The utmost cleanliness was mandatory in our kitchen,

which meant clean white aprons with half sleeves for anybody who spent any time there. But once my mother's passion for cleanliness was bettered by a cook who covered the whole kitchen floor after each washing not with newspaper, but white wrapping paper to keep it clean. All possible kitchen surfaces were similarly covered. The cook herself looked like an operating-room nurse with white stockings and shoes, a long, longsleeved white coverall and a gauze mask over her nose and mouth. Every single strand of hair was tucked into a white cap, and she wore a white apron over her coverall, which she changed several times a day, whenever it showed a spot. This woman also sterilized our pots and pans, dishes, and silverware by boiling them long and hard. Since she insisted on a similarly hygienic getup for the other maid and even my mother when she wanted to come into the kitchen, she did not last long.

For her dinner parties, my mother used to engage two and more waiters, calculating one waiter for every four guests. They were in black and wore white gloves. Though the meals were formal, with a white, a red wine, and champagne for dessert, the menus were much simpler than those of American hostesses. The beginning was invariably a strong double beef consommé made at home, and garnished with strips of homemade crepes, served in cups, with cheese straws. Then came the fish, sautéed, or cold trout, or a whole bass, or fried fillets of sole with tartar sauce. The fish was served with nothing but small boiled parsleyed potatoes, and to this day I think that boiled potatoes are the only vegetable fit to accompany fish. The meat course consisted either of roast veal or roast beef or breaded and fried turkey breasts, a great delicacy because the turkeys were small and you had to buy the whole bird. The meat was carved in the kitchen and dished up on silver platters in over-lapping slices, with mounds of tiny vegetables arranged around the meat with a view to color: broiled tomatoes next to roast potatoes, bundles of string beans next to carrots, peas next to cauliflowerets. The vegetables were fresh and seasonable. Sometimes my mother served a green salad before the dessert, which was followed by cheese and fruit. Coffee, already poured into tiny cups, was handed around in the drawing room, together with liqueurs and cigars for the gentlemen. Nobody smoked at the table.

Among my mother's entertainments were tea parties, *Herrenabende* and *ricevimenti*. For the first, the dining table was laid with an elaborately embroidered white cloth, for in those days, all the tablecloths one ate from were white, and nothing else. As for dinner, the artfully folded tea napkins matched the tablecloth. The china was thin English bone china, I still see the little sprigs. Plates covered with hand-embroidered doilies, holding thin little cucumber, salmon, anchovy and prosciutto sandwiches, were matched by plates holding a variety of cookies. The sandwiches were speared with special pronged forks (I still have them), and the cookies seized with a kind of wide-bladed blunt scissors. We used egg scissors for our boiled eggs and grape scissors (all silver, of course) to cut the grapes at the table and wash them in the inevitable finger bowls that sat on their own doily on the dessert plate. My mother poured the tea from her two silver pots, and when she needed new tea, she rang her little silver bell, the one she used at the dinner table to call a maid dressed in black for the afternoon, with a white cap and a white organdy apron. The ladies helped themselves either to cream, lemon, or rum. I still have the little tea table rum decanter we used. I especially remember one tea party, when I was tall enough to look over the table as I emerged from under the long folds of the tablecloth. I used to hide under the table when I was small enough to do so, and pinch the legs that were so readily available. Then I was hauled out, slapped, and sent into my room.

Herrenabende, gentlemen's evenings, were those when gentlemen entertained themselves without women. I hasten to say that they were no more stag parties than ballet performances, but occasions when men talked business or politics without having to be polite to the ladies. They started after dinner, around nine, with wine, whiskey, and cigars. Neither my mother nor the maids appeared since my father let in his guests by himself. During the course of the evening my mother set out a cold collation on the dining table, so that the men could eat whenever they felt like. Here too, she never showed. The food was substantial, including cold roast beef eaten with remoulade sauce in the German manner, ham, wurst of different kinds, including the great delicacy of goose liver wurst studded with truffles, cheeses, potato salad, a mixed vegetable salad containing pickled herring, and, of course, various breads and mounds of butter rolls. No sweet was served and the drink was beer.

As much as the *Herrenabende* were a German institution, the *ricevimenti* were an Italian one, the social payoff, equivalent to the American cocktail party. Now, with the American way of life encroaching on Old World habits, few Italians still give *ricevimenti* unless for a super special occasion, and like us, pay off their social debts in what is called "un cocktail," meaning a cocktail party. But in my youth, predinner debauches were unknown, the guest getting only a vermouth or Campari before his meal, an aperitif in the truest sense of the word. It would have been unheard of to get sloshed before dinner, as we do here. *Ricevimenti* fell into two kinds: one could give afternoon *ricevimenti*, though my mother favored evening ones, which began at nine and ended at midnight. Since the guests had had their dinner, there was not much to eat or drink at a *ricevimento* though it was served with elegance.

First, black coffee was handed around by the hired waiters who were a necessity for a proper *ricevimento*. They wore white gloves and looked worldly and cynical, which was not surprising considering the sights they must have seen during their work. Next, Marsala, Strega, Benedictine, Chartreuse, and the like were served to the ladies from tiny glasses. The gentlemen were offered cognac or whiskey, with soda if so wanted, but without ice. People who did not like spirits could get lemonade or orangeade, freshly made. The alcoholic drinks were meant to be sipped, not downed, and if a man, in a couple of hours, got more than two under his belt he was lucky, but that depended on the waiters. Again, to be even slightly under the influence was unheard of. As for the ladies, they would have thought it scandalous to sip more than one little glass of sweet liqueur. For their benefit, small cakes and petit fours, all tiny in size, made the rounds on doily-covered silver platters. The moral character of a lady was not suspect if she stuffed herself with sweets, as it would have been had she sneaked three liqueurs, not that that would have been easy. The ladies could also nibble from the scores of *bonbonnières* that stood around filled with chocolates, fancy candy, and sugared almonds.

Any self-respecting family in Italy used to accumulate an appalling number of these, offered as elegant, desirable presents, but of small use. The memory of the painted, gilded, scrolled and embossed china, glass and silver *bonbonnières,* in every possible shape, from basket to cupid, shell to cupped hand, all not to be touched by children because of their precious beauty, still sends shudders of hate through me. We all react against our childhood, and my reaction was and is to have as few objects around as possible.

Another feature of the *ricevimento* of my youth, but one never found in our own home, was the rented cakes. Honor bound, I must say that this practice is passé for many years now. But in those days, in Rome, it was possible to rent a number of showy cakes from a *pâtisserie.* These were masterworks of spun sugar and butter cream sculpture, and even of romantic scenes painted on with a brush dipped in liquid chocolate. *Facevano un' ottima figura*—they made an excellent impression at anybody's party buffet. A small rental fee for the evening was charged for each of these cakes, but the host only paid for the whole cake if it actually had been cut. At the end of the *ricevimento* the caterer took the cakes back home, no doubt to rent them again the next day. Thus an ambitious hostess could be very elegant at a small cost. My mother, superior to practices of the kind, told me with glee that the more frugal hostesses of her acquaintance watched the rented cakes with terror in their eyes lest a guest should demand a slice of the rented beauty, thus ruining her chance of returning the whole cake. It was said that if you wanted to spite your hostess, the best way to do this was to ask for a tiny slice of each cake which looked as if it had been rented.

Childhood impressions last one's own life. Even if I had no part in my mother's kitchens, I absorbed her way of doing things there, as I realize anew almost every day.

Such as washing up the dirty dishes as you cook, in order to come out with a reasonably clean kitchen when the meal is ready to serve, of wearing an apron the moment I enter the kitchen, of cooking everything fresh and in just quantities to avoid warmed-up leftovers. And finally, but very centrally so, of hating men who mess around in the kitchen when they are not professionals or paid to do so, or rather, of hating those men who mess around in a kitchen and want to be admired for it.

Eggplant Antipasto

(About 1 quart)

3 cups peeled and cubed eggplant

⅓ cup chopped green pepper

1 medium onion, coarsely chopped

¾ cup sliced fresh mushrooms or one 4-ounce can mushroom stems and pieces

2 cloves garlic, crushed

⅓ cup olive oil or salad oil

1 6-ounce can tomato paste

¼ cup water

2 tablespoons wine vinegar

½ cup stuffed olives

1½ teaspoons sugar

½ teaspoon oregano

1 teaspoon salt

¼ teaspoon freshly ground black pepper

Put the eggplant, the green pepper, the onion, the mushrooms, the garlic, and the oil in a frying pan. Cover and cook gently 10 minutes, stirring occasionally. Add the remaining ingredients and mix well. Simmer covered until the eggplant is tender, about 30 minutes. Put in a dish, cover, and chill in the refrigerator overnight to blend flavors. Serve on lettuce leaves.

Tomatoes and Peppers

(4 servings)

A Roman first course or salad

6 tablespoons olive oil	Salt
2 tablespoons mild vinegar	Freshly ground pepper
¼ cup minced shallots or onion	2 large or 3 medium ripe tomatoes
1 large garlic clove, minced	2 large or 3 medium sweet peppers, preferably red
¼ cup minced parsley	
½ teaspoon ground thyme or dried basil	

Combine the olive oil, the vinegar, the shallots, the garlic, the parsley, the thyme, and the salt and pepper in a small bowl. Mix well. Let stand for 30 minutes. Peel the tomatoes by plunging them into boiling water for 1 minute and removing the peel. Cut off the blossom end. Chill the tomatoes before cutting them into medium slices.

While the tomatoes are chilling, prepare the peppers. Turn one of the top burners of the stove on to medium heat. Stand the peppers over the heat so that they will char on the side exposed to the heat. As this side is black and blistery, turn them around on all sides so that they will char all over. Under running cold water, using your fingers and a paring knife, scrape off all the burnt skin—the cold water will cool your fingers. Trim the peppers by cutting off the seeds and the membranes. Cut the trimmed peppers into 1½-inch-wide slices. Dry them with paper towel and chill them for a few minutes. On a shallow serving dish, or on four individual plates, arrange alternate slices of tomatoes and peppers. Mix the dressing and drizzle it over the vegetables. Chill for 1–2 hours before serving or serve as is.

Variation

For a fuller first course, you may add one or more of the usual Italian antipasto foods, such as chunks of tuna fish, sliced salami, anchovies, stuffed eggs.

Stuffed Tomatoes

(6 servings)

These rice-stuffed tomatoes are a typical Roman dish. They may be eaten hot or cold, as a first course. It is difficult to give exact amounts for the rice that is to stuff the tomatoes since the size of the latter varies. Roughly speaking, 2–3 tablespoons of cooked rice are needed for each tomato. If there is any rice left over, bake it alongside the tomatoes in the pan.

8 medium to large tomatoes
½ cup olive oil
¼ cup minced onion
1 garlic clove, minced
¼ cup minced parsley
Grated rind of ½ large or 1 small lemon
1 cup rice (preferably converted rice)

2 cups hot chicken or beef consommé
½–1 cup freshly grated Parmesan cheese
Salt
Freshly ground pepper
Freshly ground pepper

Cut a ½-inch slice off each tomato at the stem end. Scoop out the tomatoes with a teaspoon, taking care not to break the walls. Reserve the scooped-out pulp. Turn the tomatoes upside down to drain them. Then place them side by side in a buttered or oiled shallow baking dish, preferably one that can come to the table. Sprinkle each tomato cavity with a little olive oil, using, all in all, about 2–3 tablespoons. Strain the scooped-out pulp through a strainer and reserve. Heat the remaining olive oil. Add the onion, the garlic, and the parsley. Cook over medium heat, stirring constantly, for about 2–3 minutes or until the onion is soft. Stir in the lemon rind and the rice. Add the consommé and lower heat to simmer. Cook covered for about 10 minutes or until the rice is about three-quarters done. Cooking time depends on the kind of rice used. The rice should be creamy, but not soupy; it may even be necessary, again depending on the kind of rice used, to add a little more consommé or to cook without a cover to let excessive moisture evaporate. Remove from the heat. Stir in the Parmesan cheese. Taste and season lightly with salt (the cheese is salty) and pepper.

Fill the tomatoes with the rice. Pour the reserved tomato juice into the pan with the tomatoes, to the depth of ⅓ inch. Bake in a preheated moderate oven (350°F.) for about 30 minutes. If during baking time the tomatoes show signs of drying out, add a little more tomato juice or water. If the tomatoes are very juicy and give out too much liquid, spoon some off. The end result should be tomatoes that are moist but not soupy and not dried out. Serve the tomatoes from the dish.

Amatriciana Sauce For Pasta

(Enough for 1 pound pasta, preferably spaghetti)

A specialty of Roman trattorie. The sauce is made with pork fat rather than olive oil and quickly cooked so that the tomatoes taste fresh. The traditional cheese used with this sauce is the sharp, pungent Pecorino, but I recommend either a mixture of Parmesan and Romano, or Parmesan alone.

2 tablespoons olive oil	Salt
½ cup minced blanched salt pork or bacon	Freshly ground pepper
	1 pound cooked pasta
4 tablespoons minced onion	1–2 tablespoons butter
1 garlic clove, minced	1 cup freshly grated Parmesan and
¼ cup minced parsley	Romano cheeses,
1½ pounds ripe Italian plum tomatoes, chopped	mixed, or either one of them

Combine the olive oil, the salt pork, the onion, the garlic, and the parsley. Over medium heat, and stirring constantly, cook for about 3–4 minutes or until the onion is golden. Add the tomatoes, salt and pepper to taste. Bring to the boiling point. Lower heat and simmer without a cover 15 minutes or until the tomatoes are just cooked. At serving time, when the sauce is to be poured over the cooked pasta, stir the butter into the pasta. Serve with grated Parmesan and Romano.

Summer Spaghetti

This is a method rather than recipe with definite amounts of ingredients. The tomatoes must be very ripe and very fresh, and the spaghetti very hot. No grated Parmesan is needed.

Fresh ripe tomatoes, peeled, seeded, and coarsely chopped
Olive oil
Salt
Freshly ground pepper
Fresh minced basil or parsley

Combine the ingredients, using olive oil, salt, pepper, and basil to taste while the spaghetti is cooking. Drain the spaghetti, toss with the sauce, and serve immediately.

Garlic-Broiled Shrimp

(6 servings)

This is the "scampi al ferri" featured in many Italian restaurants. The Italian scampi, however, differ somewhat from the American shrimp. But on the whole, the taste is similar.

2 pounds medium or large shrimps
⅔ cup olive oil
2 garlic cloves, minced
2 teaspoons salt
Freshly ground pepper
½ cup minced parsley
Juice of 2 lemons
Lemon wedges

Wash the shrimps. Shell them, and with the point of a sharp knife, remove their black veins. Arrange the shrimps in a shallow broiling pan. Sprinkle with the olive oil, the garlic, the salt and pepper, and half of the parsley. Broil about 4 inches from the source of heat for about 4–6 minutes on each side, depending on the size of the shrimps. Transfer the shrimps to a heated serving dish. Sprinkle with the lemon juice and the remaining parsley. Serve with lemon wedges.

Frittata With Peppers
(3 servings)

A *frittata* is a flat, pancake-like Italian omelet. Any other suitable ingredient may be added to the eggs, such as mushrooms, onions, chicken livers, bits of cooked meats or vegetables, and the like. If the additional ingredients are raw, they should be cooked first in the usual manner; if already cooked, they are added as is. A *frittata* is a splendid way of dealing with leftovers. It is good hot or cold, and fine as a sandwich stuffing or for picnics.

2 sweet green, red, or yellow peppers	2 tablespoons water or milk
4 tablespoons olive oil	Salt
5 eggs	Freshly ground pepper
1 tablespoon flour	

Wash the peppers. Remove all the membranes and the seeds. Cut the peppers into 1-inch-long slices. Heat the olive oil in a frying pan. Over low heat, and stirring frequently, cook the peppers in it for about 5 minutes or until just tender but still crisp. Beat together the eggs, the flour, the water or milk and season with salt and pepper to taste. Pour the mixture over the peppers. Mix well and distribute evenly in the frying pan. Cook over low heat until the eggs have set and the underside of the *frittata* is lightly browned. Slice on a dinner plate, browned side up. Slide back into the frying pan and cook for about 2 minutes longer or until set. Serve immediately on a hot plate or cool to room temperature before serving.

Roman Lamb Stew With Egg Sauce

(4–5 servings)

Lamb is very popular in Rome. The meat is pale, delicate, and lean, and does not have to be trimmed of large amounts of fat as American lamb does. Lard is much used in Roman cooking, and is one of the reasons for the distinctive flavor of the cooking of Rome. This dish, which can also be made with veal, might be served with boiled new potatoes or with mashed potatoes and green peas.

3 pounds boneless lamb, trimmed of all excess fat, cut into 1½-inch cubes
¼ cup minced prosciutto or lean bacon
3 tablespoons minced onion
1 large garlic clove, minced
1 teaspoon dried rosemary, crumbled, or more to taste

2 tablespoons lard
Salt
Freshly ground pepper
2 tablespoons flour
⅔ cup dry white wine
Hot water
3 egg yolks
2 tablespoons lemon juice
¼ cup minced parsley

In a deep frying pan or in a saucepan, combine the lamb, the prosciutto or bacon, the onion, the garlic, the rosemary, and the lard. Cook over medium heat, stirring constantly, until the lamb is golden—it should not be brown. Season with salt and pepper and stir in the flour. Add the wine. Cook uncovered, stirring frequently, until the wine has evaporated. Lower the heat and add enough hot water to almost, but not quite, cover the meat. Simmer covered, over low heat and stirring frequently, for 25 minutes or until the meat is tender but not overcooked. If the dish is too dry and threatens to scorch, add a little more hot water. There should be about ½ cup of liquid left when the meat is cooked.

Beat together the egg yolks, the lemon juice, and the parsley. Remove the lamb from the heat and stir in the egg mixture. Over lowest possible heat cook until the sauce has thickened. Stir constantly and *do not boil,* or the sauce will curdle; it should be just heated through. If necessary, set the pan with the lamb on a flame-proof asbestos pad or into a larger dish filled with hot, but not boiling water.

Pork Chops With Artichokes

(4–6 servings)

A popular Roman specialty, as you find in the small family-run trattorie, the old wineshop-restaurants in the small old side streets of old Rome, near the Tiber. Serve with home-fried potatoes.

2 large or 4 medium
    artichokes
4 tablespoons olive oil
6 pork chops, trimmed
    of excess fat
    Salt
    Freshly ground pepper
2 garlic cloves, minced

1 tablespoon fresh
    minced rosemary or
    basil, or 2 teaspoons
    dried crumbled
    rosemary or sage
1 No. 2 can Italian-style
    tomatoes (about 2½
    cups)

Slice the artichokes according to directions given below. Heat the olive oil in a deep frying pan. Cook the pork chops in it until they are brown on both sides. Pour off the excess fat. Arrange the artichoke slices around the pork chops. Sprinkle with the salt, pepper, the garlic, and the herbs. Pour the tomatoes over the meat. Bring to the boiling point and turn heat to simmer. Cover and simmer for about 1 hour or until the meat and artichokes are tender. If the sauce is too thin, simmer uncovered until sufficiently reduced.

Note: This is a more-or-less dish. If you like more artichokes, put them in. Or else, use fewer pork chops—the ingredients are flexible. But do not use frozen artichokes because they cook too quickly and disintegrate before the pork chops are ready.

How to Slice Artichokes

Have ready a bowl of cold water mixed with white vinegar or lemon juice—about 2–3 tablespoons for each quart of water. Since artichokes discolor as soon as they are cut, they must be dropped into the acidulated water to keep light. Use a sharp knife.

Slice off and discard the stem at the base of the artichoke, leaving no more than about one-quarter inch. Tear off and throw away the large outer leaves. Place the artichoke on its side and cut off the tops of the leaves, with about 1–2 inches of leaf on the base. The idea is to get rid of the tough upper parts of the leaves, using only the tender bottom parts. How much to cut off depends on the size and age of the artichokes; old artichokes get tough and more leaf has to be cut off. Dip the artichoke into the acidulated water. Trim the base with a paring knife to achieve a smooth surface. Dip the artichoke again into the acidulated water. Cut it into 4 quarters as if cutting an apple. Drop the pieces into the acidulated water. Take one quarter at a time, and cut out the fuzzy bit in the middle, called the choke, just as you would core an apple. Thinly slice each quarter just as you would slice an apple, and drop each slice immediately into the acidulated water. Keep the artichoke slices in the acidulated water until ready to use. Then drain and pat dry with paper towel.

Naturally, the artichokes may also be used in quarters, but always de-fuzzed. However, American artichokes are tougher than Italian ones. Whenever a recipe calls for quartered artichokes, I cut them into eighths, unless they are very small, because they cook through better.

Veal Scaloppine Al Marsala

(3–4 servings)

White wine or a medium sherry may be used instead of the Marsala. Serve with parsley potatoes and a green salad.

2 pounds veal scaloppine, cut as thin as possible from a leg of veal, measuring about 4-inches square	4 tablespoons butter Salt Freshly ground pepper ¼ cup dry Marsala Lemon wedges

Place the scaloppine between two pieces of waxed paper. With a rolling pin, or a bottle, or a full can of fruit, pound the scaloppine to flatten them as much as possible without tearing the meat. Heat the butter in a large frying pan. Place the meat side by side in it. Cook over high heat for 2–3 minutes on each side or until golden brown. Season with salt and pepper. Transfer the scaloppine to a heated serving platter and keep hot. Pour the Marsala into the frying pan. Scrape up all the brown meat bits at the bottom of the pan. Bring to the boiling point once and pour over the scaloppine. Serve immediately, surrounded by lemon wedges.

Broccoli, Roman Style

(4 servings)

1 bunch broccoli
¼ cup olive oil
2 garlic cloves, whole
Salt

Freshly ground pepper
1½ cups dry red or white
    wine

Trim the broccoli. Cut into small flowerets. Peel the thick stems and slice them. Wash the broccoli, drain and dry on paper towel. Heat the olive oil in a large frying pan and add the garlic cloves. Cook until the garlic is brown. Remove it and throw it away. Add the broccoli and season with salt and pepper. Cook over medium heat, stirring constantly, for about 3 minutes. Turn heat to low and add the wine. Stir to mix. Cover and simmer for about 5–10 minutes or until tender. The cooking time depends on the freshness of the vegetable and the size of the flowerets. Stir occasionally with a fork, taking care not to break the pieces.

Pan-Fried Potatoes With Mozzarella

(4 servings)

Mozzarella is a Roman favorite

2 tablespoons butter
2 tablespoons olive oil
4 cups sliced boiled
    potatoes
½ cup diced mozzarella

1 teaspoon dried
    rosemary, crumbled
Salt
Freshly ground pepper

Heat the butter and the olive oil in a skillet. Add the potatoes. Cook, stirring frequently, until they begin to get golden. Stir in the mozzarella and the rosemary and season with salt and pepper. Cook, stirring the potatoes gently with a fork, until well-blended and golden.

Sweet-Sour Onions

(4–5 servings)

A Roman dish served either as part of a plate of antipasto or with boiled or roasted meats. The dish may be eaten warm or cold.

About 25 small white onions (pickling onions are best)
3 tablespoons butter
1 tablespoon flour
1 cup beef consommé or onion broth

1 tablespoon vinegar
1–2 teaspoons sugar
Salt
Freshly ground pepper
2 tablespoons minced parsley

Peel the onions. Cook them in salt water to cover until not quite tender. Drain and reserve 1 cup of the broth. Heat 2 tablespoons of the butter in a deep frying pan or shallow saucepan. Over low heat, cook the onions in it for about 3 minutes or until they are golden. Shake the pan frequently to prevent sticking. Remove the onions with a slotted spoon and keep hot. Add the remaining tablespoon of butter to the frying pan. Heat until golden, but do not brown. Stir in the flour and the consommé or the onion broth. Cook over low heat, stirring constantly, until smooth and thickened. Stir in the vinegar, the sugar, and salt and pepper to taste. Return the onions to the sauce. Simmer covered for 5–10 minutes or until tender. Sprinkle with the parsley before serving warm or cold.

Green Sauce (Uncooked)

(About 1⅓ cups)

A classic Italian sauce for hot and cold, boiled and broiled meats and seafood, hard-cooked eggs (as a first course), and cooked vegetables, such as broccoli, cardoons, cauliflower, and artichokes. With a blender, the sauce is easy and quick to make since it eliminates all the chopping and mincing.

2 tablespoons drained capers
1 tablespoon chopped onion
1 garlic clove
1 anchovy
2 cups parsley sprigs, no stems and tightly packed

1 teaspoon dried basil or fresh basil to taste
¾ cup olive oil
Juice of 2 lemons
1 teaspoon salt
¼ teaspoon freshly ground pepper

Combine all the ingredients in a blender. Blend to a puree. Or mince all the dry ingredients together on a chopping board until they are a paste. Transfer to a bowl. Slowly beat in the olive oil and the lemon juice.

Variation

Add a chopped hard-boiled egg to the sauce or ⅓ cup chopped walnuts or pignoli nuts.

Ricotta Soufflé

(4–6 servings)

Ricotta, which resembles cottage cheese but has a distinct flavor of its own, is much used in Roman cooking. The proper ricotta is made from the whey of cheese made from ewe's milk, such as provolone. In the United States, it is made from cow's milk and not nearly as flavorful as the real thing, but still much more interesting than cottage cheese.

¼ cup minced candied lemon, orange or citron, or a combination
¼ cup golden raisins
⅓ cup rum, brandy, or Kirsch

1 pound ricotta
2 tablespoons flour or cornstarch
¼ cup sugar
3 eggs, separated
2 egg whites
Sifted confectioners' sugar

Combine the fruit in a bowl and pour the spirit over it. Let stand for 15–30 minutes. With an electric beater, beat together the ricotta, the flour or cornstarch, and the sugar until the mixture is very smooth. Beat in the egg yolks, one at a time, beating well after each addition. Stir in the fruit and their liquor. Beat all the egg whites until stiff. Fold them into the batter. Turn into a buttered 1½-quart (6-cup) soufflé dish. Bake in a preheated moderate oven for about 45 minutes or until the soufflé is puffed up. Sprinkle with confectioners' sugar and serve immediately. Cream or any fruit sauce may be served with it, or any compote or fresh strawberries or raspberries.

The Roman Way With Strawberries

Since water destroys a good part of the strawberries' delicate taste and aroma, in Rome they are washed with
wine rather than water. Trim the berries as usual. Fill a
small bowl with any inexpensive dry red or white wine.
Quickly rinse the berries in the wine and drain them.
Put them into a serving bowl and sprinkle with sugar
and chill, but not excessively or the flavor will be gone.

Variation

In Rome, as in other parts of Italy, the sugared berries
are sprinkled with either orange juice, or lemon juice, or
Marsala, either before chilling or at serving time.

Granita Di Caffe Con Panna

(4–5 servings)

This is a coffee ice, not an ice cream, topped with
whipped cream. It is a favorite Roman refreshment,
served in all cafés. It is easily made at home; I find
Americans like it as much as the Romans on a hot summer's day, as an improvement over ordinary iced coffee.

1½ cups ground Italian-
   style coffee
⅓ to ½ cup sugar

6 cups boiling water
Sweetened whipped
   cream

Combine the coffee, the sugar, and the water in the top
of a double boiler. Steep covered over simmering water
for 30 minutes. Cool. Strain through a strainer lined with
a triple thickness of cheesecloth. Freeze in an ice tray
at regular freezing temperatures. Stir once or twice; the

finished *granita* should be icy and mushy rather than hard and smooth. Serve in glasses, topped with sweetened whipped cream.

The Cerro Kitchen

SALAMI SANDWICHES AND birth pains fused into one on a fine July morning in my mother's kitchen in Cerro, a village on the hilly southern shore of Lake Maggiore, opposite Stresa. I was there to expect the arrival of my firstborn, and my then husband, an Englishman, was there too to recuperate from illness. Being pregnant is called an interesting condition in Italian and well did I understand why, since the child would not arrive. Sweepstakes on the date of his birth had been taken up, and bored as I was, I had considered hiring a posse of bloodhounds to chase the reluctant infant out of the womb into the world. What made things worse was that I knew that I would not know when birth was imminent, and how right I was! I had inquired from a number of pregnant women on how they knew when they were due, but the answers had not been satisfactory. Thus I ignored the whole situation, went to Cerro instead of staying in Milan in the vicinity of the Clinica where the blessed event was to take place, and kept house with abandon because it was the first time that my mother's kitchen was mine. Prudently, my mother, during this time, had retired to one of the high Alpine resorts of Switzerland which she adored, to rest up for the great event. The arrangement suited both of us very well.

The kitchen was an old-fashioned Lombard country kitchen, part of the old Northern Italian country house that my parents had left pretty much as it was, except for adding the conventional modern hygienic amenities. The bedrooms were on the upper floor, and the downstairs consisted of two rooms: a large sala, a combination sitting and dining room, and an even larger kitchen. The sala had the sparse quality of Italy's pre-interior-decorating times: whitewashed walls, speckled tiled floor, a round table in the middle of the room with a hanging lamp and embroidered lampshade over it, six straight bentwood chairs, two bentwood rockers, and an antique horsehair sleigh-shaped sofa. Clusters of green house

plants stood in one corner and in the other, a sideboard where the table linens were kept, with a cut-glass punch-bowl and glasses on it which served no earthly purpose. A battery radio also stood on the sideboard and a vase filled with flowers from the garden. Piles of books and magazines lay on a nearby low wicker table.

The focus of the big kitchen was the hearth, which occupied almost half of one of the long walls. A gigantic hood topped the mantel shelf on which stood a wooden box with sewing materials, odd apples and quince left there to ripen, a glass holding pencils, several candle-holders, an old oil lamp, and dun-colored paper boxes filled with coarse kitchen matches. In the fireplace itself you could still see two iron arms from which dangled chains with big links: in earlier times, they had served to hold the *paioli*, the big copper polenta pots in which the cornmeal was stirred with a wooden paddle as it cooked. The firedogs topped with sphynx heads emerged from the ashes. Though we no longer used the hearth for cooking, we kept a fire going whenever there was a chill in the air, fed from a pile of wood neatly stacked in a corner. On either side of the hearth were two masonry seats, built like an entrance to the fireplace so that you sat sideways in them as you warmed yourself. Two charred and banged-up old chests stood on either side of the hearth containing the kindling for the fire and serving as benches.

In the late afternoons, after work in the fields and woods, the peasants used to come in and sit by the hearth to consult with our caretaker's wife, Rita, who looked after us. Rita was a wise woman, one who knew how to advise, to soothe and to cure; and her remedies, which she brewed herself from herbs and fruits, had a high local reputation. Usually, my mother or I would go into the kitchen at that time to greet the men, who stood up when we came in, and to offer them a glass of wine. The older women, wrapped in black shawls, came in after supper, when they had finished their day's chores. They brought their knitting, and we gave them a cup of strong, black coffee with much sugar. The young people were away from home, in the village café, or at a rustic dance or at the movies in the nearby town.

Another wall in the kitchen was taken up by a large chestnut sideboard which had seen better days in a genteel country dining room, perhaps a priest's. We cooked with aluminum and iron pots and pans; the copper *batterie de cuisine*, which my mother had banished from her Milan kitchen, was kept shining bright, but for show only. All the cooking utensils hung from nails on another wall, near the small wood stove on which we actually cooked. We also had an electric hot plate for the coffee making, which went on all day. Next to the stove was a stone sink with a banged-up marble draining board and near it, a small wooden icebox for which we bought the ice daily from an old man with a mule cart on which the ice lay covered with woodshavings and newspaper. The overhead light was a single, but powerful electric bulb. The kitchen was no thing of interior-decorated beauty, but from the lingering smell of wood smoke, cooked food, and wine you knew it had been lived in for well over a hundred years.

In the summer, the enormous kitchen table in the middle of the room was always piled high with newly picked vegetables and fruits, with a decapitated chicken in a corner waiting to be plucked and drawn, and a grocer's package of salami, proscuitto, and other cold cuts, and cheeses for our supper in another corner. How well I still see that rough, gray paper which covered the waxed paper that held the food; I've seen it nowhere else.

The cold cuts and the cheeses came from the *salu-*

meria in the village of Cerro, from a man who was a scoundrel, but an interesting one. He had come back to the village as a last resort from adventures in England and America he hinted at, but gave no details of, which under the circumstances, was probably just as well. He claimed that he had been an opera singer in these countries and he looked like a broken-down one, with gray hair touching his collar long before this was fashionable, and a dulcet baritone that he lavished on his female customers as he cheated them on the weight of their purchases. I sort of got along with him because I was known as the Signora Inglese, prone to buy 3 ettos (300 grams) of prosciutto instead of the customary 100 grams, as well as a wild selection of all available cold cuts and cheeses. But most of all, I was fond of his salami, the best salami I have ever eaten, before and since. Pregnancy is supposed to do strange things to a woman, and to me, it did salami. I consumed salami at breakfast, for elevenses, for lunch, tea, supper, and late-night snack. The salami I was passionate about was not the greasy, pepper-dotted usual kind, but a dry salami made locally—the closest cousin in New York is Hungarian salami.

On the day before my oldest boy was born I had laid on a goodly supply of this ambrosial salami as well as prosciutto crudo, mortadella, which in America is known as baloney and has no resemblance to the real thing, as well as Fontina, the cheese that makes a Piedmontese fondue, my favorite semisoft cheeses Bel Paese and Stracchino, rich, dark-green-veined Gorgonzola and smoky Provolone. All this bene di Dio, God's blessing, was meant to be consumed for supper over a period of several days, since we had our main meal at noon and ate eggs, cold cuts, cheese, and salads at night.

On that hot night in July, or rather in the early morning, I woke up with some unidentifiable pains in my innards which I took for being hunger pangs. Without waking my husband, I loped into the kitchen, cut some bread out of the bread drawer in the sideboard, and attacked the gray package of cold cuts, fishing out several slices of salami. This I consumed with pleasure, with no suspicion as to the real nature of my pangs. I ate one salami sandwich (several slices of salami between two slices of bread) and another and then another, without assuaging the rumblings in my innards. In fact, they got worse. Then the biological occurrence known as breaking of the water took place, of which the less said the better, but which convinced me that I'd better get to a doctor as soon as possible. Back upstairs I loped to wake my husband. Mercifully his sister, a solid, square lady interested in art, was also staying with us—mercifully because for that day she had ordered herself a car to take her to view some distant works of art; we didn't have a car in those days. During all of this commotion, my then sister-in-law's rented car arrived. The situation was explained to a sympathetic driver, and they set out to find the local doctor. Over vale and dale, that is, in the hilly back country, behind Lake Maggiore, this poor, serious, unmarried lady had herself driven, asking the peasants in the fields if they knew the whereabouts of the *dottore*, who had left from his home in the next village to visit rural patients. Finally she found him and brought him back to me, who had but one thought in mind, namely to get myself to Milan and the Clinica, a project with which the local doctor agreed completely. Thus the rented car, the driver more sympathetic than ever, instead of taking my then sister-in-law to the rural church fresco she had planned to contemplate, set out with the doctor, my then husband, and myself, en route to Milan.

To be on caution's side, the doctor had asked for a pair of scissors, several old sheets, and a bottle of strong disinfectant, which we provided, together with a flask of wine and one of water. Well-equipped for any emergency, we made for Milan and the Clinica where we arrived in high good spirits and no wine left in the flask. The baby was born soon after and has grown into an excellent man, from every point of view, a salami lover like the boy born after him.

That summer became memorable for many things. The ones that concern us here were the lovely food that we bought, cooked, ate, and discussed with the friends that came to stay, and the task we had set ourselves: to drink all the wines mentioned in the Italian chapter of Schoonmaker's and Marvel's *The Complete Wine Book*.

This was also the summer when I became conscious of the differences in Italian food. My mother's food was basically Roman food since she was a Roman herself, but without the excess of pork fat, garlic, herbs, and seasonings which make so much of Rome's food rather coarse. Her cooking also avoided the endless tomato sauces, and all the rich heavy dishes of Southern Italy, which she described as peasant food. She was right in many ways, for what are all those complex macaroni, meat, vegetable, tomato and meat and sauce dishes, such as the various lasagne, but the food of poor people filling themselves up as a welcome change from their usual sparse fare.

Most people, when they first start to cook, have pretty much the food they ate at home; I was no exception, as I am no exception in inheriting many of my mother's food prejudices, which have stayed with me. To this day I don't really like tomato sauces, heavy pasta dishes, snails, sweetbreads, and raw oysters. Left to myself in the Cerro kitchen, I would have cooked as I always had cooked. But there was the baby, and there was Rita, the caretaker's wife. The first obviously took up much of my time, and the second was an excellent cook who in the true manner of Italian regional cooks could not imagine any other way of cooking but her own.

To begin with, we never ate any meat or pasta, but for an occasional dish of homemade noodles with a vege-table sauce or done all'Inglese, that is, dressed merely with sweet butter and lots of freshly grated Parmesan. The secret is to have very hot noodles in a very hot dish, and very cold butter cut into little pieces. But mostly we ate soups and rice for our first courses. Since this was summer, we had light summer minestrones, all fresh vegetables, without the addition of the beans and pastas that go into winter minestrones. Rita's way was to add the olive oil that goes into the soup only when the soup had come to the first boil, and indeed, it makes a lighter dish. She also made two delicious light soups, one with rice and spinach and the other with peas and mush-rooms. Her rice dishes were marvels of invention: white risottos (not the saffron-yellow kind which is a Milan specialty) sauced up with mushrooms or zucchini, arti-chokes or peas or a mixture of all, when the dish was called a "risotto rustico," a country risotto. When we had guests she made a splendid Rice Timbale. We did not eat much meat, and then of the short-order variety, such as chicken livers with sage, thin little slices of veal cooked with lemon and herbs, roast chicken on Sunday— chicken then being still a festive dish—or rabbit. The thing I drew a line at were the little birds which local custom serves roasted with polenta as the famous polenta e osei. I don't like the murder of the innocent, and we ate our polenta with cheese. All these were summer dishes, especially the Vitello Tonnato, veal with tuna fish sauce, which sounds awful but is actually one of the best specialties of Italian cooking, wonderful for cold summer eating. The fruit came from our own trees, cherries, apricots, peaches, and pears in an orchard behind the house. We picked them ourselves.

After the baby was born, we had visitors from England, where my then husband and I lived. I remember them so well, Roger, Blaise, and Gerald, all three young as we were, enormously tall and in love with the Italian countryside as we were. Roger is still my greatest friend, Gerald disappeared in the Second World War, and Blaise disappeared in life. When Roger and Gerald drove down from England, they had asked my mother what they could bring her as a hostess present. My mother, a practical woman, wanted paper napkins which, in pre-world war, not yet reconstructed Italy, were an expensive rarity that she recognized as a simplification of life. The dear boys brought her packages over packages of paper napkins stashed away in their car. We counted them up and there were about two thousand of them.

My mother felt pure bliss, because she, as myself, hated using a napkin twice, a disgusting habit we thought, which brings back an anecdote I heard about an earlier Duke of Bedford, I believe. This nobleman, once, somewhere, saw a napkin ring and asked his secretary what the curious-looking object was. "A napkin ring," said the secretary and proceeded to explain its use in keeping one's napkin for several meals. After thinking about this matter for a while, the Duke only said: "Good God." But we could use paper napkins only during the week. On weekends, when my father came from Milan, cloth table napkins reappeared on the table, a clean one for every meal, of course, because my father would not put

up with such newfangled trash on his table. He did care
about nice things. The previous summer he had com-
plained bitterly because the proper cheese knives had
been left behind in Milan. I wasn't there, but some
friends were, and they said it had been quite an occasion, with him leaving the table in a marked manner.

I can think of two summers of my life when I was
blissfully happy all the time, happiness ordinarily being
but fleeting and instant contentment the rest. One was
the Fire Island summer described elsewhere, and the
other this one. We swam in Lake Maggiore, we climbed
the mountains that reflect in it, and we had ourselves
rowed across the lake to the Borromean Islands, in
the big lake boats covered like a covered wagon with
canvas stretched over big hoops, the oarman standing at
the helm, rowing with two big oars. The weather was
warm and sunny, but I remember foggy days, when the
white fog enveloped lake and mountains, and you glided
through it as in a ghostly world. On the Isola dei Pesca-

tori, the Fishermen's Islands, we used to eat freshly caught, deep-fried lake perch, sitting under a wine pergola overlooking the splendid baroque gardens of the main island, the Isola Bella, and the island that Toscanini called his own. Back home, at night we sat out, listening to the cuckoos and the nightingales taking turns in the shrubbery to make the night come alive with sound.

The loveliest memory of all is the very early mornings, when I nursed my baby on the balcony, overlooking the misty lake, and the sun rose behind the golden snows of Monte Rosa. I also remember one of the life's useless agonies, now, thank heaven, abolished by modern child care, namely the weighing of an infant before and after each breast feeding, to see if he had been properly nourished. My baby, and I am sure he was no exception, loathed being weighed, which made things difficult, to say the least. I still see Roger or another one of our friends trying to hold down the screaming and kicking baby, without pressing down the scale, while I weighed and calculated the input of ounces of mother's milk.

As I write this, I have in front of me the volume of Schoonmaker's and Marvel's *The Complete Wine Book* with the checkmark beside the wine we drank that summer. I do not know Mr. Schoonmaker, but I owe him a great debt of gratitude for then having opened my eyes to the pleasure of wine. So far, I had taken wine on the daily table for granted as part of the meal, giving it little thought. It never occurred to me that one would not drink a glass of wine with a meal; what wine was decided by my father, who had a good cellar. Like almost all the young people of my youth, eating and drinking were part of life, but only part.

The idea of people in their twenties being fascinated

with food and wine as they are nowadays would have been incomprehensible to me, life being so full of more intriguing things. Today, I could kick myself for this lack of interest when I think of the opportunities I missed: my father's cellar, older friends of the family and of mine in Paris and Berlin and Zurich, connoisseurs of fine food and drink who used to take me out to the best restaurants and who in vain tried to make me interested in such matters. I really had the great restaurants in these towns at my beck and call, and I did not care. As a matter of fact, I cannot remember ever having drunk any whiskey, gin, or similar spirits until I came to America in my early twenties. Of the eighty-seven major Italian wines listed by Mr. Schoonmaker, we drank our way through sixty-odd, no mean feat considering that many of the wines were from distant regions. My father was a great help in our studies; Friday nights he used to arrive from Milan laden with bottles we could not have found locally or in the nearest town. Oddly enough, I still like the wines I liked then, preferring the wines of Piedmont, Lombardy, the Veneto Tuscany, and the Emilia and Marche to those of Rome and Southern Italy.

As I said, my mother was away until the baby's birth, while my father came out from Milan to spend the weekends. He used to bring a houseful of guests with him, all people whom my mother disliked but to whom he was obliged. It's a brilliant idea more of us should adopt: Invite the people you must invite but whom your partner dislikes when your partner is legitimately away. The guests won't be offended and family peace is preserved.

The summer ended with a great garden party in honor of the newborn and of the birthdays of my mother and one of our friends. People had come from Milan and from everywhere around the lake. My father, who was fond of silly but very literary nonsense, had written a playlet for the occasion in which he figured as Nero, clad in a sheet with an off-the-shoulder effect and a laurel wreath. He was surrounded by a dozen young maidens, the daughters of friends who presented him the high point of the party, an enormous cake baked for the occasion by the fanciest *pâtissier* of Milan. In order to bring it out to the country, rather than taking the usual train, my father had to hire a car. The cake was 1 meter in circumference, that is, about 40 inches, and about 12 inches tall. I measured it as my father brought it in, not believing my eyes. It was a rich sponge, golden with heaven-knows-how-many eggs, redolent of rum, and resting on a plank covered with an embroidered cloth. A luscious pink icing covered the top and sides, with artistic decorations of glacé fruit. The cake, one to end all birthday cakes, tasted as good as it looked; no one at that party ever forgot it, almost as if it were the symbol of the last carefree summer before the Second World War.

Menu for the Cerro Birthday Party

Cold Lake Trout Mayonnaise:
whole fish covered with mayonnaise and heavily decorated with vegetable cutouts

Double-Strength Consommé:
served with cheese sticks

Cold Fillet of Beef:
served with various salads, such as mushrooms, green beans, and lettuce

The Great Cake

Fresh Fruit:
big baskets of peaches, apricots, cherries, and bananas

Coffee

Wines:
Soave (a white wine from Verona)
Frecciarossa (a red Lombard wine)
Asti Spumante (sparkling wine from Piedmont)

Green and White Italian Vegetable Summer Soup

(3–4 servings)

4–6 cups well-flavored beef broth (depending on how thick a soup is wanted)

1 large potato, peeled and cut into ½-inch dice

1 large Italian parsley root, peeled and cut into ½-inch dice (optional)

1 cup green beans, trimmed and broken into 2–3 small pieces

2 tablespoons rice

1 zucchini squash, cut into ¾-inch pieces (peeled if the skin is coarse or damaged)

1 cup shelled peas

2 tablespoons olive oil
Salt
Freshly ground pepper

½ cup minced parsley

2 tablespoons minced fresh basil leaves, or 2 teaspoons dried basil or to taste, or fresh or dried thyme to taste

Bring the beef broth to the boiling point. Add the potato, the parsley root, the beans, and the rice. Bring to the boiling point, lower heat, and cook covered for about 10 minutes. Add the zucchini, the peas, the olive oil, and salt and pepper to taste. Cook for 3 minutes and add the parsley and the herbs. Cook until the vegetables and the rice are just tender, but not mushy. Serve warm or lukewarm, but not chilled.

Spinach and Rice Soup

(5–6 servings)

Another light and easy soup from Milan

1 pound fresh or 1–2 10-ounce packages frozen whole spinach
6–8 cups well-flavored chicken or beef consommé
½ cup raw rice, any kind

Salt
Freshly ground pepper
⅛ teaspoon ground nutmeg
Freshly grated Parmesan cheese

Wash the spinach in at least three changes of water to remove all sand. Drain. With kitchen scissors, cut off the coarse stems and cut the leaves into shreds. Bring the consommé to the boiling point. Add the rice. Over low heat, simmer covered until the rice is almost tender. Add the spinach. Season lightly with salt and pepper and the nutmeg. Cook about 3 minutes longer; the spinach should be still firm. Serve with freshly grated Parmesan cheese.

Annetta's Light Soup

(5–6 servings)

An excellent soup from a Milanese friend which shows how Italians can make a few simple ingredients go a long way.

6–8 cups well-flavored chicken or beef consommé
2 tablespoons butter
⅓ cup raw rice, any kind
1 cup finely chopped parsley
¼ pound sliced mushrooms

1 cup shelled or frozen peas
Salt
Freshly ground pepper
Freshly grated Parmesan cheese

In a heavy saucepan, bring the consommé to the boiling point. Stir in the butter. Lower heat to lowest possible. Add the rice, the parsley, the mushrooms, and the peas. Check the seasoning; if necessary add a little more salt and pepper. Simmer covered for about 45 minutes. Serve with freshly grated Parmesan cheese.

Stracotto Sauce For All Pastas

(For 1 pound cooked pasta)

Stracotto means overcooked in Italian, and overcooking is the trick behind this sauce, which is one of the best in Northern Italian cooking. It is robust, but not coarse at all, and really an essence of meat, flavored with mushrooms and Marsala. The meat—beef, in this case—must be of good quality and absolutely free of fat, tendons, and other such matter. The mushrooms should be the dried imported kind, since they are much more flavorsome than our domestic variety. And, though red or white wine can be used instead of Marsala, a dry Marsala or sherry will give infinitely superior results.

1 pound good-quality
   lean beef
½ cup butter
1 medium onion, minced
1 medium carrot, minced
1 stalk celery, minced
½ cup minced parsley
1 ounce dried
   mushrooms
½ cup dry Marsala or
   medium sherry
½ cup bouillon
Salt
Freshly ground pepper
1 teaspoon grated lemon
   rind

Cut meat into tiny dice, or put through the coarse blade of a food grinder. The meat must not be ground fine—hamburger will not give the same results. In a heavy saucepan, heat butter and cook onion, carrot, celery, and parsley in it over medium heat for about 5 minutes, stirring frequently. Break the mushrooms into pieces, discarding the stems. Soak in water to cover for 15 minutes. Add Marsala, bouillon, the mushrooms, and their liquid. Season with salt and pepper and add lemon rind. Cover tightly and simmer over lowest possible heat until the meat is *stracotto*—that is, almost dissolved—stirring occasionally. This may take as much as 3 or 4 hours, depending on the meat used. But the sauce must be cooked this way for the flavors to blend. Serve over any pasta or use for linguine or similar dishes.

Note: Sometimes a peeled chopped tomato is added to the ingredients. This may thin the sauce, which should be thick. Therefore, if the sauce appears to be too thin, cook uncovered until the proper degree of thickness is achieved.

Prosciutto and Pea Sauce for Pasta
(For about 1 to 1½ pounds pasta)

Obviously, this sauce also dresses boiled rice

¼ pound prosciutto or
    Canadian or other
    lean bacon
1 medium onion
1 garlic clove
1 3–inch piece celery
⅔ cup parsley sprigs, no
    stems
¼ cup olive oil
3 tablespoons butter
1½ pounds fresh peas,
    shelled, or 2
    10-ounce packages
    frozen peas, thawed

⅓ cup beef bouillon or
    water
1 large tomato, peeled,
    seeded and chopped
2 tablespoons fresh basil
    or 2 teaspoons dried
    basil
Salt
Freshly ground pepper
Cooked pasta
1–2 tablespoons butter
Freshly grated
    Parmesan cheese

On a chopping board, chop together very finely the prosciutto, the onion, the garlic, the celery, and the parsley until they are a paste. Heat together the olive oil and the 3 tablespoons butter. Over low heat, and stirring constantly, cook the prosciutto mixture in it for about 5 minutes. Add the peas and the bouillon or water. Simmer covered, stirring frequently, until the peas are almost tender. Add the tomato and the basil and season with salt and pepper to taste. If there is too much liquid, cook uncovered to allow for evaporation. The sauce should be on the dry side. At serving time, when the sauce is to be poured over the cooked pasta, stir the remaining butter into the pasta. Serve with the Parmesan cheese.

Rice Timbale

(Timballo di Riso)

(8 servings)

2⅔ cups Carolina or
    Italian rice (do not
    use Uncle Ben's)
½ cup butter, at room
    temperature, cut into
    small pieces

½ cup grated Parmesan
    cheese
4 egg yolks well-beaten
    Fine dry breadcrumbs
    Filling (see below)

Cook the rice in plenty of boiling salted water until almost tender. Drain. Blend in the butter, the cheese, and the egg yolks. Mix thoroughly. Butter a 3-quart casserole or baking dish and coat on all sides with the breadcrumbs. The dish must be generously buttered and thoroughly coated. Spoon two-thirds of the rice mixture into the casserole. Press the rice with a spoon against the bottom and sides, leaving a well in the middle. Put the filling into the well. Spoon the remaining rice over the top and sides of the entire casserole, taking care that the meat is well covered. Bake in a preheated moderate (350°F.) oven about 1 hour or until the rice is set. Unmold carefully on a heated platter. Cut into wedges and serve with a tomato sauce.

FILLING:

2 tablespoons butter
¼ cup minced onion
1 garlic clove, mashed
1 pound ground pork
and veal mixed, or
beef mixed with pork
and/or veal
½ pound chicken livers,
chopped
⅓ cup minced green
pepper or pimiento

1½ cups cooked or canned
and drained green
peas
4 tablespoons tomato
paste
1 teaspoon salt
1 teaspoon sugar
Freshly ground pepper
1 teaspoon ground thyme
or ½ teaspoon dried
basil

Melt the butter in a large skillet. Add the onion and the garlic. Cook, stirring constantly, until the onion is soft. Add the ground meat and the chicken livers. Cook, stirring frequently, for about 10 minutes or until the meats are tender. Add all the other ingredients and mix well. The mixture should be thick, but if it looks like sticking and scorching, add a tablespoon or more of hot water, a little at a time so as not to thin it too much. Cook covered over very low heat for about 10 minutes, stirring frequently.

Risotto Alla Milanese

(4–5 servings)

Unlike a pilaf, a risotto is not dry, but creamy and made by a different method. Do not use converted but long-grain rice, or the imported Italian rice found in Italian groceries.

4 tablespoons butter
¼ cup chopped beef
   marrow or 2
   tablespoons butter
¼ cup very finely
   chopped onion
2 cups long-grain or
   Italian rice (do not
   wash the rice)
½ cup dry white wine

About 5 cups boiling
   chicken consommé
½ to ¾ teaspoon saffron,
   steeped in 3
   tablespoons chicken
   consommé
3 tablespoons butter,
   cut into pieces
⅔ cup freshly grated
   Parmesan cheese

In a heavy saucepan, heat together the butter and the marrow. Over medium heat, and stirring constantly, cook the onion in it until soft and golden. Do not let it brown. Add the rice. Cook, stirring constantly, until the rice becomes opaque or about 2–3 minutes. The rice must not brown. Stir in the wine. Keep on stirring. When the wine has evaporated, stir in ½ cup of the boiling consommé. The consommé must be kept boiling hot in a separate saucepan. Cook over medium heat, stirring all the time, until the consommé is absorbed. Stir in the rest of the consommé gradually, by the ½-cupfuls, as the rice absorbs it. The less consommé added at a time, the creamier the rice. The cooking time should be around 20 minutes from the time the consommé is first added, and the stirring constant.

After about 15 minutes cooking time or before the rice is tender, stir in the saffron. Finish cooking. When the rice is ready, stir in the butter piece by piece. Stir in the grated Parmesan cheese. Serve very hot, and immediately, on hot plates, with additional Parmesan cheese as a first course or as an accompaniment to Osso Buco.

Note: Risotto is a flexible dish. A lighter risotto may be made by respectively increasing the wine to 1 or 1½ cups and decreasing the chicken broth to 4½ or 4 cups. Please also note that the amount of liquid must be gauged as the rice is cooking, since various kinds of rice absorb different amounts of liquid. The end result should be rice that is creamy and not mushy to the bite. Furthermore, risotto does not lend itself to ahead-of-time cooking and reheating. It must be made at the last minute and eaten at once.

Polenta and Cheese Dish

(6 servings)

Use as a first course, with tomato sauce, or instead of rice or potatoes with a sauced meat dish.

2 quarts water	Freshly ground pepper
1 tablespoon salt	½ cup butter, melted
2 cups cornmeal	½ cup grated Parmesan
2 cups diced cheese such	cheese
as Fontina, Muenster	
or Swiss	

Bring the water and the salt to the boiling point in a deep saucepan. Sprinkle the cornmeal into it, stirring at the same time with a wooden spoon to prevent lumping. Cook over low heat, stirring frequently, for about 10 minutes. Stir in the cheese. Cook 20 more minutes, stirring frequently. The mixture should be on the soft side. Check the seasoning; add a little pepper. Turn the polenta out on a serving dish and stir in the butter. Sprinkle with the cheese and serve hot.

Osso Buco Alla Milanese

(4 servings)

This is the classic Milan dish of braised veal shanks served with risotto, the only time that risotto is served as an accompaniment to a meat dish rather than on its own, as a first course. To be authentic, the osso buco dish must contain no tomatoes and it must be finished off with gremolada, a mixture of parsley, garlic, and chopped lemon peel. Veal shanks can be ordered from the butcher, who will trim them.

2 tablespoons butter
4 veal shanks, 4 inches long and about 2 inches thick, with plenty of meat on them
2 tablespoons flour
Salt

Freshly ground pepper
1 cup dry white wine
Hot beef bouillon
2 tablespoons finely minced parsley
1 garlic clove, minced
Yellow peel of 1 lemon, minced fine (not grated)

Heat the butter in a heavy casserole or Dutch oven. It should be just large enough to hold the shanks standing upright. Coat the meat with the flour and season with salt and pepper. Over high heat, brown the shanks in the hot butter, turning over several times to insure even brownness. When browned, stand the shanks upright so that the marrow in the bones won't fall out. Pour the wine over the meat and cook without a cover for 5 minutes. Add about ½ cup hot bouillon. Simmer covered over low heat for about 1 hour or until tender. Ten minutes before the shanks are done, squeeze together the parsley, the garlic, and the lemon peel to make a paste. Sprinkle the shanks with this paste. Cover and cook about 5 minutes longer. Check the sauce. If it is too thick, add a little more bouillon. If too thin, thicken it with 1 tablespoon flour kneaded together with 1 tablespoon butter.

Braised Veal With Lemon

(3–4 servings)

There should be only a little sauce in the finished dish. Serve with a green vegetable such as beans.

2½ pound boneless veal, trimmed free of all gristle and fat, and cut in 1½-inch pieces
Flour

3 tablespoons butter
Juice of 2 large lemons
⅔ cup dry white wine
Salt
Freshly ground pepper
⅓ cup minced parsley

Coat the meat with the flour and shake off excess. Heat the butter in a heavy saucepan. Over high heat, brown the veal in it, stirring constantly. Stir in the lemon juice. Reduce heat to lowest possible. Simmer covered, shaking the pan frequently, for about 3 minutes. Stir in the wine. Season with salt and pepper to taste. Simmer covered for about 15–20 minutes or until the veal is tender. Stir frequently. If necessary, to prevent scorching, add a little hot water, a tablespoon at a time. Before serving, sprinkle with the parsley.

Venetian Liver With Onions

(4–5 servings)

Obviously, this dish comes originally from Venice. But it is very popular throughout Italy and one of the best ways of eating liver. The trick lies in cooking quickly thin strips of liver.

1 ½ pounds calf's liver	¼ cup dry white wine
4 tablespoons butter	Salt
2 tablespoons olive oil	Freshly ground pepper
4 large onions, sliced	Juice of ½ lemon
very thinly	¼ cup minced parsley

Wash and dry the liver thoroughly. Cut into very thin strips, about 2–3 inches long. Heat the butter and olive oil in a frying pan. Cook the onions in it, stirring frequently, until soft and golden. Add the wine and cook for 1–2 minutes. Season with salt and pepper to taste. Add the liver. Over high heat, and stirring constantly, cook the liver until just browned. Depending on the thinness of the liver and the size of the frying pan, this should take 2–3 minutes, no more. Remove from the heat and stir in the lemon juice. Sprinkle with the parsley. Serve immediately on a *hot* serving plate, with a salad of watercress and Belgian endives dressed with a little oil and lemon juice.

To Make Little Steaks More Flavorful

An Italian method for small shell steaks, minute steaks—any kind of little steaks that are to be pan fried quickly.

Combine 2 parts of olive oil with 1 part lemon juice. Season with salt and pepper and mix well. If wanted, rub the meat with a peeled garlic clove. Marinate the meat in the olive oil mixture from 15 minutes to 1 hour, depending on the size of the steaks. Dry on paper towel before sautéeing quickly in a skillet lightly coated with olive oil.

Lemon and Mustard Sauce

(About ¾ cup)

An excellent sauce for broiled fish or fowl, and for cooked vegetables such as green beans and zucchini. The proportion is 1 part lemon to 2 parts olive oil.

¼ cup fresh lemon juice	Salt
½ cup olive oil	Freshly ground pepper
1 teaspoon dried mustard	2 tablespoons minced
1–2 garlic cloves, mashed	parsley

Combine all the ingredients and mix thoroughly with a wooden spoon.

Italian Potato and Green Bean Salad

(4 servings)

1 pound new waxy
    potatoes
Salt
Freshly ground pepper
⅓ cup olive oil
2–3 tablespoons vinegar,
    or to taste
½ pound green beans, cut
    into 1–inch pieces

2 tablespoons minced
    onion
1 tablespoon capers
    (optional)
1 dozen small pitted
    olives
6 anchovy fillets, drained
    (optional)

Cook the new potatoes until tender. While still hot, peel and slice them. Put them into a bowl and season with salt and pepper. Mix together the olive oil and the vinegar. Pour about half of the dressing over the potatoes while they are still hot. Toss gently, taking care not to break the slices. Cool. Cook the beans until they are just tender. Combine the onion and the capers with the beans. Add the remaining dressing and toss. Combine the beans and the potatoes. Check the seasoning and the dressing; if necessary, add a little more olive oil and vinegar, very little at a time. Chill. At serving time, decorate with the olives. Lay the anchovies on top of the salad in a crisscross pattern.

Rum Cake

(About 12 servings)

A flavorful, flat Northern Italian cake with a grainy texture, which stays moist for well over a week when properly wrapped in aluminum foil. Not a dessert cake, but excellent as an accompaniment to fruit dishes or for picnics.

1 cup butter	1½ cups flour
1½ cups sugar	1 cup yellow cornmeal
6 eggs	2 teaspoons baking
¾ cup fresh lemon juice	powder
Grated rind of 3 lemons	¼ cup rum or brandy

Cream the butter until it is very soft. Gradually beat in the sugar, beating well after each addition. Beat in the eggs, one at a time, beating well after each addition. Beat in the lemon juice and the lemon peel. Sift together the flour, the cornmeal, and the baking powder. Gradually beat the mixture into the batter. Beat in the rum or brandy. Butter and flour a 9" x 13" x 2" cake pan. Pour in the dough. Bake in a preheated moderate oven (350°F.) for 1 hour or until the cake tests clean. Cool to luke-warm before unmolding.

Baked Peaches

(4 servings)

The peaches must be large, ripe, and still firm. Free-stones are best.

4 large peaches
½ cup almond macaroon crumbs or ground almonds
¼ cup mixed glacé fruit, very finely shredded

8 blanched almonds
Marsala or white wine, dry or sweet

Halve the peaches. Remove the pits. Enlarge the hollow slightly with a spoon and reserve the pulp. Mash this pulp with a fork. Combine it with the macaroon crumbs or ground almonds and glacé fruit. Mix well. Fill the peach hollows with the mixture. Butter a deep baking dish which is large enough to hold the peach halves side by side, but not larger. Place the peach halves in the dish; they should just touch each other. Top each peach half with one almond. Sprinkle the Marsala or white wine over the peaches; there should be about ½ inch of wine in the dish. Bake in a preheated moderate oven (350°F.) for about 15 minutes or until just tender. Check for dryness—if necessary, add a little more wine or water. Serve hot or cold.

Fresh Chestnuts With Marsala and Red Wine

(4 servings)

A fall dessert from Lake Maggiore. Serve with heavy cream and thin, crisp cookies.

1 pound large fresh chestnuts	1 cup dry red wine
½ cup sugar	1 cup Marsala

Score the rounded side of each chestnut with the point of a sharp knife. Place the chestnuts into boiling water and simmer for 15 minutes. Pour off most of the water, keeping just enough to keep the chestnuts moist. Slip off both the outer shell and inner skin; if the chestnuts are warm, they come off quite easily. Work carefully since chestnuts break easily into pieces. In a saucepan, combine the sugar, the red wine, and the Marsala. Simmer over low heat without a cover for 3 minutes, stirring frequently. Carefully add the chestnuts and simmer until they are tender. Shake the pan occasionally so that the chestnuts won't stick. Lift out the chestnuts with a slotted spoon and place them into a serving dish, preferably a glass or silver one. Boil up the syrup for a minute or two to reduce it and pour over the chestnuts. Serve warm or cold.

Note: If no Marsala is available, use a medium sherry—the flavor, of course, will be different, but still acceptable.

Chapter 8

English Kitchens

THE TWO KITCHENS in England I've cooked in are
worlds apart, though in time, only thirty-odd years. The
first kitchen was in Billingham, in the North of England,
where my then husband worked for a giant chemical
combine. The second kitchen is in London, in my son's
and daughter-in-law's flat. The difference between the
cookery produced in these two kitchens is extraordinary.
It reflects a change in middle-class English food habits,
an internationalization that is even more amazing when
you compare it to what happened in Italy. There food
habits have not turned themselves inside out, the food
is still regional and national, and few, if any, Italians
have the interest in foreign food of the English.

In these thirty-odd years, especially during the last
fifteen years, there has been an unbelievable diffusion of
foreign foods in England while traditional English cook-

ing, so exquisite when it is good, is falling by the way-side. The trend started with the milk and coffee bars which took the young away from the pubs, went on to the Wimpy Bars with cheap and almost inedible ham-burgers, with a current profusion of pizza shops. Many of these sell cheap wine by the glass. Ah, for the fish and chips shops of yesteryear where marvelous freshly fried fish was first wrapped in waxed paper and then in layers of newspapers to keep it warm until home. With a dash of vinegar, many is the tasty meal I enjoyed for very little money. The quality of fish and chips shops' modern suc-cessors is moot indeed.

There really is no more horrible food in the world than present-day cheap English food. When it is cheap, English pizza is far more plastic than ours, with nary a flavor in its bright colors; when it is good, it is over-priced. An American over-the-counter hamburger is al-most always edible; its English counterpart seldom, if ever. Even my ten-year-old grandson, an American child starved for his native country's basic food in London, recoiled from the horrid offering in London's most ad-vertised hamburger chain; not even the French fries were edible. Gone are almost all the Lyons' tea shops and the ABC, where once, in London, you could get a good cheap meal of tea, sausages and mash, fried eggs and bacon or a bit of chips; and even the working-class cafés —pronounced cafs—the carmen's stops and truckers' lay-bys are just rotten. In the past they were not. As a poor student in London, I lived off their Cornish pasties, pork pies, and all their other pies, washed down with mugs of strong, strong, sweet tea; they sustained me many a night when I came home from classes at the London School of Economics. The English working-class people's food has not changed much, but for the worse.

It is the middle- and upper-class diet that has veered away from the food inheritance of Victorian times which persisted into the Thirties, plunging headlong into eggplant and zucchini, rose hip jams, and other goodies of the kind from southern and eastern Europe, apples and pears from Oregon, dried mushrooms from Poland, and ingredients for Mexican chilis and Indonesian curries. Now, with Britain's entry into the Common Market, English shops will be like those of Germany and Belgium, bulging with fresh Dutch mushrooms, grapes from Spain, lemons from Italy, mustard from Düsseldorf, and even more tinned and bottled French and Belgian vegetables, all beautiful to look at and almost all tasteless mush.

The Billingham kitchen was by no means a primitive one. It was part of a little house, one in a row of houses facing the old church and graveyard of what had been the heart of an old English village, but now surrounded by housing developments for the thousands employed by the "works." Only a few other old houses remained— that of the parson, the doctor, and the grocer, whose wife came to see me after I brought my firstborn son home. In the manner of North Country people, she touched a silver half crown to the baby's lips and laid it into his little hands to bring him luck in life.

Three pubs were within shouting distance from the house, a great asset for those living in it, the real estate agent had told us. Indeed they were; and many trips with the enameled hot water can with the hinged lid, used as a beer container, were made by one and all who stayed in our house. The house must have been about one hundred-fifty or two hundred years old; the passages and the kitchen still had their flagstone pavements. On the ground floor were a largish sitting room, a dining room all by itself off a little passage, a large kitchen, and a larder, facing north. Upstairs, three bedrooms and a bathroom. I remember little of the upstairs, except the sight of one of our constant weekend guests, a very tall and very aesthetic Cambridge man who used to eat chocolates in bed for breakfast and naught else.

Among the persisting nonfood memories are the vari- ties of heaters used to keep the house warm in the cold, windy climate of the North of England. Each room was heated separately; each had a fireplace. But we used only the living room and kitchen fireplaces every day. For the rest we had fixed gas heaters, electric portable heaters, a portable kerosene stove, and an electric sunshaped heater, all of them in constant use, carried about, plugged in, phased out—an eternal ado, anything except coming to grips with the fact that a furnace or central heating is better. The living room and kitchen fires were daily laid by me, first thing in the morning. I raked out superfluous ashes, made spills from old newspapers, built the fire so that it would be ready when needed. I forgot one thing: I cleaned the hearth with stove black to have it look clean and neat, as they do in the North of England. The most successful present I ever had in my life was a gas poker for the dining room. This long iron rod, with holes, was attached to a gas outlet, and it made away with the need for spills and kindling, since you just shoved it under the coals and kept it on until the coals had caught fire. The fire itself was fondled with bellows, and by holding the London *Times'* full double-spread pages over the hearth, to prevent alien drafts that hindered the flame from going up. This necessary pre-occupation with keeping warm had one salutary effect, besides my knowing how to lay a fire in my sleep. It cured me of the expensive desire so many of my friends suffer from—for a fireplace in a New York apartment. I do think a fireplace is pretty, and even useful, but I can take it or leave it.

I cooked on a fine "New World" Regulo-Controlled gas cooker, that is, a gas stove with controlled oven temperatures which, rather than being expressed by degrees Fahrenheit as in our stoves, were designated by Regulo numbers. Regulo was nothing exotic, just ordinary temperature control. All the cookbooks of the time used the Regulo marking, including the excellent *Radiation Cookery Book* which came with the stove which I still use. Radiation then not being a dirty word as it is now. It's one of the few books which really tells you everything about how to cook plain, flavorful English home fare. The stove had the outstanding feature of most English stoves: a plate warmer rack above the cooking units. American stoves lack this useful feature, which makes heating plates a nuisance since they get either too hot from the oven or too cold from sitting over a pilot light. You have to have plate warmer gadgets, all complicating life even further, but still necessary since eating hot food off cold plates is nasty.

Obviously the kitchen had a sink, a sideboard, a table and chairs. It did not have an icebox or a refrigerator because of the larder, a cool, flagpaved little room with a stone sink, a handpump, and shelves and hooks all over the walls and ceiling.

In England, especially in the North, it is perfectly possible to live without a refrigerator if you have a cool larder, which all the older houses have. You cannot keep frozen food in it, but unless there is a heat wave of 70°F. or so which lays the English low, you can keep your larder food wholesome and sweet for at least several days, even jellying aspics and gelatin desserts. In England's cool climate, your milk stays good for two to three days and so does your meat. Your smoked foods, cheese, vegetables, and fruits keep anyway, so that there is only fish which must be eaten up the day it is bought. Leftovers were also kept in the larder, each on its own little saucer topped by an inverted bowl. This to me is the most English of all English kitchen sights, still found to this day even in kitchens with ample refrigerator space.

The other very English sight that sticks in the memory is the covers that used to be put over jams and jellies and cakes in the larder, or when one had tea out of doors to keep the flies away: they were round or square wire frames coming together at the top, covered with netting weighed down at the bottom with beads. A smaller version also existed, just a square of netting edged with beads, that went over milk and cream jugs. Cake covers were always made by one's granny or aunt or godmother, or one bought them at church bazaars.

In my Billingham larder I also remember the butter sitting in a covered dish, which in turn sat in a dish of cold water. There was also the meat safe, a wire-netting box with shelves in which the meat was kept protected from flies. A flitch of bacon hung from the ceiling, off which I used to saw the daily ration; and from nails on the wall hung the lovely strings of red onions and garlic that the Basque vendors in smocks and berets used to sell from door to door in the fall.

My groceries came from the shop next door, whose lady had put the silver half crown into my new son's hands. They must have been the usual staples, since I don't remember anything special except the brown candied sugar we used for after-dinner coffee. We had been invited for supper by these nice people, unusual in a country where in those days, the classes hardly mixed, but then, I was a foreigner, and not formidable. Following local custom, we had High Tea, which is a meal— a supper—and not tea. I daresay the usual spread of potted meats and fish and shrimps, boiled eggs and cold ham, spicy watercress and sliced tomatoes and lettuce cut into wedges, Stilton, Cheddar, and local cheeses, bread, butter, and cheese crackers, and probably a bit of cake and canned fruit to round the meal. What struck me was the North Country custom of serving immediately after this meal more tea and an assortment of sweet cookies, gingersnaps, brandysnaps, cream-filled tea biscuits, digestive biscuits (our graham crackers) covered with chocolate or without, and heaven knows how many other biscuits beloved by a cookie-mad populace. Stuffed as we were, we did enjoy our tea and cookies.

The butcher was down one of the few remaining old village streets, and so was the fish and chips shop from which I fetched our supper when I did not know what to cook. Fruits and vegetables I bought a busride down in Stockton, our nearest town, where a market went up weekly in the Old High Street. The choice was tradi-

tional. In the winter, there were the usual carrots, onions, turnips, sprouts, cabbages, leeks, celery, and potatoes; in the summer, peas, broadbeans, string beans, marrow, cauliflower, tomatoes, cucumbers, lettuces, radishes, and cress. Nobody had ever heard of eggplant and zucchini, broccoli or corn on the cob or globe artichokes. The eggs were large and often still warm from the hen, and the butter, shaped in large pats, each stamped with a decorative cow, lay golden and glistening in little baskets lined with green leaves. The cream was thick and sweet, and unpasteurized so that one could make the most heavenly of all creams—clotted Devonshire cream—to eat with jam and scones for tea.

In the market there were also the cooked food stalls with pork, veal, and ham pies and Cornish pasties, the fried fish stalls and again, vivid in memory, the stalls selling cooked eels, mussels, and winkles, the latter to be picked from their shells with a pin. The meat stalls sold fresh suet for our puddings, so infinitely nicer than the ordinary prepackaged shredded suet. Suet puddings, made with a light and experienced hand, are a delight on a cold winter's day; Ginger Pudding, Marmalade Pudding, Cabinet Pudding, Treacle Pudding, Spotted Dog (with sultanas), and all the other steamed puddings are great comforters. When we scorn them today we forget that in the past, before universal central heating, foods that warmed you, like puddings and pies, were an essential part of keeping well in a cold and damp climate.

Hanging my head in shame once more, I must confess that I never achieved a light hand with suet puddings, deep dish pies (so delicious when made of mixed blackberries and apples), and apricot flans. These, and all the English food, were cooked for me by Mrs. Wilson, who came to help me twice a week. She also made excellent Bacon and Fish Rolls which we ate for supper, she baked a Piquant Mackerel and the simplest of all fish dishes, fillet baked between two plates. She taught me to make Kedgeree and the secret of perfect, creamy, melting rice pudding, which is to leave it overnight in an extremely slow oven. When it was hot, she made traditional English thirst quenchers like Barley and Apple Water and when I had a cold, Black-currant Tea.

I myself cooked Italian in the North of England because this is what pleased those around me. In those days, outside of London, in the provinces, there were none of the trattorie, tavernas, French restaurants, Indian curry parlors, and other purveyors of foreign foods which now are part of English provincial eating. A good dish of spaghetti, a risotto, osso buco (from veal shanks obtained with inordinate coaxing of the butcher, who traditionally hated veal), and the classics of Italian cuisine were a welcome change from the local English fare. What I learned was to bake cakes, mostly French and German ones, however, and lovely English fruit creams.

Our drinking habits were equally simple. Sherry was the favorite predinner drink, a habit acquired at Oxford and Cambridge by the men and women we knew. Cocktails and cocktail food were unknown to us. We drank beer with most of our meals and wine on occasions. In the evenings the men drank brandy and soda or Scotch and soda, moderate quantities and without ice, the only ice being obtainable at the fishmonger, not that anybody wanted any. When we asked people to come in after dinner like everybody else, around ten, we served coffee and tea and a variety of cakes, cookies, and even sandwiches. We were young, we had strong legs and good appetites, and our greatest pleasure on Sundays was to walk twenty and thirty miles over the nearby Yorkshire Moors, ending up in the dusk with a Farm Tea advertised with a handwritten card in the window of a farmhouse, very much like the one I described earlier.

The other English kitchen is my daughter-in-law's, in which we've cooked together. It is very different indeed, a kitchen in a modern London flat, south of Victoria, with steel cabinets and counters and no space for a table, just like an American apartment kitchen. There are a gas stove and a refrigerator, not provided by the landlord, but by the tenant. The refrigerator is waist high, with so small a freezing compartment that it will hold no more than two ice cube trays. Not only are most English refrigerators small compared to our own, they are still middle-class possessions. If you can't store your frozen foods, you don't buy them except for immediate use, and this is what people, especially working-class people do—a package here, a package there.

In the streets around this kitchen a street market goes up every morning. Most of it consists of vegetable and fruit stands piled high with eggplant and zucchini, globe artichokes, broccoli, asparagus, spinach, chard, bell and chili peppers, green plantains, and all the fruit of Europe in and out of season. What is missing, in season, is the profusion of English berries which so struck me when I came to school in England as a girl. I was not the only one from the Continent to marvel at all the strawberries, raspberries, bilberries, mulberries, blueberries, blackberries, loganberries, gooseberries, red and black currants that made English summer eating such a delight.

Today (I've checked on this) you see few of the traditional English summer berries, mostly strawberries and raspberries and a few gooseberries perhaps, and they are very expensive. Do people no longer pick them because it is not worth their while? A crying shame it is, to have to do without some of the loveliest fruit England produces. The same is true for apples. Not that there is a shortage of apples; on the contrary they abound, both in town and in the country, where handmade signs at nearly every house tell you that apples are on sale. When you go for them the lady of the house or a child will shake a tree and stuff the apples into any old paper bag that is around. Though there may or must be some, I can't remember any farmers' market stands on English roads, with their bounty of neatly arranged vegetables and fruits that we know in America. But at any London street market, you can still buy armfuls of fresh flowers for pennies.

My son and his family live in a socially and racially mixed district composed of English working-class people, Indian, Pakistani, and Mediterranean immigrants, and young English middle-class people. On the outer edges there are still the private homes of the well-to-do, but they do not shop in the neighborhood stores. The groceries reflect this racy mélange, from the Golden Syrup and shredded suet, the bacon and sausages which are staples of English working-class eating, to curry spices, olive oil, Parmesan and feta cheese, tomato paste for which, in my youth, you had to go to the Continental shops in Soho. They also sell a staggering variety of formerly unknown American-style snacks—potato chips called crisps, Cheeze-it and other savory biscuits and pretzels, popcorn, peanuts, and the like—which seem to be consumed mostly by the working-class children, on top of their steady, traditional munch of candy.

New too is the large sale of battery-fed, that is, assembly-line-produced chickens, which have as little flavor as our American ones, but are cheap. If you want poultry that really tastes as it should, you must ask for free-range chickens and pay accordingly. New too are the inexpensive wine shops, dispensing cheap sherries and wines, "plonk" as it is so suitably called. As much and perhaps even more indicative of the change in English living than the new wine shops are the bakeries of the district, where just as on the Continent, you can buy a variety of breads, French loaves and Italian rings, ryes and pumpernickels, cracked wheat, a far cry from the former white and brown cottage loaves.

In the old days, in a district like this one, if you

wanted food or drink, you went to one of the little tea shops or had "a cut from the joint and two vegs" at one of the many pubs, together with a beer. Today, there is a rash of small restaurants where kindly and mostly young people serve kindly cooked ethnic foods in a kindly manner, together with a glass or carafe of white or red plonk. The tea shops have practically disappeared and most of the pubs blare rock and roll.

In London you could always buy whatever foreign and exotic foods you wanted if you went to Harrods, to Fortnum and Mason, and to Soho. Nowadays, you don't have to—there will be small groceries and brand-new supermarkets in or near your neighborhood that will allow you to cook Turkish, or Indonesian, or plain American, as in my son's family. There is another interesting change in everyday English food—it is far more seasoned and spicier than it used to be; you notice it in the sausages, the meat pies, and the other prepared cheap foods, which used to be totally bland.

The English upper classes always ate excellent varied food, and there is nothing more delicious and careful than English country-house cooking, based upon the best meats and the freshest vegetables. Older cookbooks reflect this, and I have learned an immense amount about good food from the books of Wyvern (Col. Kenney-Herbert), Lady Jekyll, Lady Sysonby, and especially Lady Clark of Tillypronie, this latter a goldmine. Ah, here were men and women who knew and cared, and who had the leisure, the money, the ingredients, and the servants to set a superb table. From my own youth, I remember the meals in various country houses (and this at a time when food was of no great importance to me) with marvelous oddities, such as the Colonel's Clear Indian Soup, a tart gooseberry sauce served with mackerel, an oily fish, a savory Oyster Cream eaten as a first course, Cold Chicken Curry, thick mushroom stew nestling in buttered spinach and Claret Jelly with Raspberries. In those days, middle-class food was at best dull, with the few exceptions of roast beef and Yorkshire pudding. It struck me at the time, when I first went to England as a school girl, that English women simply did not care for their food and houses, compared to Continental women.

Today, when I go to England, I am as surprised at how much and how well English middle-class women have learned to cook. I think that the absence of domestic servants has largely been responsible for this change of attitude, plus the internationalization of life. English domestic life has indeed been turned upside down: I'll never forget the shock of seeing an old friend of mine, who rose to great heights in a world-embracing business, dry the dishes after dinner in a household glad to have a weekly cleaning lady.

When educated women have to cook, *volens nolens*, a proliferation of cookbooks is not far behind. Now in England, along with modern cookbooks on good traditional food there are rows of international and specialty cookbooks for posh and plain, which would have been unheard of thirty years ago. But English women do not seem to be as shackled to the letter of their recipes as American women, so that, in the hands of a good cook, a familiar dish will be coupled with an unfamiliar one, or undergo flavor or texture changes, making for more amusing food.

The modern kitchen in the modern London flat has indeed become an international kitchen. My daughter-in-law cooks American, and I have cooked Italian and Turkish for her. Her teen-age son has learned to bake cakes and cookies from a children's cookbook and my son, true to the British workingman's tradition, is the one who makes us the first, strong morning cup of tea. But for that, goodbye to good old England and her kitchen ways.

Americans have never taken properly to traditional English food as they have to French and Italian food. Food editors have told me many times that people don't like them to print recipes for dishes such as Cornish pasties, steak and kidney pie, suet puddings and the like, because they won't make them—not even try them. For that matter, I am not especially fond of these doughy morsels, so that I never make them. As I said before, this is food for people living in chilly houses in a chilly climate and used to large amounts of starches. What I like about the following recipes is that they show that there is, Virginia, another kind of cookery in England, which is as English, and lovely.

The Colonel's Clear Indian Soup

(6–8 servings)

A warming soup suited to being taken along in a thermos.

8–10 cups good strong beef consommé
1 large, tart apple, cored and sliced, but not peeled
2 medium onions, sliced
1 tablespoon grated fresh or unsweetened coconut
1 tablespoon curry powder, or curry powder to taste
3 chicken backs, or the carcass of a raw or cooked chicken

Combine all the ingredients in a large, heavy saucepan. Bring to the boiling point, lower heat to simmer. Cook covered for about 1 hour, stirring occasionally. Strain the soup. If a very clear soup is wanted, clarify it in the usual manner according to directions in a standard cookbook. Before pouring the soup into the thermos, bring the strained soup once more to the boiling point.

Lady Clark of Tillypronie's Oyster Creams

(4–6 servings)

Serve as a first course

About 2 dozen oysters and their liquid	Freshly ground pepper
1 cup heavy cream	Juice of 1 small lemon
	Parsley sprig

Bring the oysters and their liquid to the scalding point, cook for 1 minute. Cool and puree in the blender. Whip the cream until stiff. Combine the oyster puree and the cream and mix gently, but well. Spoon into small individual cups or soufflé dishes. Sprinkle with pepper and a little lemon juice. Do not salt since the oysters are salty. Garnish with a parsley sprig and serve chilled.

Bacon and Fish Rolls

This is a method; the quantity of the ingredients depends on the number of rolls wanted.

Bacon strips
Fish fillets (frozen ones
   must be thawed)

Lemon juice
Salt
Freshly ground pepper

Separate the bacon strips and lay them on a sheet of waxed paper. Sprinkle the fish fillets with lemon juice, salt and pepper. Roll them up. Roll 1 bacon strip around each rolled-up fillet. Place in a shallow buttered baking dish side by side. Bake in a preheated moderate oven (350°F.) for about 15 minutes or until the bacon is cooked and the fish flaky.

Kedgeree

(4 servings)

A dish of Indian origin, to judge from the name. It can be made with any cooked white fish, but is glorious with salmon and great with smoked finnan haddock.

6 to 8 tablespoons butter
2 cups boiled rice
2 cups cooked finnan
   haddock or other fish

2 hard-cooked eggs,
   chopped
Salt
Freshly ground pepper

Heat the butter in a flameproof serving dish until golden but not browned. Add all the other ingredients and blend with a fork. Over low heat, and stirring constantly, heat the mixture until it is very hot. Serve immediately.

Note: For a fancier dish, also traditional, hard cook the eggs and separate the whites and yolks. Chop the whites and mix them into the fish and rice. Mash the yolks through a ricer and sprinkle over the dish.

Piquant Mackerel

(4 servings)

4 mackerel, weighing about 1 pound each	4 tablespoons butter or margarine
Salt	¼ cup minced parsley
Freshly ground pepper	
4–6 tablespoons vinegar other than wine vinegar	

Make the fish ready for cooking. Cut a few gashes crosswise down each side of each fish and sprinkle with salt and pepper. Place the fish in a greased shallow baking dish side by side. Pour the vinegar over them and dot with the butter. Cover the dish with greased waxed paper or aluminum foil and tie it with string. Bake in a preheated moderate oven (350°F.) for about 15 minutes if the fish is without a head or about 25 if the head is still on. Sprinkle the parsley on top. Serve immediately or the fish will be soggy.

Lady Sysonby's Mild Cold Curry

(6 servings)

1 cup butter
2 big celery hearts, sliced
⅓ cup parsley sprigs
    without stalks,
    minced
4 medium onions, sliced
4 tart apples, peeled,
    cored, and chopped
2 medium potatoes,
    peeled and chopped
2 large tomatoes, peeled
    and chopped, or 1
    cup Italian-type
    canned tomatoes,
    drained

¼ teaspoon dried thyme
¼ teaspoon ground
    marjoram
1 bay leaf
¼ cup long-grain rice
1–2 tablespoons curry
    powder
5 cups hot chicken broth
Juice of 1 lemon
1 cup heavy cream,
    slightly whipped
¼ cup mayonnaise
1 large boiled chicken,
    boned, skinned, and
    cut into neat pieces

Put the butter into a large, heavy saucepan. Add the vegetables, the apples, the herbs, and the rice. Cook covered over very low heat until the vegetables are soft. Do not let them brown. Then stir in the curry powder. Turn the heat to medium and cook, stirring all the time, for about 2–3 minutes; this releases the curry flavor. Stir in the hot chicken broth. Bring to the boiling point, then lower heat to simmer. Cook covered for 1 hour, stirring occasionally. Strain through a fine sieve or puree in the blender. Cool. When quite cold, stir in the lemon juice, the whipped cream, and the mayonnaise. Mix well. Put the chicken pieces into a serving dish and cover them with the curry sauce. Serve with rice and salad.

Mince

(4 servings)

Generations of English children have been brought up on this surprisingly tasty hamburger dish. Serve on toast, with mashed potatoes or boiled rice or noodles and a salad.

2 tablespoons beef drippings or cooking fat	1 tablespoon uncooked oatmeal or ¼ cup fine dry breadcrumbs
2 small onions, minced	Salt
1½ pounds ground beef	Freshly ground pepper
1½ cups beef consommé	

Heat the drippings in a heavy saucepan. Add the onions. Cook, stirring constantly, until the onions are soft. Add the meat. Stirring constantly to prevent lumping, brown the meat. Stir in the beef consommé, the oatmeal or breadcrumbs, and salt and pepper to taste. Simmer covered over low heat for about 20–30 minutes.

Mushroom Stew In Buttered Spinach

(4 servings)

¼ cup butter	Salt
⅓ cup minced shallots or onions	Freshly ground pepper
	¼ cup minced parsley
1 pound fresh mushrooms, sliced	1 cup sour cream
2–3 10-ounce packages frozen spinach, thawed	¼ cup butter
	Salt
	Freshly ground pepper

Heat the butter and add the shallots or onions. Cook over low heat, stirring constantly, until the shallots or onions are soft but not browned. Add the mushrooms. Simmer covered until the mushrooms are soft but still firm, for about 5 minutes. Cook uncovered for 5 more minutes. Season with salt and pepper and stir in the parsley and the sour cream. Mix well and cook only to heat through. Do not boil. Keep hot.

Cook the spinach according to package directions and drain well. Chop the spinach coarsely. Return to heat and stir in the butter and a little salt and pepper. On a heated serving dish, arrange the spinach in the shape of a nest. Fill the spinach nest with the mushrooms and serve very hot, immediately.

Gooseberry Sauce

(About 1½ cups)

Gooseberries are common fruit in England and Germany, and they can be found in America in vegetable markets catering to the foreign-born and their descendants. American gooseberries are tarter than European ones and are suited for cooking rather than eating raw.

1 pint gooseberries
½ cup water
   Handful of spinach or
     sorrel leaves
     (optional)
1 tablespoon butter
   Salt

Freshly ground pepper
⅛ teaspoon ground
   nutmeg
   If the berries are very
     sour, 1 teaspoon sugar
     or to taste

Remove the stem and blossom ends of the berries. Wash them. Cook the gooseberries in the water until they are soft. Add the spinach leaves and cook for 3 minutes more. Drain the gooseberries and reserve the liquid. Rub berries and spinach through a sieve or food mill— a blender will not pulverize their seeds. Return gooseberries and liquid to the saucepan; the puree should be the consistency of a thin batter. Add butter, salt, pepper, nutmeg, and sugar. Simmer about 2–3 minutes, stirring constantly. (If no spinach or sorrel is used, add a few drops green food coloring for the right color.) Serve with rich fish like mackerel or salmon, or with duck.

Blackberry Cream

(5–6 servings)

4 cups fresh blackberries
½ cup sugar, or more to
    taste
¼ cup water
1 tablespoon (1 envelope)
    unflavored gelatin

½ cup milk
1 tablespoon brandy,
    rum, or Kirsch
1 cup heavy cream,
    whipped

Combine blackberries, sugar, and water. Cook over low heat, stirring frequently, until soft. Strain through a sieve; there should be about 2 cups pulp and liquid. Or pulverize in a blender, although some of the blackberry pips will remain. Cool. Sprinkle the gelatin over the milk and blend. Dissolve the gelatin over hot water. Mix together the blackberry pulp and liquid and the gelatin. Stir in the brandy or other spirit and blend thoroughly. Fold the whipped cream into the blackberry mixture. Chill before serving.

Gooseberry Fool

(5–8 servings)

American gooseberries are tarter than English ones and better cooked than eaten raw.

1 quart gooseberries
1 cup sugar
1 cup water
1 tablespoon brandy
    (optional)
    Green food coloring
    (optional)

2 cups heavy cream,
    whipped, or 2 cups
    custard, the
    consistency of
    whipped cream

Remove the stem and blossom ends of the berries. Wash them. Combine berries, sugar, and water. Cook over low heat, stirring occasionally, until tender. Taste for sweetness; if very tart, add a little more sugar. Strain berries through a sieve; do not use a blender. Stir in brandy and a few drops of food coloring to make a pale green color. Cool. Fold the whipped cream or the custard into the gooseberry mixture. Chill before serving.

Summer Pudding

Delicious and easy—a method rather than a specific recipe.

Butter a deep baking dish. Line bottom and sides with overlapping slices of stale white bread, from which the crusts have been cut off. The dish must be completely lined without the smallest chinks, leaving no space through which fruit juices can escape. Cook any berries with sugar to taste to a thick compote. Raspberries are best, especially when mixed with a quarter of their volume of red currants, but blackberries and blueberries are also great. Spoon the fruit into the baking dish. Cover the fruit with a layer of overlapping bread slices— the fruit must be completely covered. Fit a plate or a saucer on top of the bread and weigh it down with something heavy, such as a large can of peaches or a bag of rice or beans. Chill overnight. At serving time, unmold the Summer Pudding onto a deep serving dish. Serve with heavy cream and sugar on the side.

Claret Jelly With Raspberries
(4–6 servings)

2 packages (2
tablespoons)
unflavored gelatin
½ cup water
½ cup fresh orange juice
2½ cups claret or other dry
red wine

Sugar
1 cup fresh raspberries
Whipped cream
Raspberries for decorating

Sprinkle the gelatin over the water and stir to dissolve. Heat the gelatin over hot water (set the bowl into a saucepan with boiling water) until it is liquid. Combine the orange juice and the claret. Add a little sugar to taste. Stir until the sugar is dissolved. Stir the gelatin into the wine mixture. Chill until the jelly has the consistency of unbeaten egg white. Stir in the raspberries, dividing them evenly through the jelly. Pour into a glass serving bowl and chill until set. At serving time, decorate with swirls of whipped cream and the raspberries.

Simnel Cake

In the old days, a great deal of good baking went on in England's farm kitchens. The Simnel is such an old, traditional English cake, with a layer of almond paste baked right into the dough. It was baked for Mothering Sunday in old England, that is, the fourth Sunday in Lent, the day when the children who lived away from home visited their parents, bringing presents for their mothers.

The following is but a variety of Simnel. I make it very often because it is so well liked and not really that much trouble. The Almond Paste should be made first.

A good quality store-boughten almond paste, such as the imported Danish variety, available in gourmet stores, is just as good as the homemade kind.

STEP 1. ALMOND PASTE:

1 cup finely ground blanched almonds	A few drops of yellow vegetable coloring
½ cup superfine sugar	½ teaspoon almond flavoring
1 small egg	

Combine all the ingredients in a bowl. Mix thoroughly and knead into a smooth paste. Set aside.

STEP 2. Preheat oven to slow (300°F.).

Use a deep 8-inch springform pan. Roll out the almond paste between sheets of waxed paper the size of the cake pan. Reserve. Butter the springform pan on the bottom and sides. Cut a circle of unglazed brown paper to fit the bottom of the pan. Place it inside and butter the paper.

STEP 3. CAKE:

¾ cup butter	1 cup currants
2 cups sugar	¾ cup shredded mixed glacé peel
2 cups sifted flour	
1½ teaspoons baking powder	4 large eggs

Cream the butter until soft. Gradually beat in the sugar, ¼ cupful at a time, beating well after each addition. Sift together the flour and baking powder and reserve 1 cup. Dredge the currants and peel with this reserved flour (this prevents the fruits from sinking to the bottom of the cake during baking). Beat in the eggs, one at a time, beating well after each addition. Stir the remaining flour into the batter. Add the fruits and mix well. Pour half of the cake dough into the prepared springform pan. Place the circle of almond paste on the dough. Top with the remaining dough. (If preferred, the cake may be divided into three layers and the almond paste into two layers.) Bake for about 2½ hours or until the cake tests clean. Cool the cake in the pan for 5 minutes. Turn out on a cake rack and cool completely. Frost with Almond Butter Icing piped through a pastry tube into the shape of rosettes and swirls. Decorate with glacé cherries and strips of glacé peel.

STEP 4. ALMOND BUTTER ICING:

½ cup sweet butter, at room temperature
⅛ teaspoon salt
4 cups sifted confectioners' sugar

2 teaspoons almond flavoring
Glacé cherries and glacé fruit for decoration

Combine the butter, the salt, the confectioners' sugar, and the almond flavoring. Beat together until very smooth and of spreading consistency. If desired, color parts of the icing with food coloring for special effects.

Old-Fashioned Barley Water

(About 3½ cups)

A traditional and surprisingly refreshing English drink once popular with Queen Victoria as well as among farmers working in the fields and invalids.

⅓ cup barley
1 quart water
Yellow peel of 1 lemon

Juice of 1 lemon
Sugar to taste

Put the barley into a saucepan and add the water and the lemon peel. Bring to the boiling point, lower the heat to simmer, and cook covered for about 30 to 45 minutes. Strain, add lemon juice and sugar to taste, and chill before serving.

Apple Water

(About 3½ cups)

Another old-fashioned and refreshing English drink

1 pound tart apples	Sugar
1 quart boiling water	Juice of 1 lemon

Wash the apples. Chop them without peeling or coring. Place the apples into a large jar and pour the boiling water over them. Add sugar to taste and the lemon juice. Stir to mix well. Cover the jar and chill for 2 hours or more. Strain before serving.

Black-Currant Tea for Invalids

(1 serving)

Nice when you have a cold and even better with a little bourbon or vodka in it.

1 large tablespoon black-currant jam	2 cups boiling water

Put the jam into a glass or a cup and pour the water over it. Stir well, add anything else you fancy in spirits, and drink as soon as cooled enough.

Chapter 9

Fire Island Kitchen

DURING THE SUMMERS, especially one of them when we rented a house on Fire Island, I learned to feed the multitudes. Fire Island is a long, narrow sandspit off the mainland not far from New York, with a number of communities which are quite different in their life-styles. Ours, Fire Island Pines, was quite a fancy one, with superb modern beach houses that had to be seen to be believed and one single grocery store which, though it was stocked with a large number of gourmet items, did not offer much in the way of family food at reasonable prices. The place sported two bar-restaurant ear-splitting rock-and-dancing establishments that had their aficionados. We were not among them, perhaps less because the life-styles exhibited at these two watering places were not quite the same as our own, than that we could not afford them. Thus we ate in, as they say, day in, day out.

237

The "we" in this case was my own immediate family of my husband and my mother, my son Tony, his wife, Gray, and their son, Julian, as well as my younger son, Julian. This core of people was extended with one's neighbors, and my husband's and my own friends and their children, and the male and female friends of my children. All of these came to stay for the day, the week-end, and for weeks and weeks. I fed them at frequent intervals because people away from home always eat more, especially at the seashore. They also sleep longer, which made for interesting situations in our rather limited beach house. Children slept in their parents' room; singles slept on available sofas, camp beds, and in sleeping bags—the sleeping bags either out on the porch or in the sand under the house, which stood on piles, so as not to be in the way of indoor traffic. Whatever, people slept long and soundly, notwithstanding the waves of household life washing over them. I remember with special affection the profound slumbers of the beautiful Lorraine who later became our cherished daughter-in-law. Looking more than ever like a Florentine madonna, on her living-room couch, she slept through house cleanings, family quarrels, continuous breakfasts in the alcove kitchen, visitors, children back from fishing expeditions, and heaven knows what.

I've expressed my views on family meals before, but with all of the people in the house I had to overcome my aversion to them. Seldom, if ever, were there less than a dozen people to feed; and I soon found out that I was going stark mad with the constant eating that went on in the kitchen. Oh, how I hated the snap-snap-snap of closing refrigerators, the clinking of ice and the scratching of soft drink cans being opened, the soft thudding of sandwich .manufacture, the sizzling of hamburgers, and all the sounds made by snackers snacking. Then the rule went out that aside from breakfast, no one was allowed to get their own food at odd times. After lunch and supper, those who wanted to could make themselves sandwiches to tide them over to the next meal. If they forgot, and got hungry, there was plenty of snack food at the village store to buy with their own money.

The breakfast of the young was simple: huge boxes of cornflakes, gallons of milk, and store-boughten cookies was all they wanted. As for vitamins and other items of nutrition, I felt that the sunshine and fresh air offered ample compensations. Besides, I had other things to do; let the parents take care of their little ones with vitamins and fresh orange juice if they chose to squeeze it, the vitamin content of any other kind being a moot quality, whatever the ads say.

I always tried to be out of the house when the young fed on their huge bowls of cereal, since I hated the sight of them slurping it down. Slurp they did. I could probably have stopped the slurping, but the effort was too fatiguing. To avoid this horrid sight my husband and I walked to the store, past wonderfully colorful co-vacationers bent on similar domestic errands. There were no roads, only boardwalks over the sand and outstandingly luxurious stands of poison ivy, which could bring untold riches to someone bright enough to find a use for it. Everybody walked, and most people dragged a red child's wagon, this being the standard way of transporting things in a carless, unpolluted environment. During the week, when many of the vacationers were working in New York to be able to afford their beach life, the wagons were chained to the iron railing along the harbor. Ferries take you to almost all the Fire Island communities, and

it's a common sight on Friday nights to see a stream of men and women pouring out of the ferry and rushing to free their chained wagons for weekend transportation of goods.

The store was at the end of the pretty little harbor, past the two restaurants, two real estate offices, and a shop of picturesque, miscellaneous clothing. A few of the lads who had danced all night had not yet had the strength to leave the deck of the more famous of the two places, lounging there, *presque tout nus*, over coffee. On the other side of the path lay moored the boats of the garment industry bosses and similar people, from New York or Long Island, who had come to observe the local color, admittedly very intensive at night. The boats, though I am sure they were endowed with the latest in engines, looked like large whales if beached whales can be a status symbol. The really big, fancy ones, prides of the Coliseum boat show, were invariably embellished with plastic shrubs lurking behind the cocktail table. Hideous, pot-bellied men in Bermuda shorts and sailing caps lounged around. From the looks of the women, one knew that they were legitimate wives, sisters, and cousins; nobody in their senses would put such unattractive women on their boat unless they had to. The store was geared to a sophisticated, well-heeled community where food was taken as seriously as houses and their decorating. I've never seen more refined domesticity than in the one-sex ménages of our village, enough to make one wish to revert to caveman living. When I think of the amount of food we bought daily, dragging it on the wagon, I still shudder with emotions of varying kinds. To boot, whoever went to the mainland brought back food too, especially meat, since it was less expensive there.

As I said before, I soon realized that with all these people in the house, the usual summer lunches of hamburgers and cheese would simply not work, both as to convenience and expense. Keeping a dozen people in daily hamburgers is an awesome task, and not one for me. As for cheese, nothing but whole wheels would have served. No, what we needed not only for supper, but for lunch as well, was good, solid, rib-sticking food, in large quantities, kettles full, the kind that keeps lumberjacks going in the cold. Thus kettles and pans full of spaghetti and meatballs and other pasta dishes, beans and sausages, pork roast and potatoes, beef stew, chickens with biscuits and thick, stomach-gripping soups emerged from my hands twice a day, not to mention an occasional beef roast when I was in an exhilarated mood, with some cash to spare. With every meal, we had salad in lieu of vege-

tables. That was another discovery of mine; it simply wasn't worthwhile to cook vegetables for so many people who did not care for them, but liked salads instead. Indeed, who needs vegetables when you spend the day in the sun and water, soaking up for free all those priceless health boosters. Dessert, however, we did have, twice a day. And twice a day, dessert was cake and fruit because that is what everybody liked and wanted, feeling deprived at the sight of puddings, or cheese, though occasionally pies were acceptable. That is, if one of the girls would bake them, for I hate making pies though I love making cakes. I made at least two cakes every day, and what with this mass production, I must confess that I used mixes. Generally speaking, I do not like convenience foods, but cake mixes are good if you don't compare them to a good cake made from scratch. Who in my family was to criticize me? Everybody was welcome to do better than me.

There are a great many different cake mixes. I went through them all, adding those personal touches the cake mix people say you should add or else you feel guilty for not putting yourself out for your loved ones. My loved ones were far too numerous for me to worry about, but I did—and I do think that extra vanilla or whatever flavoring, or a pour of whatever booze was handy, or an extra egg, or a little fresh butter improved the cake mixes no end. And then the frostings! You would think that those tall, brawny, and extremely proud-of-their-intellectual-sophistication kids would be above goo on cakes. Nothing of the sort—the more, the thicker, the better. The all-time favorite filling and frosting was the seven-minute variety with various flavorings. There never was any shortage of willing hands to beat the frosting in the double boiler for the allotted time since whoever beat could lick the pan. Do not think I was tied to the kitchen all day. Willing hands and feet were available for jobs— making the beds, sweeping the house, washing the dishes —in keeping with the principle that whoever cooks does not wash or run to the store for last-minute milk or to the liquor store for last-minute wine.

Another reason I had plenty of time for myself is that I am an early riser, like my husband. We would go down to the beach around 6 for a morning swim or walk, come home and have a grown-up breakfast of tea or coffee and bread and jam, and then go to the store for the main provisions. Shortly after nine I would start the day's cooking and then go down to the beach again before lunch. I surely cooked a great deal, finding it easier to do it myself, but then, I did not have to invite so many people to stay with me.

When you cook in large quantities, you must season, season, and season again. The trouble with much institutional, that is, quantity food, is not so much that the food is poor and ill cooked, but that it has so little flavor because of underseasoning. With seasoning, I do not mean a conglomeration of herbs and spices in one dish, which spells disaster. I do mean enough of the seasoning of which the dish is meant to taste, seasoning emerging over the unobtrusive but essential presence of parsley, onion, garlic, and even celery and carrot, which are necessary to set off the dish's master flavor. There is rosemary for roast lamb and roast pork, sage for beans, basil for tomato, bay leaf for beef, tarragon for veal, fennel for chicken, scallions for salads, thyme for soups, horseradish for cream sauces, and so on, according to taste.

The same is true for spices, though here the seasoning hand must be somewhat lighter, going in for less obvious spice and food affinities such as cardamon rubbed into veal, juniper berries cooked with pork, mustard coating for roasting chickens, cinnamon and nutmeg spicing for beef stews and ground meats, cumin or ginger for creamy foods and sauerbraten, mace for flavoring butters. Besides, there is the spicing of desserts which makes even packaged vanilla pudding interesting when a little mace or ginger is added to it—the spices that also do wonders for fruit salads, as does cardamon.

A seasoning all too frequently underestimated is grated fresh lemon rind, wonderful in meat loaves, fish cookery, and to my taste, almost everywhere. Just as a squeeze of fresh lemon juice will give life to any vegetable and salad, to curries and chilis, to chicken, veal, and pork dishes.

As I said before, I do not care much for spice blends and I prefer my own combinations. But the many spice and herb blends, ready-packaged and with cooking suggestions, have their merits; they are better than no seasoning.

One of the essentials of summer beach life is a large, constant flow of wine and beer, and a lesser flow of hard liquor. Sun, surf, and sand and all the healthful, zestful summer open-air activities that go with them make for thirst, the thirst that requires great gulps and quaffs of liquid to quench it. Milk, wine, and beer were what my loved young ones poured into themselves by the gallon, leaving soft drinks and fruit juices for the little kids and punches and water for the birds. Hard liquor they loathed as something for us debauched elderly; I remember the looks of disgust at us and our contemporaries, sitting peacefully on the deck at sunset with a mild little Scotch or bourbon in hand. You would have thought that we had spent ten days in a barroom and were unwilling to come out.

The gallon jars of California wine consumed by us would have supplied lamp bases for each citizen of the Emerging Nations; beer cans, metal to line the Queen Elizabeth II with from top to bottom. All of this contributed to the cost of life in no small way, and one day, when we were particularly numerous among ourselves, I brought this up with options, as we now say, the option being that we would give up all but the cheapest food to afford the drink. Everyone agreed enthusiastically, and some of those present even went so far as to buy wine several times out of their own money. Wanting to match the exhilaration of so much fresh air and sunshine with a little exhilaration from within stands to reason. Sun and wine go together, or the good Lord would not have arranged it so that grapes will only grow when they have sufficient sunshine.

Though, as I said before, people could go to the store to buy their own snacks, I did feel that the house should be able to produce emergency sandwiches. I wish I could say that I baked my own bread or bought the better loaves, but for the most part I did not, since the young did not seem to care much. Ours were the long loaves

of the kind of bread that does twelve different things
for your bones, spread with butter, not margarine, which
I don't think worth eating, whatever people say. Again
acting on popular demand, we had salami, and salami
only, for sandwich innards, besides some kind of mouse
cheese. The salami I bought large and entire, from an
Italian grocery store in the Village, and the Cheddar I
imported in five-pound lots from Vermont. The gourmets among us also could have mustard on their sandwiches.

The virtues of salami sandwiches became once more
apparent to me through my younger son, Julian, who
spent his early youth desiring little else to eat with the
exception of hamburgers and spaghetti. By salami sandwiches he did not mean creations with butter or mayonnaise and lettuce, but stark slices of plain bread stuck
together with lots of salami slices. This he ate at all
times, his concession being on family trips when, *force
majeure*, salami had to be substituted with ham. I still
remember the astonishment on the face of the waitress
in the Mount Washington restaurant when she heard
the tiny tot refuse a ham sandwich made with buttered
bread and some lettuce. He ate salami sandwiches for
breakfast, for lunch and in between, and he thrived on
them. Nary a vegetable except potatoes passed his lips.
He had been made, and with this, I mean made by force,
to taste everything green once, but to no avail. But he
did eat lots and lots of every kind of raw and cooked
fruit, which obviously compensated for the lack of vegetables since he grew up to be an extremely healthy, tall,
and well-built man. Which goes to show that the American mother's vegetable mania is unnecessary and that
children do not necessarily pick up the habits of their
elders—my husband and I being near vegetarians by

choice. Not so the boys. But there is a note of hope for mothers who can't come to my conclusion that if a person goes vegetableless through life, so what. Julian was sent to expensive camps every summer, where he learned many things. One summer he learned to like corn on the cob, another summer cherry pie, and still another one, salads. By that time, he was too old to go to camp, so that he could not learn more of these useful accomplishments. In all fairness to him, I must say that since, he has been known to nibble the tips of fresh asparagus spears.

You may have noticed that I have not spoken of out-of-doors cookery in this out-of-doors summer, though we had a grill out on the deck where we ate most of our meals. The reason for it was that nobody except occasional guests was willing to cook outdoors. One of the myths perpetrated on a trusting public is that cooking out of doors simplifies life for the housewife and besides, is fun. It is all this when she has nothing to do with the whole thing, when the ambitious out-of-doors cook readies his own grill, brings out the food and condiments, cooks it, and cleans up afterward. Perhaps this rare male or female exists; I have come across only one. I've known, even among my nearest and dearest, some willing to turn a hamburger or steak over the coals, the way a great conductor swings his baton over a ready-made orchestra; someone else had to be the drudge—guess who? It led me to the firm and unchangeable opinion that if I had to cook, I would much rather do it wherever most convenient to myself: in the kitchen. I've checked with many women on this point, and the majority agree with me.

The only out-of-doors cook who did shine not only for the goodness of his grilled beef, but for his considerateness was a Korean friend, who did the whole bit by himself. Hours before we ate, he massaged the marinade into the strips of beef with his own hands, he assembled the bowls, the sauces and condiments, and he made his own fire to get the heat just right. He grilled and grilled for hours, handing out scores of tender and tasty strips to family, friends, and neighbors who had been attracted by the delicious odors wafting from our sundeck. I made large pots of rice pilaf to go with the Korean beef, about one of the easiest and best mass-feeding dishes.

We had picnics too, since picnics are an inevitable feature of summer life. Why we went on picnics, with a sundeck circling the beach house, the sight of the surf and the fresh air and sunshine right on the premises, I do not know, except that my people liked to eat further away from home. I have mixed feelings about picnics since I like to eat in moderate comfort, and not like the pigs, which is the way you eat on most picnics. The picnics I would have liked are the lovely ones of the French and English countryside, lovingly described by Hickey and other writers, so provocatively painted by Morland, so exuberantly practiced by Marie Antoinette and Byron, and above all, so conveniently prepared by one's menials with cold birds, aspics, roasts, fruit. and champagne. Alas, these amenities were not for me, but there were compromises with the sandwiches and beer school.

Picnic food, especially on beaches, has to be strong, lasting food and lots of it. Fortunately, the beach at Fire Island is quite the same all along the island, so that there was not the urge to find different scenery at distant places. This would have meant a lot of work, such as discovering picnic sites free of ant heaps and away from swamps and poison ivy, out of the wind, near something to do for the children (a pool or swings), plus the necessity of remembering to bring along everything, absolutely everything, as well as heaving oneself and the food there. We picnicked on the beach, near enough to the house so that extra water, salt, bread, napkins, garbage bags, and anything else that had been forgotten could be fetched in a trice. We spread a tablecloth on the sand, and if it was windy, a windbreak made from a sheet tied to two broom handles. If you want a sun shelter, you tie the corners of a sheet to the top of four poles or broom handles and stand them up in a little pile of sand to hold them straight. Our picnic food was usually a large kettle of a thick stew; experience proved chili and pasta and bean soups especially successful. In any case it must be food that can be eaten with a spoon and from a bowl; anything else is too complicated. With it, we had crackers because bread dries out too quickly. Cheese was served in hunks for the same reason and fruit and slabs of bitter chocolate made dessert. And of course we had plenty of drink: cold, light wine like a California rosé and beer, kept icy in a styrofoam ice chest.

As you can see, it would have been awkward to carry all this equipment a long way. However, sometimes people wanted to spend a day walking. To avoid sandwiches, which take a lot of time and are a nuisance to make if they are to be interesting, I gave each wanderer a food bag to carry along. Into it I put hard-cooked or stuffed eggs, slices of meat loaf, ham or whatever leftover meat was handy, cheese, crackers, cookies, dried fruits (which do not squash) or bananas, and even a few carrots and celery sticks, all with little packages of salt and pepper. To drink, they took canteens of iced tea and iced wine. If the wanderer did not want to

lug his food, he could eat it up at once, and if he was
hungry later, that was his problem. It worked very well,
and I had a peaceful day at home with my husband,
with a delicious little picnic à deux, when we ate a little
cold roast tarragon chicken or a cold steak or Wiener
schnitzel, with a tomato on the side that had been spread
thickly with fresh basil pounded with olive oil.

But even beach picnics get lethargic during a long
summer. The shot in the arm for this malaise is a costume beach picnic. We had a most memorable one
that summer on the deck of a friend, with the rule that
no one could rent a costume, that costumes had to be
made from whatever flotsam and jetsam could be rustled
up at one's beach cottage, and that nobody could spend
more than one dollar on his outfit. The results were
great. To give you some instances: Two men arrived
by water as twin streamer-hatted gondoliers. Their sail-
fish sported interesting banners with artistic, hand-
painted incidents of what had happened at some local
parties. My husband depicted what he called the futility
of all human endeavor by wearing a black bowler hat, a
striped shirt, and the bottoms of a pair of female
orange terry pajamas. One painter came as an ancient
Roman, laurel wreath and bare one-shoulder toga and
all. One youth was Neptune. A girl had a peek-a-boo
harem costume made with vividly painted canvas strips
which she had culled from abandoned beach chairs, and
another girl a shimmering aluminum foil bikini. One
of the children was the Tin Woodman encased in a
construction of cardboard boxes and one little boy wore
an enormous peon hat which reached down to his chest,
on which large, colorful eyes, nose and mouth had been
painted.

I, and I don't mind if I say so myself, was splendid,

in what my inward eye saw as a costume straight out of Fellini's *Juliet of the Spirits*, my favorite movie. An enormous, flowered sheet covered me from top to toe, with only eye slits and arm slits cut into it. On my head, over the sheet, I wore a large, black floppy felt hat, out of *La Vie de Bohème*. I walked with a cross nailed together from two boards to which I had attached a long, red sock. My exit was spectacular. The dock on which the costume picnic was held gave on the large, shallow bay which divides Fire Island from Long Island, or the mainland for all intents and purposes. I simply wandered

out into the bay—so shallow you have trouble to get out of your depth—and disappeared, getting rid of my clothes under the water and reappearing on land in a wet, but seemly beach dress.

Pasta and Bean Soup
(Pasta e Fagioli)

(8–10 servings)

The recipe for this rib-sticking soup can be halved or increased without trouble, provided the kettle is large enough.

½ cup olive oil
2 large onions, thinly sliced
4 garlic cloves, minced
1 green pepper, chopped fine
2 1-pound cans Italian-style tomatoes, undrained
½ cup minced parsley
4 tablespoons minced fresh basil or 1–2 tablespoons dried basil

2 quarts or more beef bouillon made with beef cubes
Salt
Freshly ground pepper
2 cups ditalini or small elbow macaroni
4 cups canned white or red beans, undrained
Freshly grated Parmesan cheese

In a large soup kettle, heat the oil. Add the onions, the garlic, and the pepper. Cook, stirring constantly, until the onions are soft. Add the tomatoes, the parsley, and the basil. Bring to boiling point, lower heat to very low and simmer covered for about 20 minutes. Stir occasionally. Stir in the beef bouillon. Season with salt and pepper to taste. Bring to the boiling point and add the ditalini or elbow macaroni. Cook until the pasta is almost done. Add the beans and cook until the pasta is tender. If a thinner soup is wanted, add a little more bouillon or hot water. Serve with plenty of freshly grated Parmesan cheese.

Interesting Rice Pilaf

(6–8 servings)

A filling main dish

½ cup butter or margarine
3 medium onions, finely
   chopped
⅓ cup chopped walnuts,
   almonds, or whole
   pignolia nuts
⅓ cup currants or raisins,
   plumped in warm
   water and drained
2 cups rice
4 cups hot chicken or
   beef bouillon

2 large tomatoes,
   skinned, seeded, and
   chopped
¼ cup minced parsley
1 teaspoon ground sage
½ teaspoon ground
   coriander
¼ teaspoon ground
   cinnamon

Heat the butter in a large, heavy saucepan. Cook the onions in it, stirring constantly, until they are soft and golden. They must not brown. Add the nuts and the currants or raisins and cook for 2 minutes longer. Add the rice, and over medium heat and stirring constantly, cook it for about 3–4 minutes or until it looks glassy. Add all the other ingredients and blend thoroughly. Bring to the boiling point and immediately lower the heat to simmer. Cover and cook over lowest possible heat for about 20 minutes or until the rice is tender. Turn off heat, but keep on hot stove. Remove the cover, place a clean kitchen towel over the rice and cover again. Let stand 5 minutes to absorb any remaining moisture from the rice.

Note: 1) The dish is even tastier if ½ pound of any kind of minced liver is added to it *after* the onions and

sautéed for 3 minutes. Then add the nuts and proceed
as above.

2) The amounts can be doubled and tripled provided
the saucepan to cook it in is large enough.

Creamy Moussaka

(6 servings)

A satisfying main dish, to be followed by salad and
cheese.

2 tablespoons butter
3 medium onions,
    chopped
1 pound ground beef or
    pork
¼ cup minced parsley
½ teaspoon ground thyme
    Salt
    Freshly ground pepper
2 tablespoons flour

¼ cup dry white wine or
    dry vermouth
4 eggs
1 cup light or heavy
    cream
6 tablespoons butter
    About 6 cups peeled,
       sliced potatoes
    Fine dry breadcrumbs

Heat the 2 tablespoons of butter and cook the onions
in it until they are soft and golden. Add the meat and
cook, stirring constantly, for about 3 minutes. Stir in
the parsley, the thyme, salt and pepper, and blend well.
Stir in 1 tablespoon of the flour. Stir in the wine. Cook,
stirring constantly, for about 3 minutes. Separate 2 of
the eggs. Beat the yolks with 2 tablespoons of the cream
and stir into the meat mixture.

In another skillet, heat 4 tablespoons of the butter.
Sauté the potatoes in it until they are semisoft and
golden. Butter a deep ovenproof dish and sprinkle with
breadcrumbs. Fill it with alternate layers of potatoes

and meat mixture, ending with potatoes. Dot with the remaining 2 tablespoons butter. Bake in a preheated moderate oven (350°F.) for about 20 minutes. Beat together the remaining cream with the 2 remaining eggs and stir in the remaining 1 tablespoon flour. Pour the mixture over the Moussaka. Bake for another 10–15 minutes or until browned and bubbly on top. Serve with a tomato dish such as stewed tomatoes or a tomato salad.

Meat Loaf

(6–8 servings)

The grated Parmesan cheese makes any meat loaf more flavorful, and the hard-cooked eggs inside make it prettier and more nourishing.

3 pounds ground beef, lean cut
1 teaspoon salt
½ teaspoon freshly ground pepper
2 teaspoons dried basil or ground thyme
Grated rind of 1 lemon
½ cup grated Parmesan cheese

½ cup fine dried breadcrumbs
¼ cup minced onion
¼ cup minced parsley
1 large garlic clove, mashed
3 eggs, beaten
3 shelled hard-cooked eggs

In a deep bowl, combine all the ingredients except the hard-cooked eggs. Mix thoroughly with hands. Check the seasoning. Place the meat on a 10" x 12" piece of waxed paper. Pat it out to cover the paper. Place the hard-cooked eggs lengthwise on the meat. Roll up into a meat loaf and remove the waxed paper. Line a baking pan with aluminum foil and place the meat loaf in it.

Bake in a preheated hot oven (425°F.) for 10 minutes.
Lower heat to moderate (350°F.) and bake for about
1 hour and 15 minutes or until baked through. If the
meat loaf looks very dry, baste it with a little dry white
or red wine. Let stand in a warm place for 5–10 minutes
to settle the juices and make for easier carving.

Peter Hyun's Korean Beef

(4 servings)

The national name of this marvelous dish is *Bul Kogi.*
It is probably the most popular Korean meat dish. The
quantities can be increased at will, but the proportion
of the ingredients should be kept.

2 pounds sirloin, rib or
   flank steak, trimmed
   of fat and gristle and
   thinly sliced on the
   bias
3 scallions, chopped
4 garlic cloves, mashed

5 tablespoons soy sauce
2 tablespoons sesame oil
¼ cup sugar
2 tablespoons sherry
¼ teaspoon freshly
   ground pepper

Score each piece of meat with an X. Combine all the
other ingredients in a bowl. Add the meat, and with the
hands, massage the marinade into the meat, coating it
thoroughly. If possible, marinate the meat for 2 hours
or overnight in the refrigerator. Grill in the usual
manner.

Roast Leg of Lamb

(12 servings)

Pork may be roasted in the same manner

1 leg of lamb, weighing about 6–7 pounds, trimmed of fat and fell	Freshly ground pepper
	3 garlic cloves, sliced
	4 tablespoons olive oil
1 lemon	2 tablespoons crumbled rosemary or ground thyme
2 teaspoons salt	

Cut the lemon into halves and rub the meat on all sides with the lemon; sprinkle the lemon juice over the lamb. Rub in the salt and pepper. With the tip of sharp knife, cut little pockets into the meat. Insert a slice of garlic in each. Place the lamb into a baking pan. Massage the olive oil into it and sprinkle the rosemary or thyme on it, on all sides. Cover the pan with aluminum foil and let stand at room temperature for 2 hours. Or keep in the refrigerator overnight, but let it stand at room temperature for 2 hours before roasting.

Preheat the oven to moderate (350°F.). Place the lamb, still covered with the aluminum foil, into the oven. Roast for 1 hour. Then remove the foil and roast for 1 to 1½ more hours, depending on how well done the lamb is to be. Baste occasionally with the pan drippings. The finished lamb should have a well-browned surface. Let stand in a warm place for 10 minutes before carving. Serve on a large platter decorated with watercress.

Cheap Instant Chili

(4–5 servings)

1 tablespoon salad oil
1 pound lean ground
   meat
1 small onion, minced
1 1-pound can kidney
   beans, undrained

1 1-pound can Italian-
   type tomatoes
Salt
Freshly ground pepper
Chili powder

Heat the salad oil in a large saucepan. Add the meat and the onion. Cook, stirring constantly, until the meat is browned; pour off excess grease. Add the beans and the tomatoes. Stir in the salt, pepper, and chili powder to taste; mix well. Simmer covered over low heat for about 10 minutes or until heated through.

Stewed Potatoes

(4–5 servings)

Good with any roast meats or cold cuts

2 pounds potatoes,
   peeled and cut into
   ½-inch cubes
4 bacon slices, minced
2 tablespoons butter
1 large onion, thinly
   sliced

1 garlic clove, mashed
1 1-pound can Italian-
   style tomatoes
Salt
Freshly ground pepper

Dry the potatoes on paper towel after washing them. Heat together the bacon and the butter. Add the onion and garlic. Cook, stirring constantly, until the onion is soft. Add the tomatoes, potatoes, and salt and pepper to taste. Mix well. Cook covered over low heat, stirring frequently, until the potatoes are tender. If necessary to prevent sticking, add a little water from time to time.

Note: If you have any leftover peas, add them to the dish. Or cut up a few mushrooms and add them to the potatoes.

White and Red Bean Salad

(8–10 servings)

½ pound dried Great Northern beans

½ pound pink or red beans

1 onion stuck with 3 cloves

¼ pound bacon, in one piece, sliced, or a ham butt

2 teaspoons salt

1 medium red or yellow onion, minced

1 small garlic clove, minced

¾ cup olive oil

⅓ cup wine vinegar

1 tablespoon fresh minced basil or 1 teaspoon dried basil

Freshly ground pepper

Boston lettuce

2 medium tomatoes, in wedges

⅓ cup minced parsley

Soak the beans in water to cover overnight. Transfer to a kettle. If necessary, add more water to barely cover the beans. Bury the onion stuck with cloves and the bacon in the beans and add 1 teaspoon of the salt. Bring to the boiling point. Simmer without a cover for about 35–45 minutes or until the beans are barely tender. Do not overcook the beans, they must still be intact.

Meanwhile, blend together the minced onion, the garlic, the oil, the vinegar, the basil, the remaining teaspoon of salt and pepper to taste. Mix thoroughly.

Drain the beans and remove the onion and the bacon. Put the beans into a bowl and pour the dressing over them. Mix thoroughly. Let stand at room temperature for 2–4 hours. Make a bed of Boston lettuce leaves in a salad bowl. Pile the beans on top of it. Garnish with tomato wedges and sprinkle with the parsley.

Texas Hot Pepper Cornbread

(6–8 servings)

A San Antonio friend taught me this recipe

2 eggs
1 cup sour cream
⅓ cup salad oil (do not use olive oil)
1 cup cream-style canned corn
1 cup cornmeal
3 teaspoons baking powder

1 teaspoon salt
¼ pound Cheddar cheese, diced fine or shredded
¼ cup diced green or red hot chili peppers, seeds removed

Beat the eggs and beat in the sour cream, the oil, and the corn. Sift together the cornmeal, the baking powder, and the salt. Beat into egg mixture and mix well. Stir in the cheese and the hot peppers. Pour into a well-greased, heated 9″ x 12″ baking pan. Bake in a preheated moderate oven (375°F.) for about 20 minutes.

Note: 1) When working with chili peppers, be sure not to touch one's face or eyes with the hands, because of the danger of burning. The seeds are especially hot and must be removed. Wash hands immediately after with soap and hot water. This is a simple precaution any Texas child knows from infancy.

2) If chili peppers are not available, use desired amounts of Tabasco instead.

Chapter 10

The Brazilian Kitchen

AT ONE TIME of my life, I kept house in a tiny town in Brazil, in the interior of the state of São Paulo. I will at once say that this was in the late Thirties and that things have changed greatly in Brazil. But from what I am told, they have not changed that much in the small places such as the one where I lived, except for more technical accoutrements such as cars, radios, television, refrigerators, and the like. The essence of semi rural Brazilian life is still the same, and all of my life, I have kept a nostalgia for it.

The solid little bungalow in which we lived (my then husband was a chemist fumigating the orange orchards of the region) had a front porch adorned with a landscape of steep mountains behind which rose a gigantic, yellow moon that twinkled over a silvery waterfall—the whole a flight of fantasy in that region of thick red

261

earth, coffee trees, and citrus orchards. The house, rented furnished, was sparse and similar to the little modern bungalows in the small towns of southern Europe. The parlor, with a parquet floor worthy of the exotic woods of Brazil, had six wicker chairs and one rocker, arranged around a round table covered with a fancy hand-embroidered cloth. An electric bulb dangling from a cord was covered with an equally fancy hand-embroidered lampshade. More hand-embroidery lay on the little sideboard. This passion for hand-embroidered objects, endemic in Latin countries, was the bane of my childhood. I had to learn to make doilies, handkerchiefs, and borders for underwear—the fancier the better. And now, as an antidote to the age of machinery, it is considered more cultural and refined than ever.

The dining room, also parquet, was furnished with another round table surrounded by six straight chairs wearing snow-white cotton slipcovers on their backs, which made them look like spinster ghosts. In view of our temporary stay, this was just the place to eat, but to our friends in the town, a dining room handsomely furnished with preferably large sideboards and much fancy glass and silver on display was the final evidence of respectability.

The dining room led into the kitchen, on either side of which were the bathrooms with a cold shower and several tubs—one for whole immersion, one for feet, and one for hands. Here, the builder had given up plaster ceilings, glassed windows, and parquet floors and reverted to traditional practicality. There were only heavy wooden shutters at the two windows; and all the inside walls stopped about a foot below the ceiling, allowing a flow of cooling air. In the hot parts of Brazil, all the houses used to be built in this fashion. In my travels I stayed in many of these houses (modern ones are like ours), and I found that any suffering from a lack of privacy was amply compensated by the cool breeze and interesting observations on the private habits of my neighbors.

Our kitchen was even barer and lighter than the rest of the house, with a floor of hard-stamped earth and shelves on legs standing in empty tin cans filled with insecticide to discourage wandering ants. The stove, typical of rural stoves, was built as an adobe counter alongside one whole wall, ending in an oven. The iron-topped stove burnt a lot of thin, untrimmed tree branches stacked in the pantry. Sometimes, migrations of ants would wander in an aimless manner on the stove, which I doused with an insecticide called creolina, which seemed to me like a beautiful girl's name. No food was ever kept on the stove, and it was thoroughly washed down after cooking. Only the coffee maker stood on it, a tripod just under one foot high. A conical muslin bag held the coffee through which the water dripped into a blue enameled coffeepot. The system makes excellent, strong coffee, and whenever the muslin bag (washed after each use) looked dim, I bought a new one.

Just as inevitable as the coffee maker in a rural Brazilian kitchen was the water filter—two clay vessels one on top of the other, where the water passed through a filter, to be drawn from a spigot. It was covered with a chaste white net petticoat—no match for the turreted and painted models of our friends. Since the question of drinking water is one ever present in the minds of Americans, like the devil on the Puritan mind, here is what I did and what I do in foreign places. In the big cities, like São Paulo or Rome or Helsinki, I drink the tap water. In lesser cities, I ask if the tap water is good and act accordingly. In small Brazilian places, like ours, I drank filtered water. In dubious villages, mineral water. I've always come out well with this rule, but others have not. So there.

The wooden kitchen table also stood in cans of creolina to prevent encroaching insect life; the Brazilian cockroaches are stupendously big. In fact, anything that held foodstuffs stood in its creolina-filled cans. All this sounds worse than it was, especially when I think of the cockroaches every New York apartment dweller has to fight constantly and relentlessly.

The kitchen gave into a backyard full of orange trees, one luxurious banana plant, and several mangoes. From the wooden fence which divided us from our neighbors hung long twists of orange peel, drying in the sun, to be used as fragrant kindling. Brazilians, at least in the country, peel their oranges in a single strip, save the peelings, and suck the fruit. I still do the same when I live with a fireplace; the smell from the burning dried orange peel is delicious.

The backyard was inhabited by our chickens, self-supporting like all Brazilian village chickens. They are tall legged, singularly independent animals, with bare necks and tail ends, close kin to the fighting cocks which provide one of the nation's sports, albeit an illegal one and no less popular for it. As far as I could see, the chickens lived on the orange windfalls and a few handfuls of rice and beans thrown whenever one remembered. Surprisingly, they even laid a few eggs on this diet and made tough, but very flavorful eating.

Mingling with the chickens like friendly brothers and sisters were half a dozen or so black urubus, those domesticated bare-necked vultures which eat up the rural garbage and everything else scavenger birds will eat. In Brazil they perform such a valuable health service that it is against the law to shoot them. Urubus are perfectly harmless and beautiful in flight. My lasting impression of a Brazilian village is a sunlit backyard with dark green orange and mango trees, the ragged, lighter banana shrubs, where chickens and maybe a turkey or two and urubus fed together, as well as rows of urubus sitting on the kitchen fence as they did in my garden—waiting, waiting.

Our establishment also included a maid, a pretty redhead, aged eighteen, of Italian-born parents, who kept house as she would keep it later for her husband and five children—amiably, willingly, and informally, with bursts of song as she polished the floors and loud screams as she chased the chickens, to seize one for the table. Like myself, she loped around in *tamancos*, high wooden clogs which had the advantage of keeping your feet out of the deep red dust, or when it had rained, the deep red mud of the unpaved streets. I still hear our clop, clop, clop, echoing in the house. Leonor knew how to cook simple Brazilian food—rice, beans, stews, and rich, eggy cakes. I taught her pasta and sauces, roasts and cheese soufflés, though most of the time, we ate the local diet.

There was no refrigerator or icebox in the house, though this would not be so today. The town's wealthy citizen owned a refrigerator, a status symbol, because at that time it was very expensive. Leonor and I shopped daily for food, after my morning coffee and a meticulous toilet, because even in the sticks, ladies are supposed to be well groomed as to hair and nails, starched cotton frocks and for me, shoes, not clogs. The day's meat supply had come earlier, with Leonor. As in the Southern Italy of my childhood, one simply bought meat rather than a cut of meat, on the principle first come, first served. Not that it mattered much, because all parts of the beef and pork we ate our way through in a year tasted the same. But it was wise to buy the meat early in the day, before it had been set out in the open air, fly bait bar none. Before cooking, the meat was washed in water and vinegar.

The local egg situation was something else, a mystery I never fathomed. Our own chickens were temperamental layers and what with the poor meat, eggs constituted a welcome change in the diet. Either one could buy no

eggs from the various ladies who kept chickens, or several dozens at one time, all fresh and obviously newly gathered. With no refrigerator, the eggs had to be used up in a hurry, which is not easy when you take three or four dozen and have only three in the household to eat them. Never before or since have I had such orgies of sponge and angel cakes, custards and creams. I used to cook straight through all the egg dishes in the *Fanny Farmer Cookbook* I had brought along, and Leonor did her own with her cakes and cookies.

The vegetable and fruit supply came to the house, accepted by me from my rocking chair on the front porch. The marvelous vegetables—cabbages, zucchini, squash, beans, tomatoes—came from a neighboring garden run as a little truck farm by a Japanese family. Everybody worked at it, the smallest of the children weeding with patient, tiny fingers. An incredibly ribald old Brazilian woman provided the salads. She claimed to more than twenty children in her day, though we could never pin her down to the names of more than a dozen. The pineapple and avocado man also came by with his mule cart, with very fine fruit, costing a dime and less in those pre-inflation days. The bread, long Italian loaves, came with the baker's youngest boy, all of five years old.

Everything else we ate and drank, and much of what we needed for daily life, came from Abe's General Store, called *Secos e Molhados*—Dries and Wets. Just as our town resembled old Western movie towns, Abe's store looked straight out of *High Noon*. It was completely opened to the street and sold everything except fresh meat, fresh produce, saddles, yard goods, and furniture. Great sacks of coffee and rice, manioc flour and beans were piled on the floor, with large black coils of chewing tobacco and cartons with hardware, topped by pyramids of the large, coarse straw hats worn by the field hands. Large hunks of dried meat and bundles of salt cod were

stacked on barrels of lard, and piles of zinc basins stood
on cases of beer, tonic water, gin and whiskey for a
nearby English colony of hard-drinking bachelors who
ran the orchards fumigated by my husband. Whatever
could be hung from a ceiling and from brooms—elastic-
sided boots to salami—hung there. The wall shelves were
tightly packed with coarse china, pots and pans, fancy cut-
glass bowls for wedding presents, and toiletries. You could
smell some of the soaps across the store. One whole
wall was reserved for the sealed tins of butter from
southern Brazil's dairy country, cans of olive oil, vinegars,
sauces, and delicacies such as pale bottled asparagus,
canned hams, Lipton tea, and English jams. Abe also
sold Brazilian wine, good *vin ordinaire* for quaffing, hard
candy, and *pinga*, the national strong drink made from
sugar cane which is the comfort of the poor. The smell
of *pinga* hung over the store—once smelled, it is unforgettable.

Abe was the man who knew everybody and everything, and could fix whatever needed to be fixed. He and
his family, who lived in a large house behind the store,
became my great friends. They were Greek Orthodox
Lebanese—Turks as the Brazilians call them in their
prejudice. The Lebanese and Lebanese-descended colony
included cotton millionaires and poor backwoods ped-
dlers. Traditionally, the Lebanese were traders of soft
goods. Then they manufactured them or developed their
peddler's packs into stores, such as Abe's. He had come
to Brazil via Canada, where his children had been born
and schooled. But his brothers, who, like him, had fled
after the Turkish massacres, had lured him to Brazil with
tales of gold in the street and with plays upon his family
feelings. Finally, he landed in our little town with his
wife, his two daughters, and three sons, all married with

children when I knew them. He opened his own general store and installed his sons in two others—one a yard goods store and the other a shoe store. Abe and his children spoke English, though Arabic among themselves. But the third generation was truly Brazilian, knowing only Portuguese, the national language. Their house was possibly the finest in town, with a parlor with a great number of embroidered cushions, chairbacks, and curtains, a dining room with a great display of painted china and cut glass, and bedrooms handsome as to furniture and more embroidery. These were the rooms for state occasions, when company came from Rio or São Paulo. Family and guests lived in simpler bedrooms, in the kitchen, and on the porch shady with banana and other shrubs. There I used to sit with the family learning about Brazilian life. In Abe's house I took baths in the real bathtub, when the shower at home palled; and when it really mattered that a dish or a dessert be iced, I was allowed to bring it to cool in the big family refrigerator.

We lived Brazilian country-style, and Leonor cooked most of our food because that was the thing for her to do. The basis of a meal, as in the houses of the rich and poor alike, was a large dish of rice and one of black or brown beans. With it, we had two meat dishes, beef or pork, and chicken. With some difficulty, I had to restrain Leonor daily from making more meat dishes, because Brazilians love meat in all forms, and well-to-do families had three, four, and even five meats on the table, in our hinterland. We had stewed beef and fried chicken, roast pork, fried pork and braised pork, in light tomato sauces. We also had potatoes, boiled or hashed or fried; at least two vegetables; a green salad and a tomato salad; and a plate of fried eggs. But at an additional dish of macaroni in a tomato or cream sauce I balked. Everything was substantially cooked in lard and butter and served with a red pepper sauce (voluntary) that can only be described as powerfully overwhelming as tropical nature. The one thing we did not have was *farofa*, a fine powder made from manioc root, a tasteless, pure starch which Brazilians, especially poor ones, sprinkle over all of their food the way the Italians sprinkle Parmesan on pasta. I also trained Leonor not to give us *canja*, the ubiquitous Brazilian chicken soup, because I loathe all chicken soups, whatever their nationality. Liquid hen is just too much.

Of course we had dessert. The standard was quince, guava or banana paste, eaten with a fresh cheese, similar to new Muenster. We also ate cheese with other desserts, with fresh pineapple, with cooked or fried bananas, or with cornstarch pudding, following local fashion. And I do remember the fresh fruit with great nostalgia. There were bananas, tasting either of apples or peaches, to eat raw (the long green plantains were the ones for cooking), papayas, mangoes, and European-type fruit such as apples, pears, and the most beautiful strawberries.

All this does not sound very exotic, and it wasn't, except for the touches of dousing starch on starch, *farofa* on rice and beans, or frying bananas as a vegetable. Brazil is a melting pot like the United States, with settlers from all parts of Europe, Asia, and the Far East. The part of Brazil we were in was settled by Portuguese and an enormous number of Italians, which had nothing to do with the plantation and slave economy of the early settlements in the north of the country. Brazil, larger than the United States, has the same division between North and South, though the other way around.

Our South is kin to Brazil's North, where *Gone With The Wind* was also a best seller. There the food, always on the rice and beans basis, is very different, with strong, savory touches of African cooking. In Brazil's South, the food resembles Mediterranean food. Different ethnic groups who also settled there contributed Polish, German, Ukranian, and other dishes. Some of the food, such as you find in the fine restaurants of Rio and São Paulo, has evolved into a superb national cuisine, as I found out later. In our part of the country, as described, the food was homey, but incredibly abundant. The food on our own table was always sufficient for at least six, though there were only two of us in the household. But people dropped in for the midday meal, which was served around eleven, following local rural fashion. In Brazil, hospitality is immense. At first, we were formally invited, with much fuss, and reciprocated. Then we just went and ate with people, or they came to eat with us, sans-façon. We had no meal at night since my husband was away at his work, and I out visiting or at home boiling myself an egg.

Anyhow, the food seemed to be gone at the end of the day. What was leftover was collected by a Franciscan monk from a nearby monastery, who came around in a little mule-driven cart with large pots. Every day, he made his rounds of the town to collect surplus food for the poor, of whom there were many. They lived almost exclusively on rice and beans, prepared with as much lard as they could afford, doused with manioc flour, with meat as a treat. Aside from a few leaves of lettuce, they never ate greens; this terrible diet seemed all the worse considering that we were living in an immensily fertile region where just a few seeds dropped into the ground would come up with a bounty. Aside from bananas, mangoes, oranges and a little fruit, they hardly ever ate fresh foods.

In everybody's experiences, some stand out boldface. Two come to my mind when I think of Brazil—first the hospitality of the people. About everybody I knew, from well-to-do, less well-to-do, and downright poor people, always set the table for more people than their own family, in case a visitor should drop in at mealtime. The other is the sight of a waiter in a good restaurant peeling an orange to smooth perfection in front of your eyes and depositing it tenderly on a slice of fresh pineapple for a marvelous dessert.

Brazilian food is extremely varied, reflecting the ethnic backgrounds of her many settlers: from the Portuguese and the African slaves who came together, to the Italians and Japanese in São Paulo, and the Poles and Germans in the South. Aside from this, there is the influence of French cooking, as in all civilized nations. The range of Brazilian food is described totally admirably in *Brazilian Cookery: Traditional and Modern*, by Margarette De Andrade, published by Charles Tuttle. This book not only gives authentic Brazilian recipes (different from the usual European recipes cooked in Brazil) but it also tells of their background, their history, and their circumstances. I highly recommend it to anybody interested in a civilization that is not as well known in America as it should be.

As to the food I myself cooked in Brazil, it was basically the Italian kind which I cook for us anywhere. The ingredients were all readily available, since many settlers of Italian descent lived in our little town. Personally, I don't like very exotic food, though I will eat it once.

Thus, the recipes that follow are not an anthology of Brazilian food, but the dishes which I've cooked myself and still cook.

Fresh Tomato Soup

(4 servings)

Easy—no canned tomato soup equals it

2 tablespoons butter
1 large mild onion, thinly sliced
1 pound tomatoes, peeled and coarsely chopped
¼ cup minced celery
2 tablespoons minced carrot
¼ cup minced parsley
Salt
Freshly ground pepper
6 cups water
½ teaspoon dried thyme or basil, or fresh thyme or basil to taste
2 tablespoons rice
Fried bread croutons (optional)

Heat the butter in a large saucepan. Add the onion and cook, stirring constantly, until the onion is golden; do not let it brown. Add the tomatoes, the celery, the carrot, the parsley, and salt and pepper to taste. Cook covered over low heat for about 15 minutes or until the vegetables are very soft. Strain through a fine sieve or puree in a blender. Return to the saucepan and add the water and the thyme or basil. Mix well. Bring to the boiling point, add the rice and simmer covered for 10 minutes or until the rice is tender. Check the seasoning. Serve with fried croutons.

Note: The rice is not obligatory. The soup should be very well seasoned.

Soused Fish

(Fish in Escavèche)

(4–6 servings)

A method you find everywhere (from Belgium to Brazil) devised by people who have to eat rather dull fish. I like it very much, but there are other variations. The idea is to make the fish piquant.

4 green peppers, chopped
3 medium onions, chopped
4 medium carrots, chopped
3 bay leaves, crumbled
¼ cup olive oil
⅔ cup cider vinegar
1 cup water
1 teaspoon salt
½ teaspoon dry mustard
⅛ teaspoon Tabasco or other hot pepper sauce
2–3 pounds white fish fillets

Combine all the ingredients except the fish in a saucepan. Mix well. Bring to the boiling point. Lower the heat and simmer covered for 20 minutes. Meantime, broil or fry the fish as usual. Pour the hot sauce over the fish, or puree the sauce first in a blender. Serve hot or cold.

Fish With Lime Juice

(4 servings)

A Brazilian method to liven up the usual dull fish. You can use lemon, but lime is better.

1 pound fish fillets or any dressed fish	Freshly ground pepper
	Grated rind of 1 lime
Juice of 1–2 fresh limes, freshly squeezed	2 tablespoons butter
	2 tablespoons salad oil
Breadcrumbs	1 egg, lightly beaten
Salt	Lime wedges

Cut the fish into good-sized, bite-sized pieces. Place them on a large plate or platter. Sprinkle with the lime juice. Let stand in a cool place for about 1 hour. If it will be kept in a refrigerator, cover the fish with plastic wrap or all the other foods will smell of fish. Dry the fish before frying. Combine the breadcrumbs, the salt and pepper, the lime rind. Heat the butter and salad oil together. Dip the fish pieces into the egg and then coat them with the breadcrumbs. Sauté until golden brown. Serve hot with wedges of fresh lime.

Shrimp Carurú

(4–5 servings)

A Brazilian dish of African descent. For sources of manioc meal see Feijoada Completa, page 280. Dried shrimps are available at many Chinese grocery stores. This recipe comes from *Brazilian Cookery: Traditional and Modern* by Margarette De Andrade.

1 tablespoon butter
1 tablespoon chopped
    onion
1 tablespoon chopped
    parsley
1 tablespoon chopped
    green pepper
1 fresh tomato, peeled
    and chopped
1 pound fresh shrimps,
    shelled and deveined
1½ cups sliced okra

¼ pound dried shrimps,
    ground to a powder
    in a blender or
    mortar
1½ tablespoons manioc
    meal
1 grated fresh coconut
    (see below)
½ cup dendé oil or
    peanut or salad oil
Salt
Freshly ground pepper

Heat the butter in a casserole. Add the onion, the parsley, the green pepper, and the tomato. Over medium heat, and stirring constantly, cook for 2–3 minutes. Add the fresh shrimps and cook for 3–4 minutes. Add the sliced okra. Mix together the dried shrimps and the manioc meal. Grate the coconut and remove the thick milk. To the residue add 1 cup boiling water and remove the thin milk. Blend the thin coconut milk and the dried shrimp–manioc meal mixture to a paste. Stir it gradually into the shrimp–okra mixture. Simmer over very low heat until the okra is tender. Just before serving, stir in the thick coconut milk and the dendé oil. Season with salt and pepper. Serve with rice and beans.

Note: The dendé oil contributes to the typical flavor of this dish. If it is not available, I would suggest leaving the oil out altogether, as I have done. The dish is still good.

Chicken With Wine, Saffron and Almonds

(5–6 servings)

This is a dish of Portuguese origin. Serve with rice and a green salad.

1 4–5 pound stewing chicken, cut into pieces, all fat and skin removed
Salt
Freshly ground pepper
Flour
¼ cup olive oil
¼ cup butter
1 medium onion, minced
2 garlic cloves minced
2 cups dry white wine
Hot chicken consommé
1 bay leaf, crumbled
1–1½ teaspoons saffron
20 blanched almonds, chopped
2 tablespoons butter
½ cup fresh white breadcrumbs
2 hard-cooked eggs, sliced
¼ cup minced parsley

Sprinkle the chicken pieces with salt and pepper. Coat with flour and shake off excess. Heat the olive oil and the ¼ cup of butter in a large, heavy casserole. Cook the chicken pieces in it until golden brown on all sides. Add the onion and the garlic. Cook, stirring frequently, until the onion is soft. Pour off excess fat. Add the wine and just enough chicken consommé to barely cover the meat. Check the seasoning and if necessary, add more salt and pepper. Add the bay leaf. Bring to the boiling point. Lower heat to simmer. Cook covered for about 45 minutes; cooking time depends on the age of the bird. The chicken should be almost, but not quite tender. Skim the fat off the chicken and the cooking liquid.

Dissolve the saffron in 2 tablespoons of the cooking liquid. Stir the saffron and the almonds into the chicken dish. Simmer for 15 more minutes or until the chicken

is tender. If the sauce looks too thin, cook uncovered
to reduce. If it is too thick, add a little more wine or
consommé. Heat the 2 tablespoons butter in a small
frying pan. Sauté the breadcrumbs in it until crisp and
golden. Transfer the chicken to a hot deep serving dish.
Pour the sauce over it. Top with the breadcrumbs and
the egg slices. Sprinkle the parsley over the breadcrumbs
and egg.

Brazilian Chicken With Orange

(3–4 servings)

Serve with Brazilian rice and a salad

1 2½ to 3-pound frying chicken, cut into pieces	½ cup blanched almonds, ground fine
½ cup olive oil	½ cup orange pulp
1 cup fresh orange juice	½ teaspoon ground ginger
1 cup dry white wine	Salt
½ cup raisins	Freshly ground pepper

Remove all the fat and the skin from the chicken. Heat
the olive oil in a frying pan. Over medium heat, brown
the chicken pieces in it on all sides. Transfer to a shallow
baking pan. Combine all the other ingredients in a bowl
and mix well. Pour over the chicken pieces. Bake in a
preheated moderate oven (350°F.) for about 45 minutes
or until tender. Baste frequently.

Fried Steaks

(4–5 servings)

A flavorful way of tenderizing the tough meat of rural Brazil applicable to our economy steak cuts.

2 pounds economy steak (chicken, chuck, round, shoulder) Salt	Freshly ground pepper About ½ cup fresh lemon juice 2 tablespoons cooking fat

Trim the meat. If it is in one piece, cut it into four or more pieces. Rub salt and pepper into the meat, on both sides. Lay it in a shallow dish. Sprinkle the lemon juice over it and make sure that both sides are coated with it. If necessary for thorough coating, use a little more lemon juice. Let the meat stand in the refrigerator for 2 hours or overnight. Drain and reserve marinade. Heat the fat in a skillet. Quickly brown the meat on both sides. Turn down heat and pour the reserved marinade over it. Cover and simmer over low heat until the meat is tender; cooking time depends on the meat.

Note: For a more substantial and very Brazilian dish called Bife a Carvalho, horseback beef, place a fried egg on each helping.

Feijoada Completa

(6–12 servings)

This is the official dish of Brazil. Like all traditional dishes in any country, cooks have their own variations on the national theme. A *feijoada completa* means a complete bean dish, and this indeed it is. In this country, a *feijoada* would make a good and different party dish, since it cannot be made in small quantities.

The jerked beef ingredient can be found, with the pig's feet, at butchers catering to Latin American and Spanish-speaking people. At a pinch, it can be left out of the dish, making it less authentic. Manioc meal may be found in Spanish-speaking groceries or at Casa Moneo, 218 West 14th Street, New York City. Don't waste any tears if it is not available, because it is pure, bland starch and alien to the American taste.

This recipe comes from Margarette De Andrade's *Brazilian Cookery*.

5 cups black beans
1 pound jerked beef or dried beef, in one piece
1 small smoked tongue
½ pound Canadian bacon
1 pound chorizo or fresh pork sausages
1 pound corned spareribs
1 pound smoked sausages
2 pigs' feet
1 pound lean beef (round) cut into 2 pieces
¼ pound lean bacon
Salt
1 tablespoon lard or shortening
2 large onions, chopped
3 garlic cloves, crushed
1 chopped tomato (optional)
1 tablespoon chopped parsley (optional)
1 crushed hot pepper (optional)

1. Pick over beans, wash and soak overnight in cold water.

2. In separate pans, soak the jerked beef, the tongue, and the Canadian bacon overnight in cold water.

3. Next morning drain the beans (if any liquid remains), cover with fresh cold water, and cook for about 2½ hours in a covered saucepan, adding as needed, sufficient water to keep the beans covered. When the beans are cooked and tender, remove ¼ cup of the bean liquor and set aside to cool and to be used in preparing the special hot sauce served with the Feijoada.

4. Meanwhile, as the beans are cooking, prepare the meats, always removing them from the liquid in which they were soaked:

   a) Drain the jerked beef, cover with cold water, bring to a boil, and simmer for 1 hour or until fork tender. Remove, cut into 1-inch strips and set aside.

   b) Parboil the tongue in fresh, simmering hot water water long enough to be able to remove the skin, drain, and set aside.

   c) Separately parboil the Canadian bacon, the spareribs, the smoked sausages, and the pigs' feet, drain and set aside.

   d) Prick the fresh pork sausages, parboil them in a little hot water, drain and set aside.

5. Place all the meats, except the fresh pork sausages, but including the beef and bacon, in a very large saucepan. Cover with lukewarm water, slowly bring to a boil and simmer covered until the meats are tender (about 1½ hours).

6. Drain the meats and add them to the beans with the pork sausages. Simmer until the meats are very tender and the beans are soft enough to mash. Season with salt.

7. About ½ hour before serving melt the lard or short-

ening in a large skillet and sauté the onions and garlic in it. If the tomato, the parsley, and the crushed hot pepper are desired, they also should be sautéed at this time.

8. Add about 2 cups or ladles of the beans to the onion mixture and mash with a wooden spoon or a mallet.

9. Pour about 2 cups of the bean liquor over the mixture, simmer until the mixture thickens and then return to the pot containing beans and meats.

10. Simmer until thoroughly blended, about ½ hour.

11. Taste and correct seasoning and serve.

To Serve:

Remove the meats from the beans and slice so that each person may have a small portion of the various kinds of meat. According to long-established custom, the tongue is placed in the center of the platter and the smoked meats at one end while the fresh meats are arranged attractively at the other end of the platter. Moisten the meats with a small ladle of the bean liquor. The beans are served in a soup tureen or deep serving dish. The guest helps himself to an assortment of meats and places a serving of Brazilian Rice (below) to one side of the plate. The beans with their rich sauce are ladled over the rice while manioc meal is sprinkled over the beans or meats. Sliced oranges and Couve à Mineira (page 285) accompany the Feijoada as well as a special hot sauce— Môlho de Pimenta e Limão (page 286)—to which some of the bean liquor is added. Brazilian rum (cachaca) may be served with this meal. Or to my mind, a good imported beer.

Brazilian Rice

(4–5 servings)

With a dish of black beans, this comes to the table almost every meal. For poor people, rice and beans are the meal.

2 tablespoons lard or bacon fat (do not use butter)	1 bay leaf
	2 cups long-grain rice
1 small onion, minced	2–3 cups boiling hot water
½ garlic clove, minced	Salt
3 medium tomatoes, peeled and chopped	Freshly ground pepper

Heat the lard in a heavy saucepan. Add the onion and garlic. Over medium heat, and stirring constantly, cook for about 2 minutes or until the onion is soft. Add the tomatoes and the bay leaf. Cook for about 3 minutes longer. Add the rice. Cook, stirring constantly, until the rice has absorbed the tomato mixture. Cover the rice with the boiling water; the amount depends on the size of the saucepan and on the kind of rice used. Season with salt and pepper. Bring quickly to the boiling point. Lower heat to very low. Cover the saucepan and cook until the rice is tender, about 15 minutes, and until all the water has evaporated. Do not stir. Taste a few grains to see if the rice is cooked. If not, add another ½ cup of boiling water. When the rice is ready, remove from the heat and uncover. Let stand for 3 minutes or so to allow any remaining steam to evaporate. Turn out on a hot serving dish.

Brazilian Black Beans

(6 servings)

Most Brazilians eat them almost every meal, but Americans might consider this dish as an alternative to potatoes and other starches. The beans should be just slightly soupy.

1 pound dried beans, washed and drained	2 bay leaves
3 tablespoons lard or bacon fat (do not use butter)	2 teaspoons salt
	Freshly ground pepper
	1 slice smoked ham or 1 smoked ham bone (optional)
1 large onion, minced	
1 garlic clove, minced (optional)	1-2 tablespoons mild vinegar (optional)

Cover the beans with water. Bring to the boiling point. Boil for 2 minutes. Remove from the heat, cover, and let stand for 1 hour. Or soak beans overnight and drain. Heat the lard in a large saucepan. Cook, stirring constantly, the onion and the garlic in it until the onion is soft. Add the beans and their liquid, the bay leaves, the salt, the pepper, and the ham or ham bone. Bring to the boiling point. Lower heat to lowest possible. Simmer covered for 2 hours or until the beans are tender. Check for moisture; if necessary add a little more hot water. Remove from heat and stir in the vinegar.

Couve à Mineira

(Kale or Collards Mineira)

(4 servings)

This dish reminds one of American Southern cooking.

4 cups finely shredded kale or collard greens
Boiling salted water

¼ cup bacon fat
Salt
Freshly ground pepper

Wash and drain the greens. Plunge them into the boiling salted water and drain immediately. Heat the bacon fat in a frying pan and cook the greens in it until they are limp. Season with salt and pepper to taste.

Hearts of Palm

Hearts of palms really come from palm trees. They are pale, bland, and somewhat similar in taste to artichoke hearts, though blander still. The canned variety, which is readily available in the United States, hardly tastes different from the fresh kind, which must be blanched first before being used in a recipe.

I suggest slicing canned, drained palm hearts and adding them to any mixed salad. Or they may be served with a well-flavored mayonnaise, such as mustard mayonnaise, as a first course, on a bed of sliced tomatoes or shredded lettuce. Serve also in a well-flavored white sauce as a hot vegetable, or with a tomato sauce.

Môlho de Pimenta e Limâo

(Pepper and Lemon Sauce)

(About ½ cup)

This is a hot sauce. Malaguetta peppers can be found in Latin grocery stores or at Casa Moneo, 218 West 14th Street, New York City. Another of the recipes found in *Brazilian Cookery: Traditional and Modern.*

3–4 malaguetta peppers
½ teaspoon salt
1 medium onion, sliced

1 garlic clove (optional)
½ cup fresh lemon juice

Put the peppers, the salt, the onion, and the garlic into a blender and puree. Or pound together in a mortar to make a paste. Stir in the lemon juice. Let stand 1 hour before using. Do not make up more sauce than you will use because the sauce cannot be kept—it will ferment.

Coconut and Papaya Custard

(6–8 servings)

A little more or a little less of coconut or papaya does not make a great difference in this recipe. But the coconut should be fresh, not preserved.

3 cups mashed, ripe
  papaya (about 1 or
  2 papayas)
1½ cups freshly grated
  coconut (page 287)
4 eggs
4 cups milk or 3 cups
  milk and 1 cup light
  or heavy cream

½ cup sugar
Grated rind of 2 oranges
Juice of 1 orange
Whipped cream, with
  sugar

Spread the papaya on the bottom of a 6-cup (1½ quarts) baking dish. Sprinkle the coconut on top of it. In a bowl, beat together the eggs, the milk, the sugar, the orange rind, and the orange juice. Pour over the coconut–papaya mixture. Set the bowl in a pan with 2–3 inches of water. Bake in a preheated slow oven (325°F.) for about 1 hour or until a knife inserted near the edge of the dish comes out clean. Cool on a rack, then chill before serving with whipped cream.

How to Grate Fresh Coconut and How to Make Coconut Milk

How to Grate Fresh Coconut

When buying a coconut, shake it and make sure it is full of liquid.

Preheat the oven to hot (400°F.). Over a bowl, and using an ice pick or a screwdriver, puncture 2 of the 3 smooth dark eyes of the coconut. Drain the coconut liquid into bowl. The average coconut yields about ½ cup liquid. Reserve. This is *not* the coconut milk.

Place the drained coconut in a baking dish. Bake it in the hot oven for about 15 minutes. Remove it from the oven and transfer it to a chopping block. The coconut may or may not have cracked. While it is still hot, crack the heavy shell with a hammer or a meal mallet. Most of the shell will fall off the meat. Pry the remaining shell loose with the ice pick. Cool the coconut. Grate it over a fine grater as you would grate cheese. Stir in the reserved coconut liquid.

Another way is to cut the coconut meat into 1-inch pieces. Place the pieces in a blender with the coconut liquid. Blend over high speed for 1 minute or until finely grated.

How to Make Coconut Milk

Proceed as above, but do not add the coconut liquid to the grated coconut. Heat the grated coconut in the top of a double boiler over boiling water. Heat the coconut liquid. Add the hot coconut liquid to the hot coconut. Remove from heat. Let stand for 15 minutes. Line a fine sieve with a triple thickness of cheesecloth. (The cheesecloth lining prevents the coconut from taking on a metallic taste from a metal sieve.) Pour coconut and liquid into the sieve and let drip for 10 minutes. Then twist the cheesecloth and squeeze out as much liquid as possible. This is the *thick* milk; a coconut should average about ¾ cup.

To make the *thin* milk, return cheesecloth with squeezed coconut to the sieve. Heat as much water as specified for thin milk in the recipe (2 cups thin milk = 2 cups water). Pour this amount of water over the coconut. Let stand and drip again for 10 minutes, then squeeze out what liquid there is. This amounts on the average to 2–4 cups thin milk.

Note: Frozen coconut milk, popular on the West Coast and in Hawaii, is being gradually introduced into East Coast supermarkets. This frozen milk is uniform in thickness, but most useful.

Packaged shredded coconut is usually heavily sweetened, though health stores sell unsweetened varieties. A uniform milk (though not a thick or a thin one) can be extracted from it. I prefer using hot milk rather than water in doing this, to the amount specified in the recipe. Treat the packaged shredded coconut as the fresh, by placing it in a triple layer of cheesecloth.

Fresh Pineapple With Pistachio Nuts

(6 servings)

1 large ripe pineapple,
   cut into small
   wedges (see below)
¼ cup Kirsch
   Sugar

⅓ cup shelled pistachio
   nuts, coarsely
   chopped
Grated rind of 1 orange

Put the pineapple into a glass or silver serving dish. Add the Kirsch and sugar to taste; toss. Sprinkle with the pistachio nuts and the orange rind. Chill. Take to the table as is and toss again at the table.

How to Cut Up a Pineapple

Lay the pineapple on its side. Cut off the leafy crown and the base with a large, sharp knife. Stand the pineapple on end and cut it lengthwise into 4 pieces. If the pineapple is very large, cut it into eighths. Cut off the prickly rind of each piece, cutting deeply enough to remove the eyes. If there are any traces of brownish eyes left, remove them with the point of a paring knife. Cut the triangular core away from each piece. Lay each piece on its side and cut it crosswise into wedges of the desired thickness.

Avocado Cream

(3–4 servings)

This simple and excellent Brazilian dessert deserves to be better known in this country.

3 ripe avocados	Juice of 1 lemon
6 tablespoons sugar	

Peel the avocados and remove the seeds. Cut the flesh into pieces and put it in a blender with the sugar and the lemon juice. Puree and transfer to glass serving dish or sherbet cups. Chill well before serving.

Note: Or sprinkle the avocado flesh with the lemon juice to prevent discoloring and press through a fine sieve into a glass serving dish. Stir in the sugar and chill.

Chapter 11

Lapp Kitchen

IN ALL MY life I've never achieved a first, except for
one glorious time: I was the first person to prepare an
American-type Christmas dinner in Karajosk in Norwegian Lapland. The dinner was to be served to the
Lapp relatives of a Danish friend who had married a
Lapp artist and lived up there in the Far North, where
he produced beautiful drawings and etchings. The Lapps
are excellent artists.

The dinner came about because my friend, in a moment of I don't know what, had ordered herself a frozen
turkey from a gloriously illustrated mail-order catalog
promoting the sale of imported frozen American poultry.
No doubt she was carried away by the sight of those
giant bronze birds, surrounded with all the traditional
accoutrements of potatoes, sprouts, creamed onions, and
cranberry sauce, with the heartwarming decorations of
the American Yuletide setting off the ceremonial offering
of the season. But she had never seen a frozen turkey
before, let alone cooked one, when Providence brought
me to her a few days before Christmas, after the bird

had arrived in the mail, to the respectful surprise of the mailman. As I came into her house a few moments after the bird had been delivered, I saw it lying on the kitchen table, so cold, so white, so bare, and so frozen.

What was I doing in Lapland at Christmas time? Traveling around for an article called "Norway in Winter," and gratifying a lifelong curiosity—to see if the famed twenty-four-hour night of the far northern winter is really black all the time, or illuminated by a little daylight. The contrast between day living and night living is one that has fascinated me since I was young, when I first went to Norway and saw the Midnight Sun above the Arctic Circle. I noticed then, as on subsequent visits, that when the Midnight Sun is up, people sleep very little and with difficulty. Would the reverse be true in winter?

I have deeply loved Norway since I first saw the country as a young woman. The straightforward friendliness of the people, the fact that they don't speak elliptical or false words, the overwhelming beauty of the fjords in the south, the glacier-covered mountains in the middle, and the island-scattered coast of the far north won my heart from the first. I also like the unfussy food made with the freshest local ingredients. Although I never had a kitchen of my own in Norway, I cook Norwegian food at home since the family and our friends find it pleasant. There has never been any difficulty with the language. English is taught in all Norwegian schools so that Americans can find their way easily. I learned some Norwegian because I like to be able to follow the conversations around me— and even put in a word of my own—and also because I like to read the literature of a country in the original.

Karajosk is an old Lapp settlement and not at all what one might think a Lapp settlement looks like. No tents, but modern wooden houses which look remarkably like New England ones, except that the siding is vertical rather than horizontal and that the wood is painted in bright shades of blue, yellow, red, or green—bright colors being more cheerful in a land where it is so dark in winter. A stream runs by the town; there are pine and birch trees on the hilly countryside. The hotel is a new, very comfortable inn, and like all of Norway above the Arctic Circle, so well heated in winter that you wish you were in a bathing suit.

A lot of snow lay on the ground, but the wooden sidewalks were swept clean. Christmas was in the air, what with lights strung up in the streets and the bustle with what seemed all the Lapps in Christendom out on a shopping spree. The Lapps there had plenty of money to spend, hardly surprising considering that they were Reindeer Lapps, the elite of their people. There are also the Sea Lapps, living along the coast of North Norway as fishermen; the Lake and River Lapps, who combine fishing, trapping, and hunting with a little meager farming; and the Forest Lapps, who raise a few reindeer but who mainly depend on hunting, providing Norway's gourmets with a supply of ptarmigan, a northern grouse which is delicious to eat. The Reindeer Lapps are the ones we associate with the picturesque costumes and a picturesque nomad way of life.

The new look of Karajosk is part of the Norwegian government's effort to settle the Reindeer Lapps into a way of life better suited to present times rather than their old nomad ways. Part of this effort is the rationalization and modernization of reindeer breeding. This is a very remunerative occupation, not only for the meat, which is even more expensive than steak in America, but also for the skins and antlers, so that the temptation to overextend the herds is great. But the countryside is just so big and can support just so many reindeer without starving the herds.

The first sight of a reindeer herd is surprising. I had been taken into the countryside by my friend's husband to see some animals that he wanted to draw. (There were no language difficulties; the Lapps speak their own language and Norwegian, and the educated ones, English.) My eye had pictured large animals, the size of deer bucks. Instead, the reindeer were small, reaching barely to my shoulders, their antlers out of proportion to the size of their bodies. What also struck me was the complete stillness of the hundred or so reindeer as they stood close to each other, without a movement. They were in their gray winter coats but for one, splendid white animal, prized by the Lapps the way white elephants were once prized by the rajas of India. To my great joy, and the joy of all of my family when they heard the tale, I was given a sleigh ride with the white reindeer. His owner's son, a fifteen-year-old boy, drove the sleigh with abandon as I hung on. I remember the utter delight of chasing over the hillocks of the gently rolling country, way into the snowy horizon.

The Reindeer Lapps of Karajosk, short, squat people, who were shopping energetically for glass, china, rugs, and all the other paraphernalia of a Western Christmas, lived a compromise life between the old and new. The men operated from their modern Norwegian houses, going out to tend to the herds in the winter, while the wives and children stayed in town, the latter going to the special Lapp schools instituted by the government in an effort to preserve Lapp culture from total assimilation to the Norwegian way of life. In the summer the whole family took to the summer pastures, living in their tents, drying the skins of the animals on wooden scaffolds, and weaving the bright ribbons that distinguish the tribes from each other. But this was winter. In the cold inland climate, the temperature was well below zero, but so windstill that the smoke plumes from the house chimneys stood erect like pencils against the dark sky next to the TV antennas. Even the Norwegians wore the traditional Lapp costume as the most rational clothing for those latitudes—leather trousers stuck into fur moccasins and the familiar blue tunic, which is light and warm and which allows you to move and work freely. With the Lapps, the color and the details of the costumes, as well as the caps, tell of the wearer's district of origin.

The school for Lapp children, where they are educated not to forget their own cultural and linguistic traditions, was a long, two-story wooden building. Below were the schoolrooms, above the dormitories, because there is no way for the children from the distant settlements to commute; they come for the term and go home for vacations. The Christmas tree was tall and bright with candles and

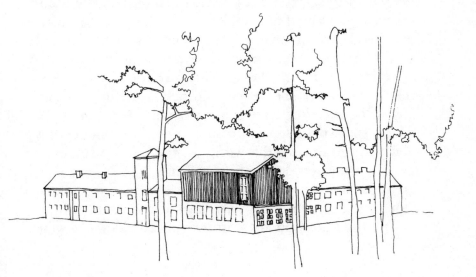

the children tremendously excited, but very self-controlled. They received their gifts, to be opened at home, we sang carols and danced around the Christmas tree, Norwegian-fashion. We had a fine meal of reindeer meat, of which the tongues, boiled and very tasty in their broth, were the privilege of the teachers and myself. Then we wrapped the children into multiple layers and blankets topped by furs, for the snowmobiles had no heat and the temperature had sunk to some 20 below zero. Their faces were equally protected against the cold with shawls and mufflers; you saw only their bright black eyes dancing with pleasure at the thought of Christmas and freedom.

In the afternoon I went to my Danish friend's house to tackle the turkey dinner. First we went shopping for the turkey's accessories. The enormous bird, now thawed, barely fitted into the electric oven of a very modern white enameled range. We decided on an onion and sausage stuffing since this was to be a typical American turkey dinner, with mashed potatoes, alas white only, since sweet potatoes were unknown, gravy, creamed onions, braised carrots, green beans with almonds, and the Scandinavian equivalent of cranberry sauce, lingonberry sauce, which is made of smaller, tarter, and tastier berries and best when preserved without cooking. I did not have to concern myself with dessert since my friend had baked the seven traditional buttery and rich Christmas cookies any self-respecting Norwegian woman bakes for Yule, which she would serve with a compote of cloudberries and with cream. All the berries of the Far North—blueberries, strawberries, raspberries, lingonberries—are delicious beyond compare but none more so than the golden cloudberries which grow only beyond the Arctic Circle.

The foodshops off the narrow wooden sidewalks were

jammed. They looked much like the shops of the small towns of the American North and West in winter, hazy with the breath of the people, sawdust on the floor to absorb the wetness they brought in, staples in big sacks, frozen-food counters and shelves, and shelves with canned goods. In this Norwegian winter, the world covered with snow, the sun hidden from November until February, I considered canned foods with new respect. We in America today look at canned foods with a very blasé air. Yet the excellent, generally inexpensive products of modern canning have revolutionized the diet of the North. We Americans think canned peaches the most ordinary of foods, to be eaten when there is nothing better. In Scandinavia few peaches, if any, will grow because of the cold; until they were canned and marketed within the reach of everybody, a peach was a rarity. The same goes for apricots and pineapple; all these fruits are featured in the desserts of luxury restaurants.

In the past the only fruits available in the North were the seasonal berries, apples, pears and plums, and the dried fruits (hence the prevalence of prunes in so much of Scandinavian cooking); but modern canning has brought not only a wealth of fruits, but also of vegetables to Scandinavia. I remember an older Norwegian woman who told me that she had never gotten over the miracle of green beans in the middle of winter, thanks to canning. And now deep freezing has brought even more new vegetables: broccoli, for instance, had never been heard of before. In the little towns of North Norway where the newspaper stores sell fruit as well, it is touching to see how a child will put down his pennies for apples and oranges, courtesy of modern transportation from the Continent.

We bought reindeer sausage for the stuffing, the only

available sausage; we bought canned milk for the cream sauces; onions; green beans (canned); almonds; and for

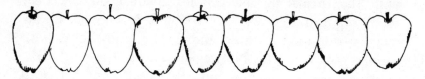

a very special treat, we bought a box of the excellent Norwegian King Haakon chocolates. I remember the shock of the cold as we came out of the hot stores into the dark. We were well protected, my hostess in her Lapp tunic and cape, the flaps of her red cap drawn across her face—that's what the flaps are for. I wore several layers of woolen tights and pants, topped with sweaters and skirt, and a heavy gray woolen cape that originally belonged to my Italian grandfather, who wore it shooting in the cold winter Lombard marshes. My feet were stuck in Lapp moccasins lined with sedge grass, which keep you so warm and let you glide so smoothly over snow still deep and clean in spite of the busy traffic. My head and face were swathed with a red and white checked wool square, the kind the Lapp women wear over their tunics. Back home we warmed ourselves with endless cups of coffee as we worked on the dinner. It was the day before Christmas Eve, the Christmas of the North, when my friend's in-laws were due in from the country. They were old-fashioned Reindeer Lapps who had not wanted to settle in town, preferring their ancestral ways, but who had consented to come for Christmas dinner to their son's house.

Preparing the dinner was the last thing of all the preparations for the greatest and deepest of Norwegian feasts. Candlesticks with thick and thin, white and colored candles stood everywhere waiting to be lit for the guests. The lovely black iron stoves, precise copies of their baroque models and marvelous heaters, shone with stove black; the furniture smelled of beeswax; all the curtains and sofa cushion cases had been freshly washed. Plants of pink begonias, the Christmas roses of the North, made us glad; we had brought them in from the flower shop wrapped in dozens of newspapers so as not to catch cold. Norwegian houses, in spite of their sparse furniture, are full of colorful accessories, the more color, the better: It is a buttress against the long darkness, just as the red and blue of the Lapp costume, the bright colors of the hand-embroidered cloths and the doilies which are as much a part of Norwegian furnishings as a bed. The Christmas tree with its candles was ready too, and so were the presents and the plates with the cookies. The wine, a Bordeaux from a good year, had also arrived from Hammerfest, the nearest town with a liquor store in that sparsely populated part of North Norway.

There is no need here to describe the makings of a Christmas dinner. Finally we put the turkey into the oven, covered with a kitchen towel soaked in butter to keep it from drying out and browning too quickly. It was to cook all night at a very low temperature to be ready when the guests came. I helped my hostess set the Christmas table with her best embroidered tablecloth and her precious Copenhagen figurines. A last cup of coffee and a last cookie and I went out into the night back to my hotel.

I heard later that the Christmas dinner had been successful. The guests liked it, the huge turkey leaving them literally speechless. But on the whole, they thought it an alien meal.

Now I knew what I had come North for: the winter

day in the Far North is not pitch black but dark gray; it is lighter between ten in the morning and two in the afternoon, though still not light enough to dispense with electric lights indoors and outdoors; and people sleep a normal number of hours in the winter. The night through which I walked was pitch black except for the northern lights. I had seen them before, looking like the straight beams of many searchlights scanning the sky for lost aircraft. That last night in Karajosk, the northern lights were different and fearsome: curling banners of vivid electric blue, yellow, orange, and pale green, bright enough to dim the thick blanket of stars. A sight as ghostly and disturbing to me as it must have been to the Lapps of old. Finally their colors faded to nothing and the stars reappeared in the black of the sky.

I left early the next morning on a bus to Hammerfest, where I was to take the Coastal Express boat down to Tromsø, where friends were expecting me. Though the snow was several feet deep, the roads had been cleared and went on being cleared as it went on snowing. Oh, shades of New York City, where snow strikes panic! We arrived in Hammerfest on time, to find a city busy with the very last-minute shopping before the stores closed early—this was Christmas Eve, the day of days of the Holy Season. In the harbor, jammed with every kind of fishing boat, all the ships wore Christmas trees on their masts and funnels—the lovely Norway Christmas custom. So did my own boat, on which I spent the nicest Christmas I ever had away from home. The crew had decorated the ship with streamers and ornaments, and put up a great big Christmas tree in the dining room—with lovely white candles. The steward carefully explained to me that the big dinner would be around six, and that the captain would personally fetch me for it. Thus, in the afternoon, I primped as seldom before; I really wanted to be at my best, feeling, so to speak, that I was representing the United States at a foreign national holiday. I also wrapped the box of cigars and the bottle of whiskey which were to be my presents to the captain.

At five o'clock sharp there was a knock on my door. The captain, in full regalia, gave me his arm and escorted me to his cabin for a predinner sherry. I was touched to see an enormous pot of flowering pink begonia—the kind which in Norway is called Christmas rose—and a small Christmas tree.

When we went in to dinner, the crew were already at the long tables. The captain and I sat in the middle with the officers on either side.

We started our meal with the traditional rice porridge, which is standard Christmas fare throughout Scandinavia. On our ship, which belonged to the Bergen Line, the meat was a dish of very excellent Pinnekjøtt, spiced ribs of mutton that are a Christmas specialty of the Norwegian West Coast. Incidentally, Norwegian lamb and mutton are absolutely marvelous, tasting like the celebrated French pre salé lamb. The dessert that followed consisted of canned pineapple with some delicious buttery cookies. After dinner we all sang Christmas carols.

What touched me most about this Christmas was that we all did our best to make the occasion a festive one. No doubt everybody was sad within himself, not being at home for Christmas. But no one showed it, and everyone went out of his way to make the burden an easy one for everyone else. It did convince me that making an effort for Christmas is one of the most worthwhile things in the world, even if it is only made for people who basically do not concern us much.

Mixed Herring Salad
(5–6 servings)

The quantities can be increased at will. This makes a good dish for a buffet.

2 salt herring (from specialty or fish store)

1½ cups cooked beets, cut into ½-inch dice

½ cup cooked peeled potatoes, cut into ½-inch dice

2 cups lean cooked meat (beef, pork, or veal) cut into ½-inch dice

2 apples, cored but not peeled, cut into ½-inch dice

1 dill pickle, cut into ¼-inch dice

2 tablespoons capers, drained

2 hard-cooked eggs, chopped

1 teaspoon freshly ground pepper

1 cup heavy cream, whipped

3 tablespoons white vinegar

1 teaspoon prepared mustard

½ teaspoon salt

1½ tablespoons sugar

3 hard-cooked eggs

1 cup minced parsley

Wash the herring. Soak overnight in equal parts of milk and water to cover. Drain, dry, and cut off tail and head. Remove all bones and skin and cut into small pieces. In a deep bowl, combine the herring, the beets, the potatoes, the meat, the apples, the dill pickle, the capers, and the chopped eggs. Season with the pepper and mix well. Into the whipped cream, stir the vinegar, the mustard, the salt, and the sugar. Blend thoroughly. Add this dressing to the herring mixture and toss lightly until blended. Pile the salad in the shape of a pyramid on a serving platter. Separate the yolks and the whites of two of the hard-cooked eggs. Slice the third egg into 8 lengthwise slices. Chop the yolks and the whites separately; they should be fine. Surround the salad with alternate mounds of chopped egg yolks, minced parsley, and chopped whites, separating the eggs with the parsley. Arrange the egg slices on top of the salad in the shape of a blossom.

Leif Borthen's Chicken With Sour Cream
(3–4 servings)

The gentleman is a noted Norwegian journalist and a sophisticated cook. Serve with parsleyed new potatoes.

1 3 to 3 ½ pound frying chicken, cut into serving pieces	2 cups milk
	¼ cup dry sherry
	¼ cup minced parsley
1 teaspoon salt	½ cup sour cream
½ teaspoon freshly ground pepper	Mushroom caps, sautéed in butter
¼ cup butter	Broiled tomato halves
¼ cup cognac	Parsley sprigs

Remove the fat and skin from the chicken pieces. Rub with salt and pepper. Heat the butter in a large, heavy frying pan. Brown the chicken in it on all sides. Pour the cognac over the chicken pieces and flame. When the flame has died down, add the milk. Simmer covered over lowest possible heat for about 35–45 minutes or until the meat is tender. Baste occasionally with the milk, which will clot. Add the sherry and parsley and cook 3 minutes longer. Transfer the chicken pieces to a hot platter and keep hot. Stir the sour cream into the pan juices and pour the sauce over the chicken. Garnish with the mushroom caps, the tomatoes, and the parsley sprigs.

Note: This dish has a good deal of sauce because the Norwegians like cream sauces. Buttered noodles are also good with it.

Reindeer Pot Roast With Mushrooms, Tomatoes, Grapes, and Pineapple

(8–10 servings)

A gala dish I enjoyed at the Grand Hotel in Tromsø, the capital of North Norway. Like venison, reindeer meat is dark, lean, and tangy. It is usually marinated before cooking.

1 5-pound reindeer roast, boned and rolled
1 quart dry red wine
1 large onion, sliced
1 celery stalk
10 peppercorns
1 tablespoon salt
2 bay leaves
½ pound bacon or ½ pound salt pork, blanched and cut into slices

½ cup butter
1 cup sour cream
½ cup heavy cream, whipped
Paprika

GARNISH:

1 pound mushroom caps, sautéed in butter
6 tomatoes, cut into halves and grilled
½ pound purple grapes, stemmed

1 cup diced pineapple (fresh or canned) sautéed in butter

Place the meat in a deep bowl, but do not use aluminum. Combine the wine, the onion, the celery, the peppercorns, the salt, and the bay leaves in a saucepan and bring to the boiling point. Boil for 3 minutes and cool. When cold, pour over the meat. Marinate for 24–48 hours in the refrigerator. Turn meat several times a day. Drain and wipe dry. Strain marinade and reserve.

Wrap the bacon or the blanched salt pork slices around the meat, tying them with string. Heat the butter in a large heavy casserole or Dutch oven. Brown the meat on all sides. Pour off excess butter. Reduce the heat to lowest possible. Pour half the marinade over the meat. Simmer covered for about 2–3 hours or until the meat is tender; cooking time depends on the age and toughness of the meat. To test for doneness, lift meat and prick with skewer; it should not draw blood. Baste occasionally with the pan juices or use a little more of the marinade. When done, transfer the meat to a hot platter and keep hot. Remove the string and the bacon or salt pork.

Skim the fat off the pan juices and stir in the sour cream. Swirl around and heat through but do not boil. If you like a thicker gravy, stir in 1–2 teaspoons of flour mixed with 2 teaspoons water into the pan juices and cook over lowest possible heat for 2–3 minutes, to get rid of the raw flavor of the flour. Slice the meat and arrange in overlapping slices on a large serving platter.

Stir the whipped cream into the gravy, heat through but do not boil and drip a little gravy over the meat slices. Sprinkle with paprika. Surround the meat with the mushroom caps in rows and alternate mounds of grilled tomatoes, grapes, and pineapple. The arrangement should be decorative. Serve the remaining gravy separately. Accompany the dish with Browned Potatoes.

Pinnekjøtt

(Norwegian Spiced Rib of Mutton)
(6 servings)

The modern version of a traditional Christmas dish of the West Coast of Norway. It is served with mashed potatoes and mashed yellow turnips.

4 pounds ribs of mutton, trimmed of fat	2 tablespoons sugar
¼ cup brandy	1 tablespoon freshly ground pepper
4 tablespoons salt	4 cups boiling water

Make sure that all the fat is off the meat. Rub the meat thoroughly with the brandy, the salt, the sugar, and the pepper; in fact, massage them in. Set the meat on a board and dry it out in the open or in a drafty place for 3 days. Dry the meat with paper towel. Set the oven to hot, at 450°F. Cut the meat into strips. Place the strips in a roasting pan and brown in the oven for 15 minutes. Reduce heat to moderate (350°F.) and pour boiling water over meat. Cook for about 1½ hours, basting every 10 minutes with pan drippings and more boiling water, if needed. If the meat looks as though it is drying out, cover with buttered aluminum foil or buttered brown paper—do not use waxed paper.

Piquant Pork Roast

(5–6 servings)

Serve sliced on a hot platter, surrounded by alternating mounds of buttered peas, buttered carrots, and Browned Potatoes (below).

¼ cup Dijon mustard
1 tablespoon fresh or
    preserved horseradish
    (the latter, drained)
1 teaspoon anchovy paste
1 tablespoon sugar
1 pork loin, weighing
    approximately 3–4
    pounds, trimmed of
    all excess fat

⅔ cup fine dry
    breadcrumbs
2 cups boiling dry white
    wine or water

Combine the mustard, the horseradish, the anchovy paste, and the sugar. Blend into a smooth paste. With a pastry brush, spread the meat on all sides with the mustard mixture. Let stand at room temperature for 15 minutes. Place the meat on a rack in a baking pan. Cover the top and sides with the breadcrumbs. Roast in a preheated slow oven (325°F.) about 35 minutes to the pound or until a meat thermometer registers 185°F. After 1 hour roasting time, pour 1 cup boiling wine or water into the pan, but not over the meat. When the liquid has evaporated completely, pour the remaining wine into the pan, but not over the meat. Slice the meat and arrange in overlapping slices on a hot platter. If there are any pan juices, spoon them over the meat.

Cabbage With Sour Cream

(3–4 servings)

Good with all roast meats, especially pork

1 medium cabbage,
   shredded (about 4
   cups)
Water
Salt

Freshly ground pepper
⅔ cup sour cream
1 tablespoon dill seed or
   2 tablespoons fresh
   chopped dill weed

Cook the cabbage in just enough water to cover and to keep it from burning. Stir frequently. The cabbage should be barely tender. Stir in the salt, the pepper, the sour cream, and the dill seed or chopped dill. Simmer covered over lowest possible heat for 5–10 minutes. Stir frequently to prevent scorching. If necessary, add 1–2 tablespoons hot water.

Browned Potatoes

(6 servings)

2 pounds new potatoes,
   small and even-sized
2 tablespoons butter
⅓ cup fine dry
   breadcrumbs

1 teaspoon salt
½ teaspoon sugar
Freshly ground pepper

Boil the potatoes in salted water to keep them firm. When done, drain and peel. Melt the butter in a heavy skillet and brown the breadcrumbs in it. Stir in the salt, sugar, and pepper. Add the potatoes. Cook, shaking the pan constantly to prevent sticking, until the potatoes are coated with the breadcrumbs and are golden brown. Serve very hot.

Norwegian Berliner Kranser

1 hard-cooked egg yolk
1 raw egg yolk
½ cup sifted
   confectioners' sugar
½ teaspoon vanilla
   flavoring
1¾ cups sifted all-purpose
   flour

½ cup butter, at room
   temperature
1 egg white, slightly
   beaten
Sparkling sugar

Combine the hard-cooked and raw egg yolks and blend them to a smooth paste. Beat in the sugar and vanilla flavoring. Work in flour and cut in butter. Mix thoroughly; this is best done by hand. Chill for 4 hours. Set the oven at 350°F. Snip off small pieces of dough and roll them between hands into strips, each about 6 inches long and ½ inch thick. If the dough sticks, flour your hands. Shape the strips into rings, looping ends, and let the ends overlap a little. Brush each cookie with egg white and sprinkle with sugar. (Sparkling sugar, not readily available in this country, can be made by crushing sugar cubes in a paper bag with a hammer or anything heavy.) Bake on a greased and floured baking sheet for about 8–10 minutes. The cookies must not brown, but be pale gold in color.

Peppernotter (Pepper Nuts)

The fruit peel must be chopped fine, not ground, and the pepper added in.

⅓ cup butter
2½ cups confectioners' sugar
4 eggs, beaten
3 tablespoons lemon juice
1 tablespoon grated lemon rind
¼ cup chopped candied orange peel
½ cup chopped candied lemon peel
½ cup chopped candied citron

4 cups sifted all-purpose flour
1 teaspoon ground cinnamon
1 teaspoon ground cloves
¾ teaspoon black pepper
1 teaspoon anise seed
1 teaspoon allspice
1 tablespoon ground cardamon
1 teaspoon baking soda
1 teaspoon salt
½ teaspoon almond flavoring

Cream the butter and add the confectioners' sugar. Beat in the eggs. Stir in the lemon juice, the lemon rind, and the orange, lemon, and citron peels. Sift the flour with the remaining ingredients except the almond flavoring. Blend thoroughly. Add almond flavoring and mix. Shape the mixture into 1-inch balls and place on greased and floured cookie sheets. Chill overnight. Set the oven at 350°F. Bake the peppernotter for about fifteen minutes or until browned. While still warm brush with lemon icing, made by stirring 1–2 tablespoons lemon juice into 1 cup sifted confectioners' sugar, stirring to spreading consistency.

Note: The peppernuts should be shaped before chilling or the dough will be too stiff to handle.

Norwegian Dalesman Cookies

(50–60 cookies)

These cookies are rich, very delicious, and rather fragile. They are best served with a fruit dessert or a custard. They must be made with potato starch (potato flour), which can be bought in Jewish, Scandinavian, and German grocery stores.

1 cup sweet butter, at
    room temperature
1 cup sugar
1 cup heavy cream,
    whipped
1 cup potato starch
2 cups sifted flour

2 tablespoons grated
    lemon rind or 1
    teaspoon vanilla
    flavoring
1½ cups minced or
    shredded blanched
    almonds

Preheat the oven to moderate (350°F.).

Cream the butter until it is light and fluffy. Gradually beat in the sugar, beating well after each addition. The mixture should be white. Beat in the whipped cream. Sift together the potato starch and the flour. Fold it into the first mixture. Stir in the lemon rind or vanilla flavoring and the almonds. Lightly grease three baking sheets. Drop the batter in teaspoonfuls, leaving about 2 inches between cookies, which will expand during baking. Bake for 10–12 minutes until the edges of the cookies are browned. Let stand on the baking sheets for 2–3 minutes to cool a little. Remove and let the cookies cool completely before storing in airtight tins.

Chapter 12

Christmas and the Christmas Kitchen

THE CHRISTMAS KITCHEN is a kitchen of its own, not connected with any territory; it is a state of mind. Christmas kitchens are where you make them, in the Alps or the Sahara or in New York—the surroundings do not count. The Christmas kitchen is the kitchen of one's childhood, just as Christmas is the yearly re-creation of the Christmases of one's childhood, if they were happy ones. People who hate Christmas are people who had a bad childhood.

My own Christmas kitchen is a German one. It has remained so though I have become an American and made Christmas for my American husband and children. As I said before, my father was a German and my mother Italian, but we always celebrated Christmas as he had

312

as a child. It all began the first Sunday of Advent, when
a wreath was hung in the dining room over the table.
It bore four candles for the four Sundays before Christmas. One candle was lit each Sunday, and by Christmas
Day all four were ablaze. I was also given an Advent
calendar, on which the twenty-four days to Christmas
were marked by colorful little pictures, each closed with
a paper flap. Every day, I tore off one of the flaps to
disclose the picture underneath. The last, on Christmas
Eve, was the grandest one, a Christmas tree in all its
glory.

Toward the middle of the month, my mother began
decorating the house and baking luscious Christmas
cookies. She wove armfuls of firs into great swags that
went over the doors; behind each picture were other
greens, and great bunches of greens stood in tall vases
throughout the house.

The *Christkind*, Baby Jesus, brings the gifts to most
German children, though there is also *Weihnachtsmann*,
a Santa, who comes to some families, but never came to
ours. On St. Nicholas Day, December 6, I wrote my
letter to the *Christkind*, saying what I wanted for Christmas. I put it under my pillow, and in the morning it
was gone. The *Christkind* had also left silver lametta
"angel's hair" on the greens in the house, which was
wildly exciting to a child—Christmas was becoming real.
Throughout the house wafted the smell of cinnamon
and spices baking, and when I had been good, I was
allowed to come into the kitchen to help crack nuts
and cut glacé peel into little pieces, and, joy of joys, to
lick the bowls. Also, during the middle of December,
the door of the parlor was tightly locked. No one was
allowed in, because the *Christkind* needed a place to
rest as he went about. It was impossible to find out what

went on inside; I never saw a parcel being taken into the room nor the Christmas tree go in.

A German (and also a Swiss and Scandinavian) Christmas takes place on Christmas Eve. At noon of Christmas Eve I put on my best dress. My father took me out to look at the crèches in the Roman churches, big, lovely baroque extravaganzas. Then, as it got dark, he took me to the German Protestant Church for a candlelight service to sing the carols of the Middle Ages: about the rose that blossomed in the winter's night, and the Babe rocked by Mary. Then home to a darkened house, where I was told to wait in the dining room until the little silver bell, kept for this purpose only, rang three times. I can still feel my heart in my mouth as I sat

waiting for the bell to ring. And then it rang, and the doors of the parlor burst open, and there was the tall tree ablaze with candles.

Our presents were not piled under the Christmas tree, nor were they wrapped. They were set in individual heaps on little tables or on the sofa or piano. Part of each heap was the *"Bunte Teller,"* a brightly colored dish laden with apples and raisins and comfits and cookies and candies. But we did not rush to our presents as we came into the room. First, by candlelight, my father read the Christmas Gospel. Then we sang "Silent Night" and "O Tannenbaum." Next we embraced each other wishing a Merry Christmas. And then, we went to the presents.

Later on there was a simple supper. During the supper and at the big noontime dinner on Christmas Day I was allowed to get up from the table whenever I wanted, to play with my new toys; getting up from the table during a meal any other day was a heinous offense. We used to have roast goose for Christmas dinner, because that was what my father had as a child. But there was no set meal, like a turkey dinner, and to this day, for Christmas the Germans eat what they like best and think the most festive—goose, venison, wild boar, chicken, roast veal. But there must be *"Hausgeback-enes,"* something baked at home, for without it, Christmas wouldn't be Christmas, even here in New York.

My mother liked to bake, but she was no baking demon like some Germans, and for that matter, Scandinavian women who start baking early in December and go on to the very last moment. My mother produced four or five kinds of cookies, the recipes of which I still have in her own handwriting, with such family titles as "the crumbly cookies Otto [my father] likes so much," "the peppernuts from the beautiful Swedish lady," and "the French macaroons from the lady at *La veille d'un crime* [at the eve of a crime]." This French lady, always called by us by that name, had a daughter who had made an unfortunate marriage to a Persian. Her mother felt that she had to avenge her, telling us—she was a family friend—repeatedly that she was at "the eve of a crime," namely doing in her son-in-law. We put this intention down to her excitability and never thought she would manage to get to Persia to do so. But she did—shot her son-in-law—was discharged for I don't know what reasons, took her daughter back to France, and remarried her to a prosperous provincial lawyer. It all goes to show, I suppose.

There are very few Christmases in my life when I did not make a tree and bake a number of goodies, old ones from home, new ones I discovered myself as I have traveled around for my cookbooks. My schedule is simple: in November, I make a pile of fruit cakes—white ones—for ourselves and to give away. Swathed in brandy-soaked kitchen towels, and watered, or rather brandied once a week, they are lovely heralds of the good things to come. Ten days before Christmas, I start baking in earnest, and though each year I try to make some new cookies, I always seem to fall back on the old, familiar ones which my friends like and expect from me. Ah, the lovely smells of Christmas, the butter and fruits and spices perfuming the air! As my mother before me, I prepare *Bunte Teller* for all family and friends. They even look like hers, because in the German stores in New York's Yorkville you can buy big imported German star-shaped paper plates made just for this purpose, and printed with the colorful Santas and Christmas trees just as they were when I was a child.

Christmas baking is my own, private thing. I know that for many families, it is a heartwarming get-together in which children and adults share lovable, creative activities, which hopefully will hold them together. I salute them: my own sons, when young, never wanted to bake a thing. Until their teens, for that matter, they vastly preferred the delicious products of commercial baking— Oreos, Fig Newtons, and the like—to any of the rich, buttery cookies that spell Christmas for me.

Christmas, in our family, is a compromise between my own traditions and those of my husband and children. We trim the tree together, but we light it only on Christmas Eve. There is no opening of the presents until after my husband or one of the sons has read the Christmas Gospel and we all have embraced each other, wishing a Merry Christmas. That is, when the sons were still at home; now they have their families and to my great and constant sorrow, we live many thousands of miles from each other. But they tell me that Christmas means a great deal to them so that the Light goes on shining through the years and over seas and across continents.

At Christmas time, we now gather under our tree the lonely among the people we know, and those who like a quiet, old-fashioned Christmas. We follow the old ritual of my husband reading the Gospel under the tree and we still wish each other a Merry Christmas before we open our presents, though we don't sing. There is little drinking, nobody seems to want it. On Christmas Eve, we have a simple supper which I prepared earlier in the day so as not to be distracted by mundane worries. The big dinner is on Christmas Day, à l'Americaine, for all who want to come to our house. And for each who sets foot there is a gift, however small, and a *Bunte Teller*, just as it was in the old days, at home, before I was home to others.

My Most Painless Christmas Dinner

Everything was prepared beforehand and the eight guests loved it. With the two exceptions that follow, the recipes are good, standard recipes found in standard cookbooks.

Cream of Barley Soup

Cold Roast Sirloin
    Remoulade Sauce
    Sour Cream Horseradish Sauce

Dilled Carrot Salad

White Bean Salad with Lemon French Dressing

Raw Mushroom and Endive Salad with Lemon French
    Dressing

Mixed Tossed Green Salad

Watercress Salad with Mustard Egg Dressing

Flaming Plum Pudding and Brandy Hard Sauce

French Bread and Pumpernickel, Salt Butter

Note: I could have dispensed with the Mixed Tossed Green Salad, which could not stand up to the other, more interesting salads.

Cream of Barley Soup

(4–6 servings)

3 tablespoons butter
¼ cup medium barley
1 celery stalk, minced
1 medium onion, minced
6 cups hot vegetable or
　　chicken bouillon

Salt
Freshly ground pepper
1 cup light cream

Heat the butter in a large kettle. Add the barley, the celery, and the onion. Cook, stirring constantly, for about 2–3 minutes. Add the bouillon and salt and pepper to taste. Bring to the boiling point and lower heat immediately. Simmer covered over very low heat for about 30 minutes. Puree in a blender. Before serving, stir in the cream and heat through, but do not boil.

Note: This soup can be made thicker or thinner, according to taste. For a thicker soup, use about ⅓–½ cup barley; for a thinner soup, more bouillon.

Sour Cream Horseradish Sauce

(About 1 cup)

1 cup sour cream
　Grated fresh horse-
　　radish to taste—begin
　　with 2 tablespoons
1 teaspoon sugar

Salt
Freshly ground pepper
2 tablespoons minced
　　parsley

Combine all the ingredients and chill.

My Father's Favorite Cookies

(Makes about 40 cookies)

⅓ cup butter (*must be*
   butter)
½ cup sugar
1 egg
2 egg yolks
1 teaspoon mace

2 cups sifted all-purpose
   flour
¼ teaspoon baking
   powder
Colored sprinkles or
   chopped nuts

Cream the butter until soft. Gradually beat in the sugar; beat until fluffy. Beat in the whole egg and one of the egg yolks, beating well after each addition. Stir in the mace. Sift the flour with the baking powder. Beat in the flour mixture, a little at a time. Knead the dough with your hands until smooth. Form into a ball, wrap in waxed paper, and chill for 1–2 hours. Turn on the oven to 350°F. With your hands, roll out little pieces of the dough into 3-inch pencil-thick little sticks. Form into S-shapes or the shapes of any other letters. Put on greased and floured cookie sheet and let stand at room temperature for an hour. Beat the remaining egg yolk with 1 tablespoon of water. Brush the cookies with a pastry brush dipped into the egg mixture. Dot with the sprinkles or the chopped nuts. Bake for about 12–15 minutes or until the cookies are just beginning to turn golden brown.

Nurenburgers

(About 5½ dozen)

2½ cups sifted all-purpose flour
1 teaspoon ground cinnamon
1 teaspoon ground allspice
¼ teaspoon ground cloves
½ teaspoon baking soda
1 cup strained honey
¾ cup light brown sugar, firmly packed

1 egg, lightly beaten
1 tablespoon lemon juice
1 teaspoon grated lemon peel
½ cup chopped nuts
½ cup chopped citron
Blanched almonds for garnish
Diced candied lemon peel for garnish

Sift the flour with spices and baking soda; set aside. In a large saucepan, mix the honey with brown sugar. Heat to the boiling point; cool. Stir the egg, the lemon juice, and lemon peel into the honey mixture. Gradually add the flour mixture and mix well. Blend in nuts and citron. Wrap in waxed paper and chill the dough at least 8 hours or longer. Roll to ¼-inch thick on a lightly floured board. Shape with a 2-inch cookie cutter. Decorate each cookie with almonds and candied lemon peel to resemble a daisy or decorate as desired. Bake on a greased and floured cookie sheet in a preheated moderate oven (350°F.) for 10 minutes. Cool on wire racks. Store in tightly covered container at least 3–4 days before eating.

Yellow Vanilla Pretzels

(About 50 cookies)

The egg whites can be used for making meringues.

5 egg yolks
1 cup plus 2 tablespoons
   sugar
2 teaspoons vanilla
   flavoring
4 cups sifted flour

1 cup sweet butter, at
   room temperature
   and cut into small
   pieces
A few drops of yellow food
   coloring (optional)

Beat the egg yolks with the sugar until very thick and lemon colored. Stir in the vanilla. Put the flour into a deep bowl and add the butter. With a wooden spoon stir to distribute the butter pieces evenly throughout the flour. Add the egg mixture and blend with the wooden spoon. Add enough food coloring for a rich yellow color. With hands, knead the dough until it is smooth and does not stick any longer to the hands. With floured hands, pinch off pieces of dough and roll them into strips about ½-inch thick and 6–7 inches long. Place the strips on ungreased cookie sheets and shape them into pretzels. Bake in a preheated moderate oven (350°F.) for 10–12 minutes or until the pretzels start turning brown at the edges. While still warm, glaze with Thin Vanilla Icing.

Note: The dough may also be shaped into fingers or rings.

Thin Vanilla Icing

Blend together 1 cup sifted confectioners' sugar, 1½ teaspoons vanilla flavoring, and 1 teaspoon (or more) water until the icing reaches the consistency of thick cream.

Vanilla Crescents

(About 60 cookies)

This never-fail recipe came out years ago in the *New York Times*. To my mind, it is one of the very best of all cookie recipes and long-keeping too.

The day before:
Cut 1 vanilla bean into pieces. Place vanilla bean and 2 cups sifted confectioners' sugar into a jar. Cover tightly and let stand overnight.

1 cup shelled walnuts, finely ground in nutgrinder or blender	¾ cup superfine sugar
	2½ cups sifted flour
1 cup sweet butter, softened and cut into pieces	

Combine all the ingredients in a bowl. With your hands, work them into a smooth dough. Shape the dough into a ball, wrap in waxed paper and chill for at least 2 hours or overnight. (Dough will keep in the refrigerator for 4–5 days.) Pinch off pieces of dough and shape them into small crescents, about 1½ inches in diameter. Bake on greased cookie sheets in a preheated moderate oven (350°F.) for about 12 minutes or until golden brown. Cool on sheets for about 2–3 minutes. Sprinkle the vanilla sugar through a sieve over the cookies and roll them in it. Or put the sugar into a bowl and roll the cookies in it. Store in airtight jars.

Note: Vanilla sugar is a usual baking adjunct. I always keep a jar in the cupboard. The longer kept, the more fragrant with vanilla the sugar becomes.

French Macaroons

(About 55 cookies)

(From the lady called *La veille d'un crime*)

1 pound blanched almonds, ground in nutgrinder or blender	⅛ teaspoon salt
	½ teaspoon almond flavoring
2½ cups sifted confectioners' sugar	1 tablespoon lemon juice
	6 egg whites
3 tablespoons mixed glacé fruit, very finely chopped	Halves of blanched almonds

Combine the almonds, the confectioners' sugar, the glacé fruit, the salt, the almond flavoring, and the lemon juice. Mix thoroughly, and if too stiff, mix in a little more lemon juice, one teaspoon at a time. The mixture should be solid but still pliable. Beat the egg whites until stiff. With the hands, and very gently, mix together the almond mixture and the egg whites to make a paste. Grease and flour baking sheets. With a teaspoon dipped in cold water, shape the dough into small rounds. Place the cookies on the baking sheets. Bake in a preheated moderate oven (350°F.) for about 10–12 minutes or until golden. With a spatula, remove cookies from the sheets and put on a rack or place on a cool bare surface, such as a marble-topped table or work counter. Press half an almond into each cookie while still hot.

Sand Torte

A German classic, with a fine, grainy texture and long-keeping qualities. Cornstarch is an essential ingredient. Since the cake must be beaten long and hard, it is well to use an electric beater or mixer. This is a good cake to serve with coffee or tea.

1 cup butter or margarine	1 cup sifted flour
1 cup sugar	1 cup sifted cornstarch
Grated rind of 2 lemons	1½ teaspoons baking powder
6 eggs, separated	½ teaspoon salt
2 tablespoons lemon juice or brandy or rum	

Beat the butter until soft and creamy. Beat in the sugar, about 2 tablespoons at a time, beating well after each addition. Stir in the lemon rind. Beat the egg yolks until light, then beat them into the butter mixture and mix very well. Beat in the lemon juice or liquor. Sift together the flour, the cornstarch, the baking powder, and the salt. Stir a little at a time into the batter. Beat for at least 15 minutes by hand or about 8–10 minutes with an electric mixer. Beat the egg whites until stiff. Fold them gently into the batter. Butter and flour generously a 9-inch tube pan. Bake the cake on the center rack of a preheated moderate oven (350°F.) for about 45 minutes or until it tests clean. Cool for 5 minutes in the pan, unmold and cool completely.

Note: This cake is not usually iced, just sprinkled with sifted confectioners' sugar.

Light Fruit Cake

(About 10-pound cake)

The secret of moist, flavorful fruit cake is to let the fruit soak in the spirits for days before they are put into the cake.

1 pound candied lemon peel	1 teaspoon cinnamon
1 pound candied orange peel	1 teaspoon nutmeg
	1 teaspoon mace
1 pound red and green glacé cherries	1 pound butter, at room temperature (must be butter)
1 pound golden raisins	2 cups sugar
2 cups dry white wine	8 eggs, well-beaten
2 cups good-quality brandy	1 teaspoon almond flavoring
6 cups sifted flour	
4 teaspoons baking powder	

First, prepare the fruit: If the peel and cherries are very sugary, wash off the sugar under running cold water and dry the fruit thoroughly. Cut into very small dice, about ¼-inch by ¼-inch. Do this with a sharp knife, dipped constantly into cold water. Put all the fruit and the raisins into a deep bowl and mix well with the hands. Combine the wine and the brandy and pour over the fruit. Let stand covered for at least 3 days, stirring twice a day.

On baking day, first prepare the pans: Take four loaf pans measuring 8½" x 4¼" x 2½". Using unglazed brown paper, such as paper bags, cut four pieces the size of the pans' bottom. Cut out strips to fit the sides of the pans. Now butter the bottoms and all sides of the cake pans. Line them with the precut paper pieces. Grease the paper pieces with butter. Turn on the oven to slow (300°F.).

Sift together the flour, the baking powder, and the spices. With an electric beater, or in a mixer, cream the butter until it is soft. Beat in the sugar, ¼ cup at a time, beating well after each addition. Beat in the eggs and the almond flavoring. Mix very well. Gradually beat in the flour mixture and stir until well blended. Stir in the prepared fruit and the liquor in which it soaked and blend again. Spoon the batter evenly into the four pans, filling not more than three-fourths full.

Place a shallow baking pan filled with about 2 inches of hot water on the bottom of the oven. Place the cake pans on the middle rack. Bake about 3 hours. Remove the baking pan with the water for the last 30 minutes of baking. Remove the cakes and their paper from the pans. Cool on a cake rack. Only when completely cooled, remove the paper. Wrap the cakes either in clean kitchen towels soaked in brandy, or dribble more brandy on them before wrapping tightly in aluminum foil. Store in an airtight container in a cool place for at least two weeks or longer. The cakes can be kept for months, but they should be moistened with more brandy whenever they look dry, about once a week at first and at longer intervals later.

Note: Of course the cakes can be baked in other kinds and sized pans, which, however, must be greased and lined with greased paper. These other pans, too, must not be filled more than three-fourths full. The baking times given above apply to the loaf pans; if other pans are used, bake shorter or longer, testing the cakes for doneness.

Mohnkuchen

1½ cups ground poppyseed   1½ cups sugar
  1 teaspoon vanilla   4 eggs, separated
    flavoring   2 cups flour
  1 cup milk   4 teaspoons baking
 ¾ cup sweet butter   powder

Soak the poppyseed in the combined vanilla and milk. Beat the butter until it is fluffy. Gradually beat in the sugar, 2 tablespoons at a time. Beat in the egg yolks. Sift the flour together with the baking powder. Add the flour alternately with the poppyseed mixture to the sugar-butter-egg mixture. Beat the egg whites until stiff and fold them into the batter. Bake in a greased and floured 13″ x 9″ x 2″ baking pan in a preheated moderate oven (350°F.) for 45 minutes. If desired, spread with tart jam or frost with lemon frosting. This is a sweet cake and needs a tart flavor contrast.

Note: Ground poppyseed can be bought in stores catering to people of Hungarian or Czech descent.

Chapter 13

Kitchens Here and There

BY NOW, IT is obvious to the reader that kitchens per se bore me unless they are part of a more interesting slice of life. I never set foot in anybody's kitchen out of sheer curiosity, unless there is a special reason such as helping or inspecting a piece of equipment that I propose to buy myself. The kitchen is not the room I would spend money on beyond making it into a convenient, unfussy place. By the same token, I don't go to people's houses just for the food or drink. I go because I like my hosts or because I am interested in the company. If the food is not very good nor the surroundings very pretty, I do not care if they represent the best the hostess can do; what I find unforgivable is carelessness. Equally offensive to me are guests who go to a house to take umbrage or who criticize what they get, or for that matter, talk about meals as the greatest ever or as disasters.

Since I am able to take kitchens or to leave them, they are not always the feature I remember best in a house. In the garden of my then mother-in-law near Marseille stood a water tank I shall never forget because I once spent several hours floating in it. We swam or rather bathed in this tank, getting into it by climbing a ladder. Getting out was more complicated. On the bottom of the tank stood a garden table, and on it, a garden chair, both submerged by the water. You stood on the chair to be able to grab the edge of the tank and swing yourself over it onto the ladder and descend. One had to be careful not to upset table and chair when splashing around in the cool water on a hot summer's day. But I did upset them when no one was home so that I had to float around in the water until a neighbor heard my cries for help. He came with a long builder's ladder which he lowered into the tank to the sodden body in it. As for the kitchen, I should remember what it looked like but I don't, though the cook taught me for the first time to make a proper fruit compote—just that, and nothing else. But it stuck in my mind that first, you make a syrup of equal quantities of sugar and water, flavored with a vanilla bean or lemon or orange peel or a stick of cinnamon. Next, you cook the syrup over low heat for 5–10 minutes. Then you poach the fruit in the syrup, a few pieces at a time. If the fruit is very juicy, you reduce the syrup before pouring it finally over the poached fruit.

At one time a kitchen in Annapolis was part of my life. What I remember best about that one was an intensive odor of sulphur. The occasion was a giant party for some seventy-five guests, for which the cook stuffed 150 eggs. The cook was a tiny old black lady whom no one, including her grandchildren, had ever seen with-

out a hat on her head. There she sat fully hatted in the kitchen, with an enormous bowl of hard-cooked egg yolks in front of her which she was mashing. The odor of sulphur that arose from those yolks almost overwhelmed me as I fled. But I can't remember what the eggs were stuffed with. Any reader who doubts my veracity has only to repeat the experiment; he or she will live to regret it. (In those days, eggs were cheap.)

I don't particularly remember any Swiss kitchens except hotel kitchens, which struck me as models of organization and super cleanliness. Neither do any German kitchens surface to the mind, for a very good reason: I never cooked in one. Though my father was a German, I have never lived in Germany except in hotels or pensions; our home was in Italy. Surely I must have gone into a German kitchen at one time or another, but since I don't recollect anything in particular, I imagine that German kitchens look pretty much like our own.

Professionally, I have worked in a few kitchens not my own, on assignments from national magazines, when I had to supervise the photography of local foods in their home surroundings. This, I may add, is one of the rare times when food for photography is food for eating. Away from the home base of a photographer's studio and its kitchen, it is not possible to gussy up foods nor is it necessary since they will be photographed normally, without excessively hot lights. Of course, they have to be dished up prettily besides being made as sturdy as possible. As the editor of the article, I did not have to cook the food. This was the job of the home-economist cook who had either come from New York with me, or had been hired locally. The third member of the team was the photographer, who had also come from New York, with his assistant. On these location jobs, you have to find somebody who will be kind enough to let you use her kitchen. All you can do to compensate the person for the fuss and bother is to offer a small gift, if it is a home or a school or a church kitchen. If you use a motel kitchen, which also happens, you have to borrow and buy extra equipment because there is never enough of it. Most of these kitchens are just kitchens, though some can be lovely. The one I admire most is a kitchen in San Antonio, Texas, which I got to see in the course of an article on Texas food. Like the rest of the house, it was furnished with the most beautiful artifacts of Mexico's folk art—pots and pans of museum quality. They were made of ceramic, and alas, rather fragile, but we still cooked in them. The shapes varied depending on the part of Mexico they came from. But what a variety of shapes, and how functional they all were! The pots I liked best came in different shades of browns and rust and they were not painted because they served for cooking. Pure and simply, they were works of art, and unforgettable.

A kitchen which for once I did visit out of sheer

curiosity was a professional kitchen—that of Sabena
Belgian World Airlines in the Brussels airport. Sabena
has good food, as I knew from experience both in tourist
and first-class, and I had been impressed that the first-
class meals were served with the flourish found in Belgian
restaurants, Belgium being a gastronome's paradise that
at times even surpasses France. The Sabena kitchens
were all that you expect a modern restaurant kitchen to
be, only many times bigger and with some seventy chefs
and helpers, including five butchers, aside from dish-
washers and the like; in season the staff comes to some
300 people. The whole place was beautifully organized
and shining.

Cooking for an airline means basically cooking the
food until it is half done since the heating up does the
rest. However, what makes all food outstanding is its
freshness, and freshness has been what I have particularly
noticed about Sabena's airborne meals. In Belgium it is
not too difficult to get really fresh produce from the
farms that are never far off, and from the nearby North
Sea. You can count it, and cook it just before it is put
on the plane. Cold dishes, and Sabena excels at fancy
aspics and the like, never spend more than one day or a
night in the refrigerator. To insure further freshness, the
trays that go onto the planes are filled at the last possible
moment, to prevent the food from going stale.

The food that was being prepared was lovely—like any
fine French food. But what interested me mostly was
the composition of the menus, which is a complicated
affair. Sabena planes go all over the world, and you have
to take food habits different from ours into account; for
instance, on flights going to Muslim countries, no pork
products are served. You have to break a flight down into
its component routes and look at the timetables, taking

into consideration that some passengers may be along for the whole trip and others for only part of it—yet they all have to be not only adequately, but also elegantly fed. When you fly from Brussels to Singapore, leaving in the evening for Vienna, you are first served (first-class) a cold buffet with Beef Wellington and Chicken Suprême, various salads, cheeses, and fruit, to be washed down with champagne. In the morning, on the Teheran-Bombay stretch, there is an ample breakfast with eggs, sausages, cheeses, and the like to sustain the travelers who came aboard in Vienna or Teheran, as well as those who came from Brussels. The meal between Bombay and Bangkok is what is called a lunch—consisting of little cocktail bits, a sauced-up dish of Dover sole, a choice (or both) of guinea hen or venison, assorted vegetables and salads, a choice of six cheeses, a fancy ice cream dessert, and fruits. To sustain life between Bangkok and Singapore, a snack of canapés, petits fours, and fruit salad is served to the travelers. All this to be consumed with good French wines and champagne, liqueurs, beers, soft drinks and hot drinks, not to mention the cocktails and apéritifs. Some of the menus are changed daily, others weekly or monthly or by the season, always taking into account that the food must harmonize with the countries flown to and the character of the passengers flying on the different routes.

I asked the Catering Manager of the Sabena kitchens what determined his choice of foods for the various menus. The answer was: the timetable and the route; the type of airplane since the facilities vary on the various kinds of jets; the material, that is, the possibility of buying locally to replenish the galley. Obviously, in Monrovia the choice will not be the same as in New York or Rome. Finally, there is the capacity of the airborne personnel; it takes a very experienced steward or stewardess to serve some of the fancy dishes served on the major Sabena flights.

Finally, I asked about complaints. Yes, there were always some complaints, which would be followed up on the spot and later, in the kitchens. In the majority of the cases, however, it turned out that the complainers had come aboard uneasy and unhappy, and that their complaints were based on their own states of mind rather than on actual Sabena shortcomings.

Chapter 14

My Favorite Kitchen

At this stage of my life, my favorite kitchen is the one I do not have to be in.

Index

337